Mythology in Our Midst

A Guide to Cultural References

Amy T. Peterson and David J. Dunworth

Illustrations by David J. Dunworth

Greenwood Press
Westport, Connecticut • London

Library of Congress Cataloging-in-Publication Data

Peterson, Amy T.
   Mythology in our midst : a guide to cultural references / Amy T. Peterson and David J.
Dunworth ; illustrations by David J. Dunworth.
      p. cm.
   Includes bibliographical references and index.
   ISBN 0–313–32192–2 (alk. paper)
   1. Mythology, European.   2. Civilization, Modern.   I. Dunworth, David J.   II. Title.
BL689.P48   2004
201'.3—dc22   2004040433

British Library Cataloguing in Publication Data is available.

Library of Congress Catalog Card Number: 2004040433
ISBN: 0–313–32192–2

First published in 2004

Greenwood Press, 88 Post Road West, Westport, CT 06881
An imprint of Greenwood Publishing Group, Inc.
www.greenwood.com

Printed in the United States of America

The paper used in this book complies with the
Permanent Paper Standard issued by the National
Information Standards Organization (Z39.48–1984).

10 9 8 7 6 5 4 3 2 1

Amy would like to thank her husband Brian, whose limitless support and encouragement provide her with inspiration, and her daughters Fiona and Nora.

David would like to thank his wife Melissa and their son Aidan for allowing him to be part of their pantheon.

∾

Contents

Illustrations

Introduction

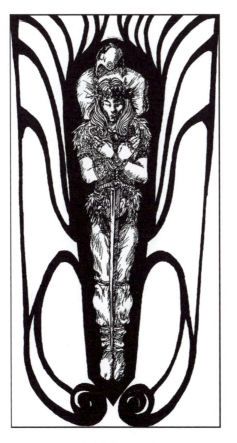

Balder's Funeral

Myths are a blend of fantasy and reality. Myths are stories that are not literally true. If they were, archaeologists would have found at least one set of giant bones or at least a unicorn horn or two. At the same time, myths are not completely false. Although literally untrue, there is a stronger current of truth that lies beneath the surface words of a myth. This current of truth flows through the power of symbols, actions, and reactions that have a very deep meaning for all people, regardless of race or age and in many cases even the period of time in which they live. Myths tell stories, but the meanings of the stories and the effects they can have upon our daily lives can range from mundane to life changing. The level to which we are affected is, in many ways, due to our personal background and the amount of effort and attention we invest in a myth.

This book outlines some of the connections between myths and our everyday lives. Few people realize how commonplace mythical references are in our lives. Every time someone uses words like academy, cereal, and echo, myths have touched our daily lives. Whenever people purchase products like Nike shoes, Olympus cameras, or Saturn cars, they patronize companies with names derived from myths. This text aims to reveal many of these unrecognized references, and their impact.

Each entry begins with a retelling of the myth. Then, through the course of the entry, the myth's relationships with popular culture, psychology, literature, art, and words are explored. In addition to the entries, this text includes appendices that list the references to mythology in the calendar, solar system, words, biology, and companies.

In the retelling of myths in this book, the popular or most well-known version is commonly relayed in the entries. The well-known versions of classic Greek and Roman myths are often different from the original versions of the myths, because they were erroneously translated or altered to be more palatable to late-nineteenth-century and early-twentieth-century Western values. In these cases, the original versions of the myths are described in the entry in addition to the more popular version of the myth.

In each entry, there is a description of the myth's influence on our modern culture. In this description, the myth is connected to modern aspects of our culture, such as a movie, word, or work of art. In some cases the connection may already be obvious to the reader, like in Disney's adaptation of the myth of Hercules. In other instances the relationship between the myth and the cultural aspect may not have been apparent until, upon reading the entry, the reader becomes initiated to the twists and turns the myth has taken to arrive into our modern culture.

Additional information regarding the influence of myths can be found in the appendixes. The reader may peruse the listing of brand names and common words that are associated with myths. Many elements in nature and in the solar system have been named after mythological people, creatures, and places; a listing of these items appears in the appendices. Another appendix lists the mythological origins of our names for the months and days of the week.

The book is organized alphabetically by the title of the myth. Readers may explore the myths in sequence, read the myths that interest them, or use the index to read myths that include specific themes. The appendices may be used as a starting point from which to explore the myths as well.

Myths flow like a river. They may change course slightly due to a translation or retelling. They might run slightly dry due to disuse and disinterest or flow heavily, pulling symbols and objects from the surrounding areas and incorporating them into the tale. Regardless of the strength of their flow, they always reach the same end point. That end point lies within the mind and soul of the person hearing the myth. The meaning of the story will unfold for the audience at the level that the person is able to understand it. Specialists argue over the meaning and purpose of myths with the same fervor that myths are told. There are many schools of thought when it comes to the meaning and purpose of myths.

Throughout the ages, mythology has had just as many detractors as it has had fans. Even some of the early Greeks, whose mythology is arguably the most well-known group of myths in Western civilization, saw them as a distraction from the real world of politics and academic pursuits. Myths were commonly reenacted on stage, or used as the background for contemporary morality plays. The Greeks did not invent myths by any means.

There is enough proof from earlier cultures to say with a great amount of certainty that myths have been around since the advent of the spoken language. Primitive cultures shared stories and myths that explained the moon, tidal patterns, and the movement of the stars. They usually had myths explaining their own existence as well as the animals and plants that they were so reliant upon. So, when scholars delve into these concepts without accurate historical records, they can choose to look at the myths as a kind of primitive science fiction that the elders of a tribe made up or consider them the product of an intense and complicated ritual system.

Still others have decided to look at myths as literal or metaphoric representations of reality as they perceived it. These differing schools of thought branched off to include the spheres of anthropology, theology, science, psychology, literary criticism, and numerous other fields of study. Today, hundreds of differing descriptions of myth exist and not all of them will agree. Myths explain and teach.

Myths provide codes of behavior for the individual and for society as a whole. They reflect the social, political, and private state of humanity and they beckon people to a long forgotten past that everyone can share in as equals. Myths use that past as a springboard of commonality. Feelings that are experienced by all people in any given time period are expressed in myth. The human condition is put on display and humanity has a chance to view it, dissect it, and learn vicariously through an ancient hero or tragic love story.

Myths do not point out the differences between people; they are in fact like a song that all people instinctively know the music to. Each person may add a few new words to the song, but the melody stays constant. Myths reveal what human beings have in common. We are all terrestrial bipeds with opposable thumbs that have tool making capacity, a sense of the future, and the imagination and hubris to think we can alter that future as we see fit.

By subscribing to a particular myth or set of myths, an individual finds a ground from which to make sense of his or her life. Myth tells them where they are in the grand, universal scheme of things, why they are there and in what direction to head to make more sense out of life. It shows us what our relationships should be with our god(s), our fellow humans, our neighbors, and our families. Myth can serve us in so many ways. Clearly, myth is far more than "a story that isn't true."

Throughout the history of humans, individuals have been filled with the ability to imagine and create because myths have played a vital role in many of the artistic endeavors. From the earliest rock carvings of fertility goddesses to video games, movies, and television shows, myths and mythical figures as old as humankind continue to extend into our culture. This text will illustrate that myths are far more prevalent than you might think. The song of myth is still playing and now, directors, television producers, authors, and artists are singing along with the melody.

Many individuals and schools of specialists have attempted to classify and rigidly define myths. Although an admirable task, it is one that is doomed to fall short of its intent. Myths, although classifiable, cannot be adequately defined in a holistic sense. It is the very act of attempting to define myths that brings an added sense to their inner meaning as well as the personal meaning they impart to the individual. The same can be said of a song. If 100 people are asked why a particular song carries special meaning for them, the 100 answers will more than likely be just as different as the individuals themselves. Perhaps the feelings evoked by the music will be similar and cause specific emotional responses, but the reasons behind those emotions are personal and based on events relative to the life of the individual.

Perhaps the more effective and worthwhile work on myth is the study of the meanings that the myths impart on the individual and the societies that subscribe to the myth. In looking at the individual interpretation of myths, each person has a series of memories based on the events that they have experienced. Within these memories are groups of experiences that are similar to one another and have particular meanings for each individual.

Certain words, colors, symbols, smells, and combinations of all of these, can trigger the memory of these past events. Myths are also full of symbols and imagery that can awaken these memories in everyone. Most people are not aware of these effects because, in many cases, the symbols go unnoticed by the conscious mind and affect people at an unconscious level.

Sigmund Freud utilized this idea as it pertained to dreams in his patients. He believed that certain latent aspects of the self expressed themselves through symbols and actions in our dreams. Freud believed that many of these expressions were of a sexual nature that had been repressed. He separated the mind into three distinct forces: the Id, the Ego, and the Super Ego. The Id is our primal force. It drives our most basic desires (e.g., food, sex, sleep). The Super Ego is a combination of social pressures and the authority figures as perceived by the person. Finally, there is the Ego. The Ego is, in the simplest sense, the "me-ness" of the person. The Ego is a kind of mediator between the Id and Super Ego. Freud believed that when certain desires become repressed, the Id would express itself in different ways. The Ego can sometimes translate these expressions into symbolic figures, actions, or situations in dreams or fantasies on the part of the patient.

Freud recognized that some of these fantasies were similar to mythological tales. He tried to prove that myths were larger expressions of repressed fantasies within cultures. One of his protégés, Carl Gustav Jung, took a different position from his mentor that eventually led to their split. Jung believed in the existence of an unconscious area of the self that our waking conscious mind cannot penetrate. That unconscious self participates in a collective unconscious that encompasses all that is or was. In simple terms, the collective unconscious is something that each individual can access, but it remains largely unknown. Occasionally, it comes to the surface when certain stimuli present themselves to an individual.

According to Jung, the collective unconscious would often express itself in the dreams of his patients. Jung had his patients draw pictures of their dreams and tell stories about them. He began to notice a series of recurring events, characters, and symbols in the dreams. Certain characters always presented themselves during particular periods of growth, pain, or reflection on the part of the patient. The drawings were strikingly similar and the actions were usually the same. Jung referred to these recurring characters and symbolic actors as archetypes. He believed that these archetypes are not only shared by all people, but also that they are and will always be present. He began to show that these archetypes are also visible within the mythological constructs of the various cultures of the world.

Jung's work has been supplemented by others like Joseph Campbell and James Hillman. Both have added to the collective understanding of mythology and also made mythology a subject for the masses again. Joseph Campbell's description of the hero myth brought a light to mythological studies at the end of the twentieth century. James Hillman has brought mythology to the individual as a source of wisdom and self-reflection. Most important is the fact that both of them, and their many followers, have opened a door into the world of mythology for everyone. They urge us to look around ourselves to find the myths that are present. They urge us to see that our society still lives in, and is directed by, myth.

Anthropologists such as Claude Levi-Strauss approach the study of mythology from a structuralist point of view. He looked at the culture that created the myth and only that culture as it lived by the myth. Although considered an outdated method, Levi-Strauss' works on the primitive mind and the social function of myth are beautifully written and informative. He believed in the power of myth as a strong force for social order and belief systems. Myth has always laid a foundation that spells out the behavior that is expected of a good person. If the myth does not, then it shows us what happens to those who are bad. Myth goes beyond simply telling the audience what is right and wrong. It illustrates exemplary models of valor and deceit, humility and hubris, and asks the audience to evaluate the given situation with respect to these ideals. The very values that people cling to or despise are put on display and people participate in society based on those values. Society uses those values in order to judge its individual members.

If one doubts whether myths affect our social order, they should ask any American child what Superman would do if he saw a person about to be crushed by a falling rock. The answers would be different, but the end result would be the same. By heat vision, super breath, or sheer strength, Superman would save the person. When asked why, the child would probably say that Superman is a hero and that is what heroes do. Ask that same kid if he wants to be a hero and the response will probably be a big "Yes!" Movies, television, and comic books provide Western society with a wide range of heroes and villains to choose from. Each provides us with a model for action.

Hidden within the pages of a simple comic book lies the heroic equivalent of any classic myth. The modern retelling of the story of Hercules by Walt Disney provides children with a certainly flawed, but genuinely good-hearted hero. No matter what generation you come from, the media has thrust forth a heroic and villainous icon for you to evaluate and integrate as you see fit. The cowboy movies of the 1940s and the science fiction epics of today all feature heroes and villains. The outfits are different but the essence remains.

Each culture around the world has its own mythology with characteristics that reflect the culture and its values. For example, the mythology of Australia is closely linked with the natural landscape and the Aborigines who first inhabited the land. Its myths focus on explanations of the natural terrain as well as events in the human life cycle, and subjects like natural disasters are often a theme of Australian myth.

The Aztec civilization, which lived in central Mexico during the fifteenth and sixteenth centuries, spread myths about grand gods who warred among themselves. The days of their calendar were associated with gods, as were their colors, numbers, and directions. People were seen as the servants to gods, and the Aztec religion often involved human sacrifices to the gods. The idea of predetermined fate was another important element in Aztec mythology.

Heroism, magic, and romance are common themes in the Celtic myths, which were orally passed down from generation to generation. These myths were perpetuated by medieval Irish and Welsh monks who documented the stories in writing. By blending history with magic and adventure, the Celtic myths are some of the most exciting.

The gods of Egyptian myth are inextricably connected to nature. These gods controlled natural phenomena, and the pharaoh who ruled the land was believed to be part-god. Few of the Egyptian myths have survived from ancient times.

Finnish mythology centers on the stories of heroes and gods. Many of the myths are recorded in the Finnish national epic, called *Kalevala*. The title of the epic means "land of the descendents of Kaleva," which is an imaginary region. The *Kalevala* has helped create a national identity for the Finnish people.

Greek and Roman myths have probably had the most impact on the modern Western world. The pantheons of gods seem to have humanlike weaknesses, which make people identify with their stories. The existence of the gods explains natural phenomena and provide soap opera–style plotlines that entertain almost any audience.

Hindu myths unfold over the central theme of reincarnation. Just as the individual soul is continually reborn, the universe is repeatedly destroyed and renewed. Modern Indian life is colored by Hindu belief and myth. Art, plays, religion, and thought are all affected in some way by the Hindu myths.

The Incans of Peru mixed fact with myth to create an official state history. These myths were not written but were carefully memorized and recited by professional storytellers. Although Spanish conquistadors largely destroyed the Incan culture, they did record what they had learned about Incan mythology. Incan myth was comprised of deities who governed over the forces of nature that function in the sky.

After centuries of orally transmitting myths, the Japanese recorded their myths in the eighth century for the imperial court. In Japanese myths, every element in nature has its own spirit or god. Thus the pantheon of gods is enormous. Many of the Japanese myths center around heroes such as Hachiman (the patron of warriors) and the sun goddess Amaterasu.

The people of Micronesia, in the southwest Pacific Ocean, created a great variety of myths. Some of the common themes included the creation of the world, heroes, the features of the landscape, and travels between the sky and the earth. The main characters of these myths were creator gods, heroes, tricksters, and ancestral spirits.

Native American myth is not a single unified body of myths, but sets of myths developed by the different tribal groups. Behind each of the myths is the concept of spiritual forces that exist in every aspect of the natural world. Trickster stories are common in Native American myth, as are heroes and animals.

Norse myths come from people who spoke Germanic languages. These groups extended through Western Europe and Scandinavia. Battles are a central theme in Norse myths. Sometimes they involve heroic warriors or kings, and other times they are between the gods. Many modern fantasy writers, such as J.R.R. Tolkien, use Norse myths as an inspiration for their work.

The conflict between good and evil is central to Persian mythology. Two powerful gods, Ahura Mazda, the god of light, and Ahriman, the god of darkness, are key figures in the ongoing battles between good and evil. Each of the gods has an army of spirits to help fight their battles, and each person, plant, and animal has the freedom to choose which god to follow.

In Siberian mythology, the earthly realm is viewed as the middle tier in a series of three, five, or seven worlds. A tree connects the multiple worlds together. Shamans play a central role in this mythology, because it is believed that they can climb the tree and move from one world to another.

The modern world has its own myths as well. Superheroes abound, taking a variety of forms from men with bat or spider powers to the three energetic sisters imbued with the power of "chemical X" known as the Powerpuff Girls. Benevolent characters like Santa Claus bestow gifts on well-behaved children.

The sources of myth are varied and numerous, but this book focuses on myths that are relatively well known in Western culture. They range from well-known Greek and Roman myths to the lesser known but equally potent Norse Myths. Also included are myths that are representative of a particular motif expressed in the myths of many cultures. Such myths are referred to as "universal myths." They emerged in cultures that had little or no contact with one another or existed in different time periods. The myths closely resemble one another, with a similarity in characters, environs, and situations. These myths lend credence to the concept of a collective unconscious because they express the same idea in mind, but do so with a flavor that is distinctive of their own culture.

There are many instances of universal myths. For instance, the concept of the Earth Mother and Sky Father is so predominant in all of the Western myths, as well as a few modern religions, that it reveals an agreement among almost all cultures as to which sex controls each sphere. This similarity cannot be simply coincidental and must have a meaning. Anthropologists, theologians, and sociologists argue as to the true meaning behind the similarity, but this text will focus on the agreement of the different cultures.

There are universal myths that span the entire globe and break down the East–West cultural divide. The scope of this text will not include the influence of Eastern myth on Western civilization. Instead, the focus will be on individual and universal myths in Western society.

Sometimes universal myths are hard to recognize because the symbols that they use have different meanings in the culture that originated the myth. This may make the universal translation quite complicated. Therefore it is as easy to mistakenly identify a myth as universal. It may have similar symbols and actions to another myth, but the meaning to that particular culture could be the opposite of another.

For example, the brash young fighter who goes against tradition to fight a warlord would be praised in the West for his in-your-face humanity, whereas that same hero might be seen as dishonorable and not in control of his anger in the East. In one case, the fighter is a hero; in the other version, he is an example of what a hero should not be. Are these myths the same? No. They do not send the same message, nor do they impart a sense of social order in the same way. But will the telling of this myth have the same affect on the warriors in their own culture? Will the Western hero thrive because of his brashness? Will the Eastern hero learn that his ways are not the ways of a good warrior? In the end, does the reader become better suited to deal with his or her own environment, based on the actions of the character? All these questions begin to scratch the surface of the importance and power of myth.

Although the myths selected for this book vary in origin and subject matter, they each contribute to modern language and art forms in recognizable ways. The myths were selected based on their influence on modern Western culture. Most of the myths will be familiar to the average reader because they are popular Greek and Roman myths. Other myths may not be well known, but their contribution to modern culture is great. Several of the myths, such as the "World Tree," are universal myths that are one myth told in a variety of forms in different cultures.

It is our hope that, by reading this text and connecting the myths of cultures past to modern culture, a reader might not only recognize the archetypes and symbols that are present in the advertising, movies, books, and other media of current culture, but also recognize some of the mythical aspects in his or her own life. Each of us has a vision of a hero, a villain, a trusty companion, and what paradise should be. We may have even been spoon-fed images by sources of which we were unaware. When we see that those sources are derivative of the great classical myths, maybe it is time to realize that these are stories we all share because they have a deep meaning for everyone. They are not stories that were relevant only to ancient people in faraway lands; they are our stories as well. Every day, in many ways, we live part of them. We watch the world and interact with others, and all the while mythology is in our midst.

Adam and Eve

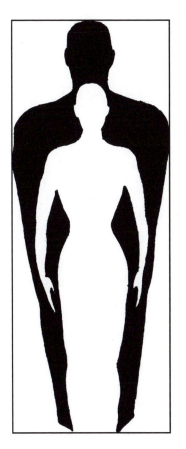

Adam and Eve

The story of Adam and Eve is fairly well known and quite similar to other "first couple" myths. After having created the earth and the animals, God created Adam. As the Bible tells it, God then created Eve from one of Adam's ribs. Hebrew mythology tells quite a different story. According to these myths, Adam had a wife before Eve. Her name was Lilith and she saw herself as the equal of Adam and not to be lorded over by him. Having been given the honor of naming and lording over all the animals, Adam was apparently not very happy with having an equal. Eventually, Lilith left Adam to pursue freely her own interests. This radically changed the idea of Eden, which according to the Bible is a place of bliss. Perhaps God realized that Adam couldn't handle having an equal, so he created Eve from his rib, essentially providing Adam with a legitimate right to her ownership.

Adam and Eve lived in a state of pure innocence and wanted for nothing. They had no cares or worries. They basked in the sun without clothing for they knew no shame. They did not need work because the gardens provided them with all that they needed. On a regular basis, God showed them that he loved them and asked nothing of them except that they love him back. God went with them through the garden as they named all of the creations. They came upon a tree in the garden that held beautiful fruit. God told them in a loving voice that they may have anything they wish in the garden except the fruit of the tree they were facing. They should never eat it for they would not please him if they did. Both of them agreed and they went about their blissful existence.

According to the Bible, Eve happened upon the tree one day and was staring at the fruit, when a serpent slithered up the tree's trunk and spoke to her. In the Hebrew myth, it was Lilith in the form of a serpent. The serpent asked Eve why she had not tried the fruit yet and she answered that God had forbidden it. The serpent answered that God didn't want them to eat the fruit because they would have the knowledge of good and evil. If they had that knowledge they might become equals to God. The serpent said that God may not want equals.

Eventually, Eve was tempted and tasted the fruit. Adam happened to be strolling by and Eve offered him a taste. At first reluctant, he then took a bite. Instantly they both noticed that they were naked, became ashamed, and hid themselves. God appeared and asked them why they had done what he asked them not to do. They answered that the serpent had tricked them. God cursed the serpent to be forever hated by the sons of man, but he also cursed Adam and Eve. He evicted them from paradise and told them that they would have to work for food and experience pain and death as well. They did encounter all these things, but they managed to have children and die at a very old age. They lived the rest of their lives ashamed for having fallen from God's grace.

If taken literally, this story can be understood as the beginning of humankind and the reason why we age, get sick, and die. It can also serve as a lesson as to who really is the highest authority. If viewed as a metaphor, this story and the symbols it contains can serve as an allegory for what it means to be a human being. Adam and Eve were innocent, naked, and completely unaware of what the world was like outside of Eden. They felt nothing but love from their father and were provided with everything they needed. This sounds very much like an infant that is being cared for by a nurturing parent. A child is given what it needs and is showered with love and affection, but it is unaware of the work that goes into providing that environment.

The eating of the fruit symbolizes a break from God's will. By eating the fruit Adam and Eve gain the knowledge of what is good and what is evil; they become aware. This edible symbol provides a concrete moment of awakening, as opposed to the gradual movement toward self-awareness into which a child grows. Children at some point in their development become aware that they are naked. They come to know when they are doing something that is wrong and become scared of the consequences. Clearly they are at a different level of thought and being than an infant. With that knowledge comes a great deal of new and interesting paths to follow, but they are paths that must be crossed without the full attention of your parents, and they are sometimes painful. Your parents can no longer shield you. You are on your own. This process continues as you gain knowledge, until eventually you leave your home, or are asked to leave depending on your behavior. Leaving home means that you have to pay your own way, get a job, and become a little more aware of your environment.

One of the interesting conundrums that a reader of this myth can encounter is the confusion over God's orders. If Adam and Eve had no idea of good or evil, how could God tell them not to eat the fruit and expect that they would know it was wrong to disobey? One answer may be that the process is simply a natural expression of the human condition. We will always be confronted by paradoxical situations, but it is our ability to choose that makes us, if not lovable, at least extremely interesting to watch.

The social issues that the story of Adam and Eve brings to the surface are numerous. Contemporary feminists point to the stereotyping of women as lesser beings in this passage of the Bible as a major contributor to the lack of equality experienced over the last few millennia. The Roman Catholic Church still prohibits women from becoming priests, although it allows women to become nuns that are separate and given less power within the church. Outside of the Church, the Western world seems to be making a change toward a more balanced view of the sexes, with the Eastern nations lagging behind.

The idea of woman being created by man may be more of a sexual fantasy than an attempt to establish a hierarchy. This concept can be seen in the movie *Weird Science*, in which two high school boys create a perfect woman that will do what they want. Even the science fiction classic *Metropolis* features a man-made female android that surpasses its maker's expectations.

The concept of Adam and Eve has been used as an allegory for the ongoing "battle of the sexes." In the 1949 film *Adam's Rib*, Katharine Hepburn and

Spencer Tracy star as competing lawyers in a marital dispute. In the movie, Hepburn shows Tracy that women should be treated with respect and not merely an afterthought. The story of Adam and Eve has inspired artists, writers, and composers. During the Middle Ages, Adam and Eve became a favorite subject in art. Even Michelangelo could not resist depicting the couple when he painted the Sistine Chapel in Rome. Likewise, John Milton was so inspired by the story that he wrote the epic *Paradise Lost* in 1667. Another more modern example is when Iron Butterfly garbled the words to their song "In the Garden of Eden" and it became the rock classic, "In-A-Gadda-Da-Vida."

Adam loaned his name to several familiar phrases. The lump in a man's throat is called an "Adam's apple" in reference to the chunk of the forbidden fruit that stuck in his throat. Gardening is often referred to as "Adam's profession." The word "Adamic" describes someone who is naked and free, like Adam. In the world of plants, there is an "Adam's apple tree" and an "Adam's needle." The latter of the two refers to the spines on the yucca plant and comes from the idea that Adam and Eve sewed together fig leaves to cover themselves.

The myth of Adam and Eve has contributed other phrases to our vocabulary as well. For example "Eve's curse" is used to describe menstruation. Any tempting but forbidden person or thing is called a "forbidden fruit," and the phrase "original sin" is used to refer to any controversial relationship.

As a story of human frailty, Adam and Eve transcends the boundaries of Judaism and Christianity. Similar stories exist in the Islamic tradition and as far back as the ancient legends of Mesopotamia. Its timeless quality ensures its place as part of our modern culture as its characters emerge in our everyday lives.

Aphrodite

ი

Like many of the Greek myths, the tale of Hephaestus and Aphrodite seems to be taken from the plot of a modern soap opera. She was the insatiable, lustful beauty and he was the ugly, crippled artisan. The couple's marriage was a union of opposites and characterized by infidelity.

Aphrodite was the Greek goddess of love, lust, and mating. Her unusual birth predated the Olympians. She was born out of a rivalry between Cronus and his father Uranus. The son cut off Uranus' genitals and threw them into the sea, which gave rise to foam. Aphrodite emerged from the foam, and her name literally means "out of foam."

The newly formed goddess floated on the sea until she landed on the island of Cythera, which was too small for her liking, so she set out again until she reached the island of Cyprus. When she set foot on the island, grass and flowers emerged beneath her feet. In some myths, she is called Cythereia or Cyprus in reference to the two islands. Sandro Botticelli painted an iconic image (*The Birth of Venus*) of Aphrodite, coyly standing in a shell covering her nakedness with her flowing hair and delicate hands. The story of her landings on the islands may be a reference to the possible Phoenician origins of Aphrodite. The islands had been the domain of the Phoenicians, and Aphrodite may have been based on Astarte, the Phoenician goddess of women, fertility, and the tides.

Once ashore, Aphrodite did not lead an industrious life. Instead, she began engaging in the activities for which she became known: having sex and making Olympians fall in love with mortals. Her magic girdle made the wearer desirable and gave rise to the idea of love potions. Interestingly, from her name comes our common term for a love potion, "aphrodisiac." The term is derived from the Greek word "aphrodisiakos," which means "sexual." When the word aphrodisiac first appeared in 1719 it referred to "lust." Aphrodite has inspired music as well, including a 1906 tragic opera titled *Aphrodite* by Camile Erlanger.

Aphrodite's indulgent lovemaking practices involved many lovers and generated controversy and intrigue on Mount Olympus. For instance, Hera disapproved when Aphrodite slept with Dionysus, the god of wine and revelry. Hera showed her displeasure by deforming their son, Priapus. He was ugly, but his enormous genitals made him a natural choice to become the god of male fertility. In ancient Greece, a stone statue of Priapus was used to deflower brides before marriage. The Greeks believed that the ceremony served two purposes: to ensure that the bride would be fertile, and to avoid the superstitions and shame surrounding the "blood of the first night." Priapus' legacy lives on in the modern word "priapism," which refers to the unfortunate condition in which the penis remains persistently erect without sexual excitement.

Not all of Aphrodite's affairs were her idea. When Hermes fell in love with her, she spurned him. Hermes went to Zeus for help and in an odd plot Zeus sent an eagle to steal one of Aphrodite's sandals. To get it back, she had to sleep with Hermes. This single encounter produced a double-sexed child called Hermaphroditus. In other versions of the myth Hermaphroditus is born as a normal child, and he does not transform until the water-nymph, Samacis, captures him. When she prays to the gods never to allow their two bodies to separate, they grant her request literally. As a result, Hermaphroditus becomes half-man, half-woman. By the fourteenth century the term "hermaphrodite" was used to describe animals and humans who have physical characteristics of both sexes. By the seventeenth century, it was expanded to refer to effeminate men and masculine women.

Many Greek Olympians inspired the ancient Roman gods, and Aphrodite was no exception. Her Roman counterpart was Venus, the goddess of love, whose beauty and seductive powers matched those of Aphrodite. The famous statue of Venus with missing arms, known as the *Venus de Milo*, is actually a depiction of Aphrodite.

Like Aphrodite, Venus' name is found in modern words. For example, "venom" once meant "love potion" before its meaning evolved to describe poison. "Venerate," another word that is derived from Venus, means to worship. The second planet from the sun is named after the attractive love goddess, and the high area along the planet's equator is known as Aphrodite Terra.

When Aphrodite married Hephaestus, she wed a man who was very different from herself. He was an industrious and gifted craftsman who served as the god of smithing and destructive fire. Another goddess, Hestia, cared for hearth fires.

According to the myth, Hera was jealous of Zeus' giving birth to Athena. She planned to even the score by conceiving and giving birth to her own child without the assistance of Zeus. Unfortunately for Hera, the product of her envy was Hephaestus, who was ugly and sickly. Embarrassed by her imperfect child, she hurled him from Mount Olympus. He landed on the island of Lemnos, but the fall broke his leg and crippled him. Not all versions of Hephaestus' birth are the same. For example, in some versions of the story, he was born lame, and in Homer's version he was the son of both Hera and Zeus.

On Lemnos, Hephaestus learned to craft metal with renowned artistry. His workshop was said to be deep inside the volcano of the island. This seemed logical to early Greeks, who witnessed the island's volcano spew smoke and fire much like a forge. To account for volcanoes elsewhere, Greeks reasoned that Hephaestus had established an extensive network of workshops. Hephaestus' Roman counterpart was Volcanus. His name is the origin of the word "volcano" as well as the term "vulcanization," which refers to Charles Goodyear's groundbreaking nineteenth-century process that strengthened rubber.

At his workshop, Hephaestus forged the powerful weapons of the gods. For Zeus he crafted thunderbolts that the king of the gods would hurl across the sky. For Poseidon, he created a trident and for Hades he forged a cap that would render the wearer invisible. In some accounts, his craftsmanship is immortalized in the constellation of Libra. Supposedly, he forged the balance and serves as its protector.

As a way to regain entrance to Mount Olympus, he forged a beautiful golden throne for Hera. She excitedly accepted the gift and sat down, whereupon she was imprisoned by Hephaestus' handiwork. While Hephaestus gloated over his trap, the other Olympians begged for him to free his mother. Finally, he relented.

As a peace offering, Hera arranged the marriage between Aphrodite and Hephaestus, but Aphrodite did not seem to take the marriage vows seriously. Shortly after the wedding, she began to have affairs with gods and mortals alike. Then she became enamored with Ares, the god of war, and the two began to see each other frequently. One night, the couple stayed together too long, and Helios (the god who controlled the rising and setting of the sun) caught them in the act. Helios went to Hephaestus and told him of Aphrodite's scandalous behavior.

Hephaestus was infuriated and immediately developed a plan to humiliate his wife. First, he constructed a bronze net and hid it over his bed. Then he told Aphrodite that he was going to Lemnos for awhile. As soon as he had left, Aphrodite invited Ares over. When the lovers got into bed, the net dropped down, trapping them. Hephaestus invited all of the gods and goddesses to witness the couple, but instead of humiliating Aphrodite and Ares, Hephaestus only succeeded in disgracing himself. When the gods made fun of him, Hephaestus became angry and demanded the return of the gifts that he had given in exchange for Aphrodite's hand in marriage.

Poseidon, who also loved Aphrodite, convinced Ares to pay for the marriage gifts. To ensure that the loan would be paid, Poseidon offered to back the loan. He made this offer knowing that if Ares defaulted, Aphrodite would become his wife. As the gods were finagling their way into Aphrodite's bed, Hephaestus realized that he really did not want a divorce, so he dropped the matter.

While Hephaestus and Aphrodite remained married, she continued her relationship with Ares. They had three children. The sons, Phobus (panic) and Deimus (fear) drove Ares' chariot when he went into battle. Their daughter Harmonia (harmony) fell in love with Cadmus, a mortal who served Ares for killing a dragon that was sacred to the god. Harmonia and Cadmus married and he became the founding king of Thebes. Like his lover Aphrodite, Ares' influence lingers in our modern world. His Roman incarnation, Mars, loaned his name to the fourth planet and its inhabitants, Martians. His warlike behavior gives us the word "martial," which describes things that are related to war or military life.

The myth of Hephaestus and Aphrodite contains characters who continue to seep into our everyday lives. As an ancient "Beauty and the Beast," they never learned the moral of the story: to see each other's inner beauty. Instead they indulged in the very human traits of selfish indulgence, pride, and revenge.

Artemis and Actaeon

❧

Artemis and her brother Apollo were fraternal twins born to Leto, who was a daughter of the original Titans. Zeus had impregnated Leto, and his wife, Hera, was so jealous of the mistress that she sent a serpent after Leto to prevent her from finding a place to give birth. Finally, Leto's sister, Asteria, took her in, and Leto gave birth to Artemis. According to the story, Artemis helped her mother through nine days of labor before her brother Apollo arrived.

The twins were protective of their beloved mother. When the giant Tityus tried to rape her, they killed him with a hail of arrows. They again defended their mother's honor when Niobe bragged that she had more children than Leto. In response, Artemis and Apollo destroyed most of Niobe's children, leaving the distraught Niobe to weep forever.

When Artemis grew up, she became one of the Olympians as the goddess of the hunt, the moon, and wild animals. She served as the protector of harbors and roads. In addition she became associated with childbirth for her role in delivering Apollo. Artemis is a Greek goddess, and Diana is her Roman counterpart.

When Artemis turned three years old, Zeus offered her anything she wanted for her birthday. Like any three year old, Artemis had an extensive wish list. As a benevolent father, Zeus granted her every one of her desires. She received all of the mountains in the world, which would serve as her home, and thirty cities. Zeus also gave her eternal virginity, a silver bow, and a quiver of arrows that the Cyclopes forged.

There were three Cyclopes—giants with only one eye. The name Cyclopes means "round eye." They were blacksmiths and worked with Hephaestus to create the notable weapons of the gods. Poseidon's trident and Zeus' thunderbolts were the work of the Cyclops. In addition, they created the cap of Hades, which made the wearer invisible.

Artemis spent most of her time in the mountains. She was attended by nymphs, beautiful maidens who devoted their lives to her. As the goddess of the hunt, she frequently hunted with her mother, Leto, and a giant hunter named Orion. Unfortunately, Orion made the mistake of offending Gaia (the earth) by bragging he was such a skillful hunter that he could kill every animal on earth. Hera defended Gaia's honor by sending a scorpion to kill Orion. In the end, Artemis pleaded with Zeus to immortalize Orion as a constellation. Zeus complied, but he made the scorpion a constellation as well. This story is the origin of the astrological sign of Scorpio.

Artemis also appears in the myth of Hercules. For the hero's fourth labor, he was to bring the Ceryneian stag to the king. The stag was one of Artemis' favorites. After a year of hunting the stag, Hercules caught the beast in Artemis' sacred grove, where she and Apollo appeared to protect the stag. She allowed Hercules to borrow the stag if he returned it unharmed, which he did.

Artemis was often force to defend her own honor. For instance, King Oeneus of Calydon once forgot the tradition of dedicating the first fruits of the harvest to Artemis. In response, Artemis terrorized his kingdom with a wild boar. The boar continued to menace the kingdom until Oeneus finally called upon the greatest heroes to hunt down the beast.

In another threat to Artemis' honor, Actaeon, a hunter, was hunting in the woods when he saw the naked goddess while she bathed in the woods. The infuriated Artemis changed Actaeon into a deer and his confused hounds tore him to pieces.

King Agamemnon's slight against Artemis is the most famous. In a thoughtless boast, he claimed to be a more skillful hunter than Artemis. As revenge, she stranded the Greeks with ill winds at the beginning of the Trojan War. To regain her favor, Agamemnon had to sacrifice his daughter Iphigenia.

Artemis has inspired artists for centuries. In early Greek classical art, she appeared on vases, on stone carvings, in paintings, and in sculpted scenes with Acteon, Apollo, and animals. The most famous of these depictions is a Hellenistic sculpture called "Diana of Versailles," in which the goddess is posed next to a deer. Later in history, Titian painted "Actaeon and Diana" in 1559, and Auguste Renior created "Diana" in 1867.

Artemis' influence is not limited to classical art. She appeared in Walt Disney's animation classic *Fantasia* (1940), and was the basis for Wonder Woman, the comic book character. Wonder Woman's alter ego is Diana (the Roman name for Artemis) and her super powers were granted by goddesses, including Demeter, Aphrodite, and Athena.

As the goddess of the hunt, Artemis protected women and was a symbol of strength. For this reason, her name is often attached to organizations and efforts that aim to support women. An e-zine for breast cancer survivors is named after the goddess because of the legend that associates her with the Amazons, a tribe of women who had their right breasts removed to allow them to draw a bow as well as a man. A Web site and support group for survivors of domestic abuse chose Artemis as its name because of the goddess' strength and independence. ArtemisPress, a publisher of feminist and lesbian e-books, is another example of her influence.

Balder's Death

~

The Death of Balder

Balder's death is one of the most pertinent and moving myths of the Norse culture. It is a story of death and rebirth that explains the cycle of nature. It is also the story of a mother's futile attempt to escape fate. Frigga, who was the most favored among the Norse gods, wanted to protect her son, Balder. He represented all that is good, beautiful, and happy.

In the myth, Balder is troubled by dreams of his own death. After he tells his mother Frigga, she begins a mission to make him invulnerable. She asks everything on earth, from every person to each blade of grass, to make an oath not to harm or injure her beloved son. Her one oversight, mistletoe, ultimately dooms her son. The gods amused by Balder's invulnerability take turns throwing objects at him to watch them bounce off harmlessly. Meanwhile, Loki, a mischievous god, learns of Balder's weakness to mistletoe. He tricks Balder's brother, the blind god Hodir, to toss a dart fashioned from mistletoe at Balder. The dart instantly kills Balder and brings great sorrow to the world.

Balder's death is thought to symbolize the change of seasons from summer to winter. As the shining god, Balder represents summer, and he is killed by Hodir, the blind god of winter. With Balder's death, the sunny months of summer are replaced by the long darkness of winter.

The myth of Balder's death was especially powerful to the Norse who endured frigid winters with nights that could last as long as twenty-two hours. In the myth, another god, Hermod, travels to the land of the dead to bargain with Hel for the return of Balder. Eventually, Balder returns so that he can renew the world. A myth about the changing seasons occurs in almost all mythologies and cultures. A sun god dies, the world mourns bringing about winter, and the end is always the same: summer returns and the god is reborn.

Looking at this cycle of renewal on a smaller scale, it also represents the rising and setting of the sun. For this reason, this type of myth is known as a solar myth. For the Norse and other cultures that have solar myths, this story reaffirms their faith that winter will end and spring will bring new life, longer days, and renewed spirits.

Looking deeper into this myth, there are other beliefs that it explains, like fate and our inability to escape it. The Norse believed that each of us was born into this world with a predetermined future. To the Norse, fate is like a strong current that carries us from birth to death. No matter how hard we try to break free, the result will always be the same.

In the myth of Balder, he must die so that winter can occur and he can be reborn. If he doesn't die, the natural cycle is interrupted and everyone's fate is changed. Loki ensures that Balder dies by seeking out his one weakness, mistletoe, and by directing Hodir's hand with the fatal dart. He could have killed Balder himself, but instead Loki guides Hodir in achieving his destiny as the god winter. Loki becomes an agent of fate by manipulating events to their predestined conclusion.

Loki appears in many of the Norse myths as a god of mischief. He is the doer of good and the doer of evil, but he is not really a bad guy or a good guy. Instead, he acts as a balance, adapting to any situation where fate needs to be fulfilled. As the gods fight to escape their fate, Loki continues to act as the rudder to steer them toward their predetermined fate. As they struggle harder, Loki becomes more flagrant and inflicts more pain in an effort to keep them on course.

With the exception of a few myths about fate, this story is quite unique in that the main character, Balder, is not trying to escape his own fate. In the role of protector, his mother is the one who attempts to alter Balder's destiny. In this same way, the story of Achilles is strikingly similar to Balder's. Achilles' mother, Thetis, attempts to make him invulnerable to all weapons by bathing him in a sacred river. Like Frigga, she makes one terrible oversight and dips the child by his ankle, leaving him with one vulnerable spot. The terms Achilles heel and Achilles tendon are derived from this story. Both Thetis and Frigga followed their maternal instinct, but they ultimately learned that fate is a stronger force.

The power of fate is a common theme in movies. For example, in the movie *Terminator*, a cyborg from the future (Arnold Schwarzenneger) is sent to the present to kill a child who will become a powerful leader. Although the cyborg has superior strength and technology, he cannot alter that child's destiny. In *Seven*, David Mills (Brad Pitt) wants to escape fate and simply arrest John Doe, the serial killer, but Doe forces Mills to fulfill his destiny and kill his psychotic adversary. The adversary becomes an agent of fate. In *Devil's Advocate*, Keanu Reeves portrays a lawyer, Kevin Lomax, who is the son of the Devil. He is destined to father a child who will bring about the end of the world. Through the course of the film, Lomax learns that he has not directed his own life; his father has manipulated events so that he will fulfill his destiny.

The idea of predetermined destiny is not limited to movies. In Christianity, Jesus is born for the sole purpose of dying to pay for man's sins. As the story goes, he tried to avoid his fate in the Garden of Gethsemene by asking God to find another way, but he could not escape his destiny.

The story of Christ has other similarities to the myth of Balder. Just as Jesus is the son of God, Balder is the son of Odin, who is the most powerful of the Norse gods. Twelve apostles follow Jesus and Balder is surrounded by twelve other gods. Like Balder, Christ rose again to renew the world. Christians celebrate his rising in the spring, which heralds the season of rebirth. Just as Balder is the shining god, Jesus is depicted as a figure of radiance and light.

In the story of Christ, Loki's counterpart is Judas. He bears the onus of responsibility for the death of Jesus by "betraying" him to the Romans. In a sense, Judas was an agent of fate by ensuring that Christ fulfilled his destiny.

The movie *The Matrix* mirrors the story as well. Laurence Fishburne plays Morpheus, who is the leader of the resistance. He believes that Keanu Reeves' character, Neo, is the chosen one who will save all of mankind from the machines. Like Balder and Christ, before Neo could become truly important in the cause, he had to die and rise again. The role of Loki in *The Matrix* is fulfilled by Cypher, who betrays Neo to the agents. Like Balder, Neo cannot escape his destiny.

Even the fairy tales of Snow White and Sleeping Beauty parallel the story of Balder's death. In both fairy tales, the wicked queen disguises herself to harm the main character, just as Loki did. Both Snow White and Sleeping Beauty fall into deep sleeps, in which everything and everyone around them mourns. This lamenting mirrors the mourning of Balder after his death. When Snow White and Sleeping Beauty are awakened, normal life resumes, just as it does when Balder rises.

Interestingly, the story of Balder's death contributes to our superstitions about Friday the thirteenth. We derive the English word Friday from Frigga, Balder's mother. All thirteen gods assembled on Frigga's sacred day, Friday, and assaulted Balder with harmless objects. Loki, the thirteenth god, encouraged Hodir to throw the fatal mistletoe.

Although the story of Balder's death is not as well know as many of the Greek myths, it plays an important role in our modern culture. It has inspired poems like Longfellow's "Tegner's Drapa" and fairy tales like Sleeping Beauty. For many generations, it explained the seasons and it has even influenced our concept of destiny.

Bellerophon

～

The tale of Bellerophon is one of great heroic deeds and excessive pride. It stands as a lesson to those who would attempt to achieve that which is beyond their limits. The story also suggests that using the gifts bestowed on you for purposes other than intended can lead to disaster.

Bellerophon was originally named Hipponous. He was the son of Poseidon and a mortal woman named Eurynome. Her husband, Glaucus, believed that the boy was his own and so he treated him as his own son. Hipponous changed his name after he accidentally murdered his own brother Bellerus. Because of this act he was exiled from his home in Corinth, and he took the name Bellerophon because it meant "killer of Bellerus."

As Bellerophon wandered the land, he honed his skills in battle and the art of archery. Eventually he was given refuge in the city of Argos. King Proteus took pity on the handsome young man and let him stay with the royal court. All was going quite well, with Bellerophon proving himself worthy by performing many tasks for the king. He also gained the attention of the king's wife Stheneboea, who soon found herself enraptured by the beauty and bravery of Bellerophon. Eventually, while the king was away, the queen invited Bellerophon to her chambers to seduce him. Knowing that if he accepted her offer it would be unjust and dishonorable, Bellerophon refused her, but he told her that he would not tell the king about it. Stheneboea, hurt and angered by his refusal, began a plot to destroy him.

When the king returned, the queen told him that Bellerophon had tried to seduce and rape her. Proteus was enraged, but he knew that killing a guest whom he had invited into his home would bring dishonor and shame upon his family. Instead, he chose to have someone else do the deed for him. Proteus dispatched Bellerophon on a mission to bring a message to King Iobates of southern Asia Minor. Bellerophon, ever the faithful servant, did as he was told and brought the sealed envelope to Iobates.

Upon his arrival, Bellerophon was treated to nine days of rest and relaxation. He also learned that the lands surrounding the kingdom were being devastated by a beast known as the Chimera. The Chimera was an unnatural beast with the body of a lion. Atop its neck sprouted both a lion's head and a goat's head that belched flames. Its tail was a grand serpent with fangs that dripped deadly poison. (A similar description is found in *Theogony* by Hesiod. The Chimera had three heads, also, including a head of a goat that belched fire. It is often similarly depicted in art as having a strong, agile body of a lion with a tail that ends in a serpent's head.) No one could escape the beast much less defeat it in combat. Once Bellerophon learned of the devastation of this horrific beast, he felt pity for the townspeople.

On the tenth day, King Iobates read the message sent by Proteus. The message repeated the lies of the queen and instructed Iobates to kill Bellerophon. Iobates, not wanting to bring shame and dishonor upon his house, decided to order Bellerophon to kill the Chimera. Surely the young warrior would not succeed and would die. In this way, Iobates could obey Proteus and not ruin the reputation of his family.

Because the order to kill the Chimera came from a king, Bellerophon was obliged to kill it or die trying. The night before he was to leave, he could not sleep. He tried to think of strategies to defeat the beast, but none seemed to hold any promise for him. He finally drifted off to sleep and into the land of dreams, where the gods speak to man.

In his dream, he was visited by Athena, daughter of Zeus. She spoke to him of the legendary winged horse Pegasus. Today's movie viewers identify this horse with the logo of TriStar Pictures. According to the myth, Pegasus was the strongest mount known to man and was believed to be too much for any mortal to ride. Athena told Bellerophon that he would be able to ride Pegasus if he used a special golden bridle. She handed that bridle to him in the dream and told him that Pegasus was not far from where he slept. Wishing him luck and telling him that he was favored by the gods, Athena vanished. When Bellerophon awoke, he held in his hand the very bridle that he had seen in the dream. He knew that he was truly favored by the gods and his courage grew.

Pegasus knew a hero when he saw one, for Theseus, the slayer of the Minotaur, had once had the honor of using the winged horse as a mount. When Bellerophon approached Pegasus with the bridle, the horse was not afraid of the heavily armed man. Instead he accepted Bellerophon and allowed him to climb upon his back. With a few powerful flaps of his mighty wings, Pegasus gave the rarest of gifts to early humankind—flight. Knowing that he was honor bound, Bellerophon wasted no time in hunting down the dreaded Chimera.

Bellerophon faced the beast from the air, a strategy he adopted so that he would be protected from the lion's fangs and poison spittle of the snake tail. Pegasus' swift and agile flying provided protection from the flames from the goat's head. This fantastical two-headed monster inspired the modern meaning of the word "chimera," which refers to an impossible or foolish whim. It is also used to describe any monster that is similar to Bellerophon's horrific opponent. Bellerophon shot many a well-aimed arrow into the body of the beast until it fell and left him victorious. Filled with pride and the knowledge that he had performed a great service to the people of the land, Bellerophon returned to Iobates to tell him of the news.

Iobates was shocked to see the hero return and quickly devised another mission for him. Bellerophon's next task was to fight the Amazons, a race of tall warrior women who exhibited a sharpshooter's aim and a weightlifter's strength. Iobates was certain that this quest would lead to Bellerophon's death. The brave hero accepted the quest and ventured to the land of the Amazons. Unfortunately for the Amazons, they were no match for the combined might of Bellerophon and his flying mount. Just like his first adversary, the Chimera, the Amazons have entered into our modern language. Today the word refers to a female warrior or a large, strong woman.

News traveled back to the kingdom that Bellerophon was victorious, so Iobates sent half of his army to ambush the hero before he reached the borders of his land, thereby avoiding the dishonor that would befall him for failing to kill Bellerophon. Although initially surprised by the attack, Bellerophon was able to vanquish the army single handedly. By the time he reached the gates of the house of Iobates he was angry and confused. "Why have you done this to me?" he asked. "Have I not done great deeds in your name and risked my life at your bidding?" At this confrontation, Iobates had an epiphany. He realized at that moment that Bellerophon was favored by the gods. No man could have performed these impossible tasks unless it was his fate to do so.

Iobates' fear of dishonor disappeared, and he showed the letter that Proteus had written to Bellerophon. The wronged hero forgave him because he knew that the real perpetrator of the crime was the queen of Argos. Iobates hugged him and offered him not only half of his kingdom, but also the hand of his daughter in marriage. Bellerophon accepted the offer and eventually became the king of Proteus' land when he and his wife died. Bellerophon continued to perform great deeds and ruled his people well, but somehow that wasn't enough. His greed became the cause of his downfall.

Bellerophon took great stock in the fact that he was favored by the gods and his deeds had proven that he was capable of much more than an ordinary man. The life of a king among normal men was not enough for him as his pride continued to swell. Slowly, the idea that he should visit the gods and live among them began to creep into his mind. He decided that he needed to reach the heights of Mount Olympus to be among those that favored him. It would be impossible for any normal man, for the climb to Olympus would kill any mortal. But Bellerophon would not climb to the top of Olympus, he would fly there.

Against the protests of his advisors and his wife, Bellerophon made preparations to ascend the mountain. His snobbish behavior began to anger those closest to him; he acted as if he was not one of them, but someone above them. When he left, many were glad to see him go and wished that he would never return for they were tired of feeling inferior. All the while the gods had been watching, and although he was favored and had performed great deeds, no mortal was to set foot in Olympus without being invited. Many of the gods were angered by Bellerophon's impudence, while others were amused and curious. Unfortunately, Zeus was not among the latter group.

Bellerophon mounted Pegasus and began his ascent. Although Pegasus was merely a beast, he knew that Bellerophon's folly was an offense to the gods, yet his master urged the horse upward, higher and still higher. Soon the city of the gods was in sight and Bellerophon swelled with pride instead of succumbing to the awe that mortals should feel when in the presence of such greatness. The mortal's insolence was the last straw for Zeus, and in a humbling gesture, he instructed a fly to sting the rump of Pegasus. Startled by the sting, Pegasus bucked Bellerophon from his back. The fall was sure to kill the hero, but Athena, who still had a soft spot for Bellerophon, softened the ground below him. Still, Bellerophon slammed into the ground with great force and was left crippled and without any idea of his identity. He wandered the land alone and confused, only a shadow of his former self, until he died. Pegasus continued his flight to Olympus, where he lived among the gods and was never seen again by mortal men.

Bellerophon's plight, although quite pitiable, offers a lesson to our modern society just as it did to the Ancient Greeks. This lesson cautions against hubris, or excessive pride. Examples of hubris are scattered throughout our culture as a warning to those who might succumb to greed and excessive pride. These examples are evident in movies such as *Wall Street*, in which Charlie Sheen stars as Bud Fox, a young stock broker who aspires to achieve the wealth and success of Gordon Gekko, a company takeover specialist and investor played by Michael Douglas. Like Bellerophon, Fox's desire to ascend to the level of investment gods alienates his family, namely his father. When Fox tries to rise up to his idol's level, Gekko destroys his career by reporting him to the Securities and Exchange Commission for insider trading.

History marks those who are great, not only by their deeds and abilities, but how they use them. Bellerophon's story illustrates the eternal problem of giving in to one's own greed, and it serves as a reminder of greed's repercussions. The effectiveness of the lesson can be seen in John Milton's *Paradise Lost* (1667) when he compares his own journey to Bellerophon's, but notes that he doesn't want it to end the same way.

Beowulf

◦

The tale of Beowulf is much older than the only surviving manuscript that bears the title. This manuscript, believed to have been written around 1000 A.D., is in the form of Old English and is believed to be the oldest surviving epic of British literature. Experts agree that it is an amalgamation of the feats of many great kings and warriors that were retold over hundreds of years. Oral versions of the stories were told by skalds, minstrels and storytellers who learned tales and told them in the form of songs. Over time these songs took on different forms as each skald embellished them, adding his own style and a bit of excitement to them. The tale continues to change as different cultures adapt it and retell it in their own style.

The tale is most likely based on kings and warriors from southern Scandinavia, so the story has a Germanic flavor to it. The basic premise behind the tale is the rise and fall of a hero. This would not seem very different from many of the myths covered in this text if not for the concept of aging that is infused into the tale. This concept was included because Norse mythology is particularly interested in the process of aging. For example, in one Norse myth, the gods lose the golden apples that keep them young and they become very disturbed by the effects that aging has on them. This tale may be testament to the fears and worries of the passage of time, and it poses the question: Is it better to die at the height of your success in a flash of heroism, or to die old and enfeebled? This same question emerges in the Who song "My Generation," when the band sings, "I hope I die before I get old." This issue of age and glory is timeless.

Beowulf was the nephew of the King of the Geats. Early in his life he proved himself as a warrior with his unearthly strength and prowess. He conquered many foes and went about the lands performing feats of heroism and bravery. He was particularly admired for his great feats of swimming. One spectacular tale tells of his defeat of sea monsters while swimming to the land of the Finns (Finland). Another tells of his defense of the land of Hetware and how he swam back to his ship carrying the armor of thirty opponents. It is obvious to any reader that Beowulf is an extraordinary man.

It is not long before Beowulf's uncle dies and he is offered the throne of his native land. Perhaps because he is still young and enjoys the adventurous life, or because he does not want the responsibility, Beowulf refuses the crown and gives it to Heardred, the son of the queen. Heardred is nothing more than a boy himself, so Beowulf offers to be his advisor and guardian until he becomes old and wise enough to rule on his own. This act illustrates Beowulf's sense of humility and his desire to protect the interests of his people in mind.

After some time, Beowulf learns of a trouble plaguing Denmark. For twelve years, the kingdom of Denmark had been ravaged by a terrible monster. Hrothgar, king of Denmark sent word of this man-eating beast, which could not be harmed by any weapon forged by man. Mariners told frightening tales about the monster they called Grendel. In these tales, they describe Grendel's horrifying practice of raiding Hrothgar's hall on a nightly basis and carrying people to his home in the wasteland. In the empty darkness the terrifying monster would devour his victims. Hrothgar could see no way to stop the devastation and desperately wished for aid in any form possible.

When he learned of Hrothgar's plight, Beowulf decided that he would journey to Denmark and see what he could do to stop the murders. He gathered a small group of his strongest and bravest warriors and prepared to set sail. His trip was rather uneventful until he reached the coast of Denmark. The kingdom was in a state of emergency and highly suspicious of all foreigners. Initially, the Danes thought he and his men were spies. Beowulf succeeded to convince the Danes that his intentions were honorable.

When the Danes learned that he intended to fight Grendel, he was taken to Hrothgar and treated to a hero's feast. Hrothgar told Beowulf that Grendel came at night and took his men, so Beowulf developed a strategy to defeat the beast. After the festivities, Beowulf and his men lay down in the hall and pretended to sleep. When the moon was high and all seemed quiet, Grendel approached the hall. With great stealth, the terrible beast opened the door, but no moonlight flooded into the hall because his frame was so massive that he filled the entire doorway.

Before Beowulf could get over the shock of the size and repulsive nature of the beast, it killed one of his men. At that point, the hall was a mass of confusion and terror. Composing himself, Beowulf attacked the monster. Before long, the two were locked in a hand-to-hand battle to the death. Grendel lunged forth with great clawed hands that Beowulf could barely escape as they threw each other to the ground. Finally, Beowulf grabbed Grendel's arm and, with all his might, tore it from its socket. The horrible creature howled in pain and ran from the hall to die at home, leaving a trail of blood behind him.

To celebrate their hero's victory, the Danes brought Beowulf and his men to another hall. Everyone in the kingdom believed that the horrors were over, but they did not realize that Grendel had a mother. Like Grendel, his mother was a hideous beast with unusual strength. She was devastated by the death of her son and emerged from her home in the moors to take revenge on his murderers. Upon entering the kingdom she stumbled upon the bloody, severed arm of her son. She snatched up the limb, which fueled her anger. As retaliation she kidnapped a Danish noblewoman and took her back to the moors.

The alarm was sounded and Beowulf, accompanied by his men, set off to find Grendel's mother and do away with her as well. Before he left, Hrothgar gave him the sword Hrunting, a powerful emblem of Danish rule. Hrothgar also offered words of advice against excessive pride, because he worried that Grendel's mother would be more formidable than her son in battle. Beowulf and his men tracked Grendel's mother to an underwater cavern.

Using his endurance and swimming skills, Beowulf dove into the water and located the cavern. When he surfaced in the cave, he barely had a chance to adjust to his surroundings before Grendel's mother attacked him. He tried to fight back with the sword Hrunting, but it shattered when he thrust it into her. The remains of other warriors lay scattered around the cave, and among them Beowulf found an ancient sword. He swiftly snatched up the sword and was able to destroy the monster with it. Then he found the lifeless body of Grendel and cut off his head as a trophy for Hrothgar. He was hailed as a hero in the land of the Danes, but his fame gained him greater rewards back home.

Shortly after his return to the Geats, Beowulf was saddened to hear that Heardred was killed in a battle with the Swedes. The throne was empty and he felt responsible to his country, so he took the throne and became king. His reign was one of peace and goodwill. Perhaps his reputation as a warrior deterred adversaries from starting wars with the king, for fifty peaceful years passed. After those years, Beowulf certainly showed signs of age, but all seemed well in his kingdom, until the dragon came.

A peasant had come across the dragon's treasure trove and stolen a golden cup. This affront attacked the dragon's pride, so it began to ravage the kingdom. Just like Grendel had done before, the dragon attacked at night and carried off its victims. Beowulf could not allow this devastation, so he decided to do battle with the dragon. Believing himself to be still capable in his old age, he initially refused the help of others. Luckily, his men convinced him that a retainer of warriors was befitting of such a great king.

The brave warriors approached the den of the dragon and Beowulf walked right in, shouting and calling out the dragon as if he were still a young warrior. The battle was furious, so much so that all except one of Beowulf's men fled the scene for fear. The young warrior Wiglaf stayed behind and let his duty to his aged king conquer his fear. The battle raged on until the dragon rushed upon Beowulf and shattered his sword. Beowulf wounded the dragon before it sank its fangs into his neck and released its poison into the king. Beowulf rallied his remaining strength and, together with Wiglaf, succeeded in killing the beast.

But they both knew that there was very little time before Beowulf would die. Beowulf gave his crown to Wiglaf and asked that his ashes be put in a shrine overlooking the sea. His wishes were honored and his body was laid upon a funeral pyre while warriors sang and cried in praise of their greatest king.

The tale of Beowulf is a powerful piece of prose that elegantly employs alliteration. Unfortunately it is also usually taught as an exercise in Old English and is drained of its power and life. In his 1976 book *Eaters of the Dead*, Michael Crichton alludes to this teaching practice in his retelling of the tale. He explains in the introduction that while teaching a classics course that would always include Beowulf as required reading, he and fellow teachers had tried to come up with imaginative and innovative retellings of Beowulf.

Crichton's version of Beowulf is told by an Arabic envoy who travels with a group of Vikings. The story places this group in a situation that is identical to Beowulf's, except Grendel's part is represented by a band of Neanderthal descendants led by a female witch doctor. Crichton chose names that were similar to the original ones in Beowulf—the Grendel character was named Wendol, Beowulf was Buliwyf, and Hygelac was Hyglak—and the story clearly has similarities to the original tale. It was made into a 1999 movie called *The Thirteenth Warrior* starring Antonio Banderas, which was not as successful as the book but retained much of the integrity of the tale.

The story of Beowulf has been retold in a post-apocalyptic setting as well. In 1999, Graham Baker directed a film called *Beowulf*, a science fiction update of the epic poem.

Beowulf's basic plot line has been duplicated in numerous movies of the Western genre. For example, in the 1953 classic *Shane*, the title character comes to town and stays with a settler family named the Starretts. When a nearby cattleman, Ryker, torments the family and tries to take their land, Shane defeats the enemy. In the 1985 movie *Silverado*, Beowulf's heroics are performed by a band of fighters played by Kevin Kline, Scott Glenn, Kevin Costner, and Danny Glover. In the comedy *Three Amigos*, Chevy Chase, Steve Martin, and Martin Short play film stars who help a Mexican village eliminate a band of outlaws that torment the village and abduct its residents.

Beowulf's tale of good versus evil appeals to people from different generations. It has a timeless quality that is repeated in modern stories, and it allows Beowulf to serve as our prototype for the selfless, valiant hero. Just as the medieval skalds retold the story in their own style, we continue to impart are own culture onto the tale.

The Birth of Hercules

Hercules

Before Hercules was a hero on a mission to complete the twelve labors, he had a colorful childhood. He was born out of deception and established his reputation of strength and victory early. It was an expectedly dramatic and romantic origin for an intriguing hero.

Hercules' mother was Alcmene, the daughter of King Electryon of Argos. She married her cousin, Amphitryon, but her unfortunate husband accidentally killed her father. Electryon's brother, Sthenelus, forced him into exile, so he and Alcmene fled to Thebes. Although his new wife acted loyally by following him into exile, she refused to sleep with him until he avenged the deaths of her brothers, who had been murdered by a group of pirates. Hercules promised that he would destroy her brothers' murderers.

While Amphitryon was off fulfilling his vow to his dutiful wife, Zeus stopped by Alcmene's house in the disguise of Amphitryon. He regaled her with tales of how he had avenged her brothers' deaths and then stepped into the bedroom to receive his reward. He enjoyed the fruits of his deception and did not want it to end. He convinced the sun god Helios to forgo his chariot ride of the day. According to Greek myth, Helios would harness a chariot to the sun and pull it up into the sky. Therefore he would bring dawn and dusk each day. When he unharnessed his chariot for the day at Zeus' request, the earth remained dark for thirty-six hours. It was a long, romantic night for Zeus and Alcmene.

Helios was the Greek god of the sun and the son of Hyperion. His name is the origin of the prefix "helio," so he influences several modern words. For example, "heliotropism" refers to the tendency of plants to turn or bend toward or away from sunlight. "Heliocentric" is the word that we use to describe our universe because the sun is at the center of it.

By the time Amphitryon arrived home the next night, Alcmene was worn out and unenthusiastic about his advances. They slept together, but she could not understand why he insisted on recounting the same stories he had told the night before. Realizing that something was amiss, Amphitryon went to a seer, who revealed Zeus' deception to him. Fearful of any reprisals from Zeus, Amphitryon refused to sleep with his wife again.

Soon Alcmene gave birth to two sons. One was fathered by Amphitryon, and the other by Zeus. Amphitryon's son was named Iphicles. Zeus' son was named Hercules, which meant "the Glory of Hera." Ironically, Hera was bitterly jealous of Zeus' illegitimate son. Throughout Hercules' life, she tormented him.

Zeus, who obviously had a habit of deceiving people, even tricked Hera into suckling his bastard child. The baby latched on and sucked with such force that Hera had to tear him from her breast. The milk that sprayed from her breast supposedly formed the Milky Way. Hera quickly began plotting against the future warrior. She sent two serpents to Hercules and Iphicles' cradle. Hercules showed his fighting spirit early in life by strangling the two snakes with his bare hands.

Because Hercules was the son of a god, he received training in warfare and the finer arts from the masters of these skills. He learned to drive the chariot from his foster father, Amphitryon. He also learned archery, boxing, strategy, manners, literature, and music. He also received helpful weapons from the gods, including an unbreakable shield.

The serpent incident was not the end of Hera's torment. When Hercules grew up, he married Megara and had two children. Hera drove him into a fit of madness, and in the rage, he murdered his wife and children. He was so ashamed of his actions that he asked for a way to atone for his terrible sin. The famous twelve labors of Hercules were his punishment for the crime.

The Creation of the World

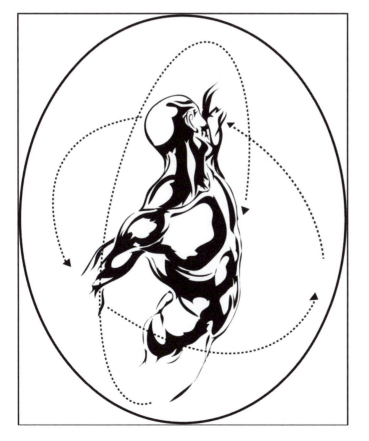

The Creation of Man

One of the functions of myth is to help humans come to grips with a past they have not experienced. Myths stretch as far back as the start of the universe and they offer a starting place to make an individual's place in history seem relevant. Every culture has a tale of its beginning, which is known as a creation myth. Everything from the well known "In the beginning . . ." to a great cosmic egg have been used to explain how the world started.

Myths that tell the story of the creation of the world are known as cosmologies. One of the most varied and interesting is that of the Norse people. Their account of the creation of the world also serves to explain the creation of the gods as well as humans. Although relatively short when compared to other creation myths, its compact size belies the complexity and richness of the tale.

According to the Norse, in the beginning, and for untold time thereafter, all that existed was a fiery heat and the cold of the void. This void was called Ginnungagap, meaning the yawning emptiness. Ice stretched as far as any eye, even the keenly perceptive immortal eye, could see. Ginnungagap grew and grew until its icy edge collided with the fiery heat of Muspell, the furnace of the universe. Muspell was believed to be both the source and the stealer of life. When Muspell and Ginnungagap collided, a great steam rose and blanketed a large amount of the universe.

Once the steam cooled, it formed the first two beings in the universe. The first one was Ymir the ice giant, who was massive and cruel. Since he was the first of all beings, he considered himself the de facto ruler of everything he saw. The second being formed from the steam was Audhumla, the giant cow that got its sustenance from licking the ice of Ginnungagap. Ymir drank Audhumla's milk to survive.

Ymir became the parent of a new race that emerged unpleasantly enough from the sweat of his armpits. These frost giants were as vile and evil as Ymir. Meanwhile, Audhumla continued to lick ice until one day she felt a bit of hair in the ice. She licked further and a day later a head was visible. Finally, a body was licked out of the ice and defrosted. This body was that of the first god, who called himself Bor, and his son Buri.

Buri was not able to create offspring alone like Ymir had, so he took a wife. He chose a frost giant named Bestla and she gave birth to three sons, Vili, Ve, and Odin. These brothers grew to become quite powerful and strong willed. Eventually, the behavior of Ymir and his band of frost giants had become so repugnant that the brothers felt it was time to act. Together they stormed Ymir's home and slew him. The universe was drenched in his blood and all but a few of the frost giants were drowned. The brothers ripped apart the corpse of Ymir and flung a great chunk of his carcass into Ginnungagap. There the carcass hardened and formed the earth.

Next they created the sky by tossing Ymir's skull upward, where it filled with his last breath. Four dwarves were created to hold the skull aloft and trap the breath within. They took his bones and threw them at the earth to create the mountains. His teeth were boulders and his blood became the water, which brought life to the barren earth. By smashing and scraping his bones together, the dwarves created sparks that shot into the top of the inside of the giant's skull. There the sparks remained and at night could be seen as stars. The sun and moon were placed in the heavens, and they would have stayed in place forever if two hungry wolves had not come looking for them. The wolves chased the sun and the moon so that they were forced to go across the sky every day.

The few giants that remained lived among the mountains and bore new children. Some were as sinister as their forefathers, while others displayed a more gentle nature. No matter how gentle their nature, they remained great warriors. Vili, Ve, and Odin ventured across the newly formed earth and eventually came upon two trees that had sprung up along the seashore. One was an ash tree and the other an elm. From these two trees they carved a man and a woman. Although beautiful to look at, they had no life within them, so Odin came forth and put his lips to those of the statues. He breathed forth and brought life to them. Vili wished for thinking, feeling beings, and so he gifted them with intelligence and emotions, while Ve gave them their senses so they could enjoy the beauty and wonder the newly created world had in store for them.

Later, Vili and Ve seem to vanish into the background, while their younger brother Odin played a larger role as the all-father, ruler of the gods. Like most all-father gods, Odin had sons and daughters with many women, but he remained married and truly in love with one, his wife Frigga. She bore him many sons and loved him dearly.

Odin became all-father to the Aesir. This group of gods lived in golden Asgard, which floats above the earth and is connected to it by the rainbow bridge Bifrost. Soon, another group of gods called the Vanir appeared. Perhaps they were the offspring of Vili and Ve, but their parentage remains unclear. At first they vied for control of Midgard, which is what they call earth. Eventually, the two groups decided to mix and get along.

The latter parts of this myth not only explain the creation of humankind and the eventual formation of the Norse pantheon, but they also provide a framework for social interaction between different groups. The Aesir, who are seen as warlike, are complemented by the Vanir, who are typically seen as fertility and nature gods. These two come together to merge their strengths. This union promotes a stronger group in an immediate sense, and it provides an example of diversity leading to better societies. One small group cannot breed among itself for very long without eventually destroying itself. Even the early gods learned, or were forced, to mix with the giants in order to create offspring.

As for the creation of the world, this is not the only myth in which the carcass of an evil being is separated into pieces and used to make the world. In Babylonian myth, the great hero-god Marduk slays Tiamat, the evil dragon, and creates the world from her body. This act, like the one performed by the three sons of Buri, illustrates the process of harnessing evil or chaos, destroying it, and reforming it into something useful. Order is brought into being and things are collected and redispersed to solve the problem. One might say that the myths of creation are really myths of problem solving.

In Egypt, there were many versions of the creation myth. In one account, the world consisted of a chaos of waters from which a primeval mound arose to establish order in the world. In another version, the creator spirit fashioned gods from his sweat and people from his tears.

In the epic Finnish myth *Kalevala*, the world is created by Ilmatar, who descends from the heavens and lives on the sea. A bird lays eggs on Ilmatar's knee, but they break when she moves. The pieces of the eggs form the sun, moon, and physical world.

Hindu creation myths also involve creating order from chaos. In one version, Purusha's cut-up body becomes the elements of the universe. Some versions describe heaven and earth as the parents of the gods.

Japanese myth describes the earth as being primeval ooze from which heaven and earth were fashioned. As gods began to populate the heavens, the youngest ones, named Izanagi and Izanami, created the islands of Japan.

In Micronesia there were several versions of the creation myth. In one account, the creator god's body forms the Earth, sky, sun, and moon. Another account describes the world as being a product of the Spider Lord, Nareau, and the younger Nareau.

The creative act is often seen as a mysterious process in our society. Artists, writers, and inventors face a world in which they are often misunderstood. Oftentimes the creative process is an arduous one that takes research and the collection of disparate pieces, followed by the careful placement of those pieces into a coherent, ordered composition that contains meaning over and above the parts. For example, industrial musicians of the late 1980s and early 1990s such as Björk, took sounds not normally considered as musical and arranged them in such a fashion as to be considered mainstream music. In the same way, Picasso and others created works that defied their contemporaries' concept of art.

Movies that study the act of creation are easy to find, but few really explore the inner mind of the creator as well as the 2001 movie *Pollock*, which tells the story of the postmodernist painter Jackson Pollock. The concept of genesis is prevalent in science fiction as well. *Star Trek II: The Wrath of Khan* (1982) focuses on the Genesis Project, which had the goal of creating a habitable planet from a barren planet.

In mythology, only gods can create a new world. Today, computer games like *SimCity* allow users to create their own worlds. Perhaps this is a sign of what is around the corner for humanity.

Cronus and His Offspring

The myth of Cronus and his offspring may be the root of the classic father-son conflict. As the father ages and becomes weaker, the son grows into manhood and becomes the physical superior of his father. This theme resonates throughout mythology and is seen in real life as well. Most cases of this theme involve humans coming to grips with the ascendance of their sons and daughters or plotting to avoid that fate. In the tale of Cronus, the audience realizes that humans are not the only beings subject to this pattern. In fact, the myth of Cronus may serve as the template for all of the tales, plays, and songs that describe this age-old theme.

To understand the full story, some details need to be explained first. According to Greek mythology, the Titans were the first beings to inhabit the earth. Giant in stature, they possessed great power and each had their own sphere of control. Cronus was the leader of the Titans. Under his rule they became cruel and used their powers without respect for the universe or its inhabitants.

In Roman myth, Cronus was represented by Saturn, who lent his name to the sixth planet from the sun. The word "saturnine" was inspired by people who were born under the supposed influence of the planet Saturn. These people were believed to be gloomy, morose, and sluggish, which is what saturnine means today. Since Saturn's rule was considered a happy, peaceful time, the word "saturnian" arose to describe a prosperous, happy, and contented period. Around December 17 each year, ancient Romans celebrated winter solstice with a festival in honor of Saturn. The revelry that took place during the celebration gave rise to the modern word "saturnalia," which means a period of unrestrained, often orgiastic revelry.

Cronus was married to his sister, Rhea. One day, Rhea announced that she was going to bear their child. Cronus consulted the Fates because they knew all that was going to happen until the end of time. Unfortunately, the Fates told Cronus something he did not want to hear: he would have a child who would be more powerful than him. In fact, the Fates told him, one of his offspring would overpower him and take his place. With this newfound knowledge, Cronus decided he would eliminate his offspring to ensure his authority and power. When Rhea gave birth, Cronus asked to see the child. Rhea handed the infant god to Cronus, and he swallowed the child whole. By consuming his own child Cronus believed he could not only avert fate, but also gain the power of his offspring.

Rhea attempted again and again to have a child. Every time she gave birth, Cronus swallowed the baby whole. Rhea became frustrated and devised a plan to keep a child. When she next gave birth to a boy, she quickly replaced the boy with a large rock. Cronus grabbed the swaddled rock and swallowed it. Rhea had secretly sent the baby to an island cave where he was taken care of by animals and spirits. The chief caretaker was Melissa, who brought the infant honey and ambrosia. Rhea named the infant Zeus, and he grew strong on the island under Melissa's care.

As Zeus grew, he was visited by Rhea and told about what his cruel father had done. She also told him about the Titans and one-eyed giants known as the Cyclops that Cronus had imprisoned and enslaved. Zeus was deeply angered by his father's ruthlessness and immediately set out to right Cronus' wrongs. He started by freeing the Cyclops and other Titans from their bondage. Next, he faced his father in combat.

Zeus grappled with his father and forced him to vomit up his siblings. They had grown to adulthood and were finally free for the first time since they were born. These newly liberated gods, along with Zeus, fled from the wrath of Cronus. Once they reached safety, they plotted to overthrow the Titans so that they would never have to live in fear again. The gods recognized the heroic actions of Zeus and declared that even though he was the youngest, he was the strongest and most capable leader of all of them. Even with his incredible might and the aid of his brothers and sisters, Zeus was not sure he could defeat his father.

Zeus and his siblings would not have to fight the Titans alone; help came from those he had freed from bondage. The Cyclops were master metalworkers and knew the secrets of magic. For Zeus, they forged a countless number of bolts that held within them the power of lightning and thunder. These carefully crafted weapons made the already formidable Zeus even more powerful.

With his thunderbolt in hand, Zeus led his siblings into battle with the Titans. The violent combat ended in the banishment of the evil Titans and the dethroning of Cronus. He was banished to Tartarus, a land that exists out of time. Similar to the concept of limbo, this infernal abyss below Hades inspired the word "tartar," which refers to someone who is violent and irritable.

The other Titans were forced to make up for their evil acts by performing services for the inhabitants of earth. The most famous example is Atlas, the Titan of strength, who was forced to carry the heavens upon his shoulders for the rest of time. The word "atlas" became the standard for books of maps when sixteenth-century cartographer Gerhardus Mercator included an illustration of Atlas holding up the heavens on the cover of one of his map books and called it *Atlas*. This strapping giant also inspired the word "atlantean," which appropriately describes something strong.

Having established freedom for his siblings, Zeus chose Mount Olympus as the home of the gods. From up high, he could watch all of the earth and keep guard over any situation. He became the king of the gods and shared dominion with his brothers Hades and Poseidon.

As Zeus grew in power, he began to acquire some of Cronus' bad behaviors. In fact, he tried to stop his daughter Athena from being born because the Fates told him that she would be wiser than him. The whole episode shows that the struggle between parent and offspring may take different forms, but it is an inevitable part of life and progeny.

Cuchulain

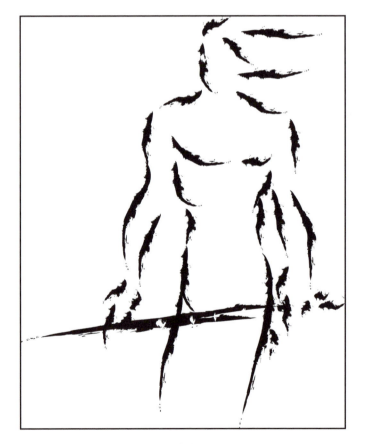

Cuchulain

Rarely does a hero command so much admiration that his entire life becomes part of the mythology of a people. The Celtic hero Cuchulain is one such hero. In Cuchulain's story, the reader becomes intimately aware of the greatest aspects of humanity as well as the pain, tragedy, and mistakes that we make as well. Cuchulain has been described as the Irish Achilles. Certainly, there are a number of legitimate reasons for this comparison; however, it oversimplifies the story of this hero.

The adventure stories about Cuchulain were first written down in the *Ulster Cycle*, which was written around A.D. 1100. Cuchulain epitomizes the concept of the Irish hero, with his skills, intellect, and ability to harness magical powers. In the stories, of which there are more than a few, the audience gets to see a boy grow into manhood and greatness, while learning lessons about right and wrong. Additionally, the very human side of the hero is revealed, such as his bashfulness around the women who adore him and fling themselves at him. The stories explain the crucial choices that he has to make, and they expose his sorrow and anger when he chooses poorly. When compared to Achilles from the *Iliad*, Cuchulain's fully fleshed out character seems altogether more real.

Bards, ancient storytellers and singers, served as historians and traveled from county to county trading stories. They are the ones who are responsible for the survival of this myth and most myths in general. As the bards told the myth, it would change as they elaborated some details and forgot others. By repeatedly telling and changing the myths, these storytellers elevated a warrior from the first century B.C. into a superhero who could single-handedly defend an entire city.

To understand the myths, it is important to know that the warring clans and families of the ancient Irish myths were just as bound by the codes of honor and law as the Greeks and Romans. Certain individuals were permitted rights based on their positions. These codes of honor helped guide the conduct of the characters in the myth.

Cuchulain's story begins with Conchobhar, the king of Ulster. Conchobhar ruled over the emerald isle, but his hold was tenuous at best. Because of the unrest and changing loyalties of various clans, the king needed a trusted and wise advisor. He chose Cathbad, a famous druid whose magic skills were only rivaled by his ability to foresee the future and advise the best course to take in a situation.

Conchobhar had a sister named Deichtire, whose beauty was legendary. She was intimate with the Irish god Lugh, who was the master of light. Lugh was a sun god whose prowess in battle was unmatched. Deichtire gave birth to a son and named him Setanta, but he was not an ordinary boy. Although he was curious and enjoyed physical activity, he could swim like a fish since birth. He also looked a little unusual. He had seven fingers on each hand, seven toes on each foot, and seven pupils in each eye. When he began to play with other children, his true abilities emerged.

The children of the town would engage in mock battles using harmless swords and javelins. Setanta had just reached the age when he could join the other children in their mock battles. As he moved onto the field, other children immediately set upon him. Setanta easily defeated them. Seeing their friends being routed by the small boy, other kids attacked Setanta. He defeated them as well. Wave upon wave of children attacked the boy, but they could not beat him. That day, Setanta defeated the entire army of children on his own. If the adults of the town were not aware of his skills, the children certainly were.

As time passed, Conchobhar's power over his people began to wane. Many saw that his nephew Setanta was the only rightful heir to the position, but the boy seemed utterly disinterested in ruling a kingdom. He was more interested in playing and practicing for battle. The adults in the kingdom had no idea of his abilities until the day he went with the king to visit with a famous blacksmith named Culann.

The blacksmith had a marvelous estate that he wished to keep safe. To ensure security, he had huge war dogs that guarded the gates of the estate. The biggest and most powerful war dog in the pack stood at the front gate. Setanta strode up to the gates and entered because he assumed he would be safe. The dog immediately attacked him and he ran to the front of the estate. Because he wore a traveling cloak, no one recognized the boy so they watched as the dog caught up to him. The audience was amazed as the boy dodged the fangs of the dog and kept it at bay with well-aimed punches. Finally, Setanta became angry and his rage boiled up within him. He seized the giant dog by the neck and smashed its head against a stone column. The audience stood in shock at the exploits of this stranger. They were doubly amazed when he removed his cloak and revealed that he was only a boy.

Conchobhar rushed to his nephew's side to inspect him for wounds but found none. Culann went to the side of the dead dog and said, "Now what shall I do? I have no great guardian for my gate. My most prized dog is dead at the hands of this amazing child." Sensing the anguish in the man's voice, Setanta came up with the only plan he could see as fair. "I will take the place of your dog, sir, until a replacement can be found. I offer this as payment for the pain I have caused," he said. Culann looked at the boy in wonder, then said to the king, "So young, and this boy already surpasses grown men in strength and in honor. I cannot accept your offer. I shall find a replacement, but your honor will be made clear this day. You shall be called Cuchulain, 'The Hound of Culann'." The blacksmith continued, "Those who were here today will know why it is an honorable title. Those who were not here will learn from the tales of your greatness, for I wager you will be great." At that moment, Cathbad had a vision: Cuchulain would be great for sure, but his life would be short.

Soon, Cuchulain became known across Ireland for his skill in battle. His fame was bolstered by his battle rage. When he became enraged, he changed into a beastly being that was horrible to behold. One eye went inward and the other bulged out and turned red. His skin became deep red and his muscles contorted beneath his skin. His hair became wild and dripped blood while his mouth grew huge and bristled with sharp teeth. He became unstoppable on the battlefield, and so great was the power of his rage that no man could come near him without fearing death. Upon return from the battlefield, Cuchulain was escorted by women and dunked in several vats of cold water. The first would explode from his heat, the second would boil over, and finally, the third would cool him off and bring him back to normal.

In his normal state, Cuchulain was adored by all the women he met. He was perfect in face and stature. Most interesting and human about him was that he was extremely bashful around woman. As the story tells it, he blushed and averted his gaze when a woman showed him her breasts. Soon, the women learned that they could curb his battle frenzy by approaching him in the nude. His embarrassment toned down his rage and allowed them to place him in the vats. The women increasingly lusted after the young hero and he gained quite a female fan club. One woman, however, hated Cuchulain with a passion, for he was gaining fame as a great force in battle. Her name was Medb, warrior-queen of Connacht and sworn enemy of Ulster, the home of Cuchulain.

Before his abilities reached their pinnacle, Cuchulain fell in love with Emer, the daughter of Fogall. Fogall's kingdom was near Dublin, so Cuchulain traveled there to ask for Emer's hand in marriage. Fogall wanted nothing to do with it, so he told Cuchulain that he had yet to prove his skills by training in Scotland with their famous champion, Domhall. This was Fogall's crafty way of getting the young man off the island and away from his daughter.

Cuchulain did as he was told, only to learn from Domhall that his training must be done under the guidance of Scathach in the Land of Shadows. He made the harrowing trip to the Land of Shadows and served under Scathach for over a year. During that time he seemed to forget Emer, as Fogall had hoped, and he became the lover of Scathach's daughter, Uathach. After a series of battles and tests of cunning with Uathach's sister, Cuchulain proved himself the better and left the Land of Shadows to return to Emer. Fogall had not expected the hero to return and was not interested in giving his daughter to the brash young warrior, so he sent a band of his best warriors against Cuchulain. Cuchulain defeated them all and Fogall killed himself in anger. With this victory, Cuchulain was considered the greatest warrior, unbeatable by anyone.

Years later, Queen Medb's forces planned to destroy Ulster and kill Cuchulain. She enlisted witches to cast curses upon him and his compatriots before staging an all out attack on Ulster. This was not the worst of Cuchulain's problems. He was racked with horrible guilt over the death of his own son. His son and he battled one another in the darkness one night, each of them stubbornly refusing to say his name. In the end Cuchulain killed his son and found out afterward who the stranger was. Furthermore, the goddess of battle, Morrigan, had fallen in love with him and he shunned her. Enraged, she turned against the hero just before the greatest battle of his life.

Even with all these things against him, Cuchulain managed to defend Ulster from the attack of an entire army all by himself. When he was wounded and lost blood, he tied himself to a stone so he could stand and fight. Eventually he died, standing with his sword in his hand. Morrigan, in the form of a crow, settled on his shoulder to proclaim him dead, and the remaining forces of Medb removed his head and right hand. Eventually, the pieces were retrieved and buried with his body.

The theme of a warrior who does his job and becomes dangerous or an outcast to his own people is a particularly painful one for many modern Americans. The veterans of the Vietnam War are a living example of that theme. Many veterans of the war tell stories of poor treatment upon their return, ranging from alienation to abuse from the general public. Like Cuchulain, these veterans were sometimes forced to commit acts that are considered barbaric in order to survive in times of war. This type of situation is portrayed in movies such as *Saving Private Ryan*, *Platoon*, and *Full Metal Jacket*. Each movie portrays its protagonist as a warrior who learns the psychological cost of warfare before returning home. Cuchulain learned the costs of war but was forced to carry on.

All too often we fail to recognize the whole person when they achieve greatness. For all his fame and glory, Cuchulain had frailties. He was a great fighter, but he had trouble controlling himself. He was handsome and powerful, but he was also bashful and easily embarrassed. He was stubborn to the point that it cost him a son, but he also won a war. He was a hero, but he was human. This lesson is relevant in today's celebrity-obsessed culture. As people are bombarded with the image of fame and perfection on a daily basis, the average person is led to believe that celebrities live perfect lives and are somehow proficient in everything. This could not be further from the truth. Just like Cuchulain, no matter what level of fame, proficiency, or authority people attain, they are still human.

Cupid and Psyche

❦

The tale of Cupid and Psyche is the basis for many "boy meets girl, boy falls in love with girl, boy loses girl" stories. It is a tale of love and the depths to which lovers will go to be together. Many people see it as an allegory for the bond between the soul and love because Cupid, the son of Aphrodite, was love personified and Psyche, when translated in Greek, means soul.

Their story begins in a kingdom by the sea. A king was blessed with three daughters, each of whom was more beautiful than the one who preceded her. They grew up and were known far and wide for their great beauty. The older and middle daughters were taken as brides by the most powerful princes in the land, while the youngest and most beautiful of the sisters remained unmarried. Her name was Psyche and her beauty was so great that there was no man who felt worthy of her attention, much less her hand in marriage.

No suitors came to Psyche's door, yet anyone she passed on the streets was enraptured by her. Crowds gathered simply to catch a glimpse of her and rumors began to spread that she was the incarnation of the goddess of beauty. Psyche was not full of pride, nor was she arrogant about her looks, but this mattered very little to Aphrodite, the beautiful goddess of love. The goddess was so angered by the reaction of the crowds that thoughts of harm and despair came to her. She would not be upstaged by a mere mortal, no matter what beauty she possessed.

Plotting a devious plan for revenge, Aphrodite called upon her son, Cupid. "Cupid, my faithful son, gather up your bow and arrows, for I have a job for you," she called to the winged god of love. Cupid answered her summons and arrived carrying his quiver of special arrows. These arrows did not harm their victims physically. Instead, they brought an aching love for whomever Cupid wished. This could be the most wonderful feeling if the love was mutual, or the most painful if not. Aphrodite ordered Cupid to make Psyche fall in love with the ugliest and meanest man in the world. Cupid was a dutiful son, so he packed up his bow and went to find the girl so that he could follow his mother's directions.

Cupid found her and snuck up to her bed, for he could not be seen or heard by mortals if he so wished. He pulled an arrow from the quiver and notched it in the bow. Just then, Psyche turned in her sleep and her great beauty startled Cupid, which caused him to fumble the arrow and poke his finger with its tip. Instantly, he fell in love with her and could think of nothing more than spending eternity with her. He suddenly snapped out of his daydream for he realized that he could not do what his mother had asked. At that moment he decided to devise a plan to have her for himself and keep her safe from his mother's wrath.

Cupid returned home and spoke nothing of the matter. Days passed and Aphrodite watched the young Psyche. No men came to see her and it seemed that she was unaffected by Cupid's work. Aphrodite planted seeds of worry in the hearts of Psyche's parents. They wished for her to be married to a great king and were becoming alarmed at the lack of suitors. They decided that they would consult an oracle, who told them that Psyche would not marry a mortal, but a thing powerful enough to overtake a god.

This news put the parents into a state of despair and worry. What manner of beast was to take their most beautiful daughter as a wife? The oracle did not answer but motioned to the mountain beyond their kingdom. Psyche realized that somehow she had offended Aphrodite. She wished only that no harm should come to her family or her kingdom. She begged her family to disown her and bring her to the beast on the mountain, but they refused until the omens came. The omens made it clear to them that they must give up their most prized princess, so they led her to the mountain and left her there to meet her fate.

When her parents had left, Psyche let herself cry. Her sadness was so great that the very elements came to her aid: the winds dried her tears and caressed her, and the dew formed in pools for her to drink. She fell asleep then and rested peacefully. When the sun rose, she awoke to find that she was no longer on the side of the mountain, but in a valley full of rolling grasses and flowers of every color known to man. Birds sang sweet melodies and in their songs Psyche heard the call of someone. The voice was hidden and beautiful. It called her forward and moved in the distance. Psyche followed until she reached a beautiful shining palace. This place was far greater than any kingdom she had ever imagined.

The voice was that of Cupid, but the god remained hidden. He said "All that you wish shall be yours. I shall love you always and with all my heart so long as you never see my true form. Do not ask to see me. Only know that when I lay with you in dark night, I love you as truly as I can. Will you abide by my offer and be my wife?" "Yes" answered Psyche. With that, numerous nymphs and sprites came to attend to the bride of Cupid. They cared for her every need and she wanted for nothing. Each night when the sun went down and the halls became too dark to see, Cupid returned to his palace and settled with his wife. She learned to love him dearly and although she asked to see him a few times, she never got the urge to break her promise.

The days turned to months and Psyche's thoughts turned to her family. She wished to ease their worries and let them know that she was not only fine, but happier than she had ever been. She worked out a deal with Cupid that allowed her sisters to visit her at the palace. She sent word to her sisters and asked them to come visit her. They came as quickly as they could and were aided by the magic winds.

When they saw the palace they were stunned by its beauty and splendor. Then they became jealous and petty. They each believed that they deserved as much as Psyche. They questioned her over and over until they found the information they needed to ruin Psyche. They asked where her husband was and what he looked like. They questioned why she could not describe him and why he wouldn't come to meet them. She explained that she had promised not to look at him or even try to see him. With this, the sisters reminded her that she was to marry something that could overcome the gods themselves. What if this beast was so ugly that it wished not to be seen? What if it was tricking her into an evil scheme? They sowed the seeds of doubt with Psyche and now she was considering a plan to get a look at her lover. They told her to wait until he fell asleep, then light a lamp and see his face. They told her to bring a dagger in case she had to slay him. Psyche was disgusted by their idea and sent them away, but the seed had been planted and the jealous sisters' plan slowly grew within her heart.

One night, in a moment of weakness, she tried to see Cupid. Instead of seeing a beast, she saw the most handsome face ever. She was so taken with him that she shook and dripped some oil from the lamp on his shoulder. This burned him and woke him up, and he looked at his love with disappointment and flew away. Realizing the gravity of her mistake, Psyche tried to catch him but found that the palace and its gardens were disappearing as Cupid disappeared in the distance.

All alone, Psyche began her journey to the kingdoms of her sisters. She told them that their evil plan had ruined her and continued on to search for her lost love. She headed for the temple of Aphrodite to make amends and try to gain her favor. Aphrodite still held a grudge and was even more angered when she saw that Psyche's beauty had not faded. She agreed to help her if she performed a few tasks. Psyche agreed but found that these tasks were intended to make her fail.

The first was to separate three types of grain into three piles. The grains filled a room and to separate them accurately would take years. Psyche began to cry as she worked in vain, but Demeter, the goddess of grain, heard her sobbing and took pity on Psyche. She sent forth a great army of ants that swarmed upon the grain pile and carefully separated the grains into three piles by the next morning. When Aphrodite came to gloat, she found Psyche sleeping next to the grain piles and became furious. She knew that the girl had received help but she could not prove it.

Following the first task, Psyche had to gather wool from enchanted sheep. She was able to do this with the aid of water spirits who felt sorry for her. For the final task, Aphrodite told Psyche to go to Hades and retrieve some of Persephone's beauty in a box. Knowing that she could not return from Hades alive, Psyche figured it was over, but she received help from an unknown source. This source revealed a way for Psyche to return alive but warned her not to look in the box. She got the box but did not heed the warning because she thought that if she were more beautiful, perhaps Cupid would take her back. So she opened the box and fell into a deep sleep.

Cupid, now healed from his wounds, found Psyche and begged Zeus to bring her back to life. In turn, Zeus asked Aphrodite to let the tests be done. He then restored Psyche to life. She was brought to Olympus and drank ambrosia, which allowed her to become immortal, and the lovers married.

In Greek myth, Cupid was known as Eros, the god of erotic or sexual love and fertility. He was depicted as a handsome young man with a bow and a quiver full of his enchanted arrows. By Hellenistic times, the image of Eros had changed into a cherubic boy with wings. Many times he was portrayed blindfolded to indicate that his shots were random. This portrayal is the one that we associate with Cupid today.

Psyche today is the word for the human spirit or soul. In psychiatry, psyche refers the concept of the mind serving as the center of emotion, thought, and behavior. The princess' name is the origin for other words, such as psychedelic and psychic.

Love stories like this are not uncommon in myth, but the fact that the woman must undergo tasks is special. Numerous tales of heroes performing great deeds for a woman's love are easy to find. This one turns the tables with surprising results. Seen from an allegorical point of view, this story is about the human soul's encounter with love and passion.

Deucalion

∿

It does not pay to anger Zeus. Take the story of King Lycaon. In arrogance and disrespect for Zeus, Lycaon had his sons sacrifice a human child and offer it to Zeus. This outraged the god and he killed the sons and turned Lycaon into a wolf. Unfortunately, Lycaon's contemptuous behavior had done its damage by informing Zeus of the degree to which humankind had degenerated. He decided to wipe the slate clean by destroying humankind with a flood.

Luckily, not all of mankind would be annihilated by the flood. Prometheus learned of Zeus's plans and warned his son, Deucalion, of the impending disaster. Because Deucalion and his wife Pyrrha were good and pious people, Prometheus instructed them to save themselves by building an ark. In some versions of the myth, the couple learned of the flood through an oracle of Themis. The couple wisely took the advice, built a boat, and filled it with provisions.

Zeus created an intense, crashing thunderstorm that destroyed all of the crops. Then he enlisted Poseidon's help to overflow the rivers, which washed away houses and buildings. Rapidly the rivers and seas obscured the landscape and entire cities lay beneath the water. All of the land animals perished and the birds drowned because they had nowhere to rest. Suddenly Deucalion and Pyrrha were the only ones left in the world.

After nine days and nights, the couple landed on Mount Parnassus near Delphi. The rain continued until Zeus realized that the only survivors were Deucalion and Pyrrha. Since he had rid the earth of the disrespectful humans, he stopped the rain and allowed the rivers to recede. The couple thanked Zeus by offering a sacrifice to him. This act did not go unnoticed. Zeus sent Hermes to speak with them. He learned of their loneliness and desire for other people. They learned through Zeus or another oracle that they could repopulate the earth by throwing the bones of their "great mother" behind them. They interpreted "great mother" to mean the earth, and her "bones" to be stones. As they threw the stones behind them, the ones that Deucalion threw transformed into men, and the ones that Pyrrha threw became women. Animal life spontaneously sprang from the earth once the moisture evaporated.

In this restored world, Deucalion and Pyrrha began a family. Of their four children, their son Hellen became the founder of the town Hellas in Thessaly. The inhabitants of the town were the ancestors of the Greeks, and Hellen's offspring became the leaders of the Greek tribes. Of his sons, Dorus ruled over the Dorians, Aeolus followed his father and ruled over Thessaly, and Xythos reigned over the Peloponnesians. Xythos' sons, Achaeus and Ion, loaned their names to the Achaean and Ionian tribes of Greece. In brief, the descendents of Deucalion and Pyrrha became the leaders of the early Greek world.

The Greek story of Deucalion's flood and the Hebrew story of Noah's Ark are quite similar. Like Deucalion, Noah was instructed to build a boat to endure an impending flood that would be sent by a god to punish humankind. Interestingly, most cultures have their own stories of a Great Flood, in which a god sends a flood to punish humans for misbehavior and a pious person or couple is saved from destruction by being instructed to build a vessel. The flood destroys the sinful race and a new, more pious race is begun by the survivors.

The ancient Sumerian culture's flood story can be found in the epic of *Gilgamesh*. Before the Sumerian gods flooded the overpopulated earth, the god Ea spoke to Utnapishtim in a dream. Ea instructed him to build an immense ark and fill it with "the seed of all living creatures." After six days and nights of rain, Utnapishtim, his family, and the animals bobbed along the surface of the water-covered earth. When the ark came to rest on the top of a mountain, Utnapishtim sent three birds in search of land. When the last bird did not return, they emerged from the ark to repopulate the earth.

The Hindu version of the flood myth revolved around Manu, who was the first human. He kindly saved a small fish from a larger fish, and in return, the small fish warned Manu about a looming flood and instructed him to build a boat and load it with representatives of each species of animal. The fish led Manu to a mountain, known as Manu's Descent, where Manu was able to survive the flood that washed away all of the living creatures.

In a final example, the Aztecs told the story of a man named Tapi, who lived in the Valley of Mexico. He lived a virtuous life, so the Creator warned him of the flood and gave him a plan of escape. Tapi's neighbors thought he had gone insane when he built a boat for himself, his wife, and a pair of every animal. When the valley flooded, Tapi and his passengers were the only survivors.

Deucalion is an example of a universal myth. The story exists in most cultures, but the details are slightly different. Deucalion may have a different name in the Babylonian version and the survivors may save themselves by floating in hollow reeds in the Navajo version, but the emphasis of the myth is the same: humankind is eradicated for bad behavior and only the pious can escape the flood to restart humanity.

Dionysus

The story of Dionysus can be seen as a mirror that reflects the best and worst humankind has to offer. Dionysus symbolizes the connections between heaven and earth, life and death, ecstasy and madness, and mortality and life everlasting. Often overlooked in the grand scheme of Greek mythology, the character and stories of Dionysus are quite potent and have had a lasting effect on the culture and belief systems of Western society. As we learn more about this paradoxical character, we will see how his role changes and how that role can be seen as the root from which a great world religion sprouted.

There are commonly two versions of the story of Dionysus' birth. Each leads to the same result: the explanation of his title "the twice-born." The fact that these two separate stories exist only adds to the paradoxical nature of Dionysus.

The first story tells of one of the many trysts between Zeus and a mortal woman, Semele, who became pregnant with Zeus' child and attracted the anger of the ever-jealous Hera, the wife of Zeus. Zeus had come to know Semele by never truly revealing his whole self to her. It was a known fact that no mortal could truly gaze upon the father of the gods in all his glory. The sight of him would be too much and the mortal would be destroyed by his radiance. Therefore, Zeus carefully covered himself and made sure that it was dark, and Semele never peeked at him. He was very careful because he loved her and did not wish to harm her. Hera felt quite differently about Semele, especially when she found out about her pregnancy. She hatched a plan to rid the world of Semele and the unborn offspring of her unfaithful husband.

Hera took the form and manner of one of Semele's nursemaids and gained her confidence. She asked Semele if she had ever truly seen her lover's face. Semele explained that she was never to look upon the face of her lover, for he said bad things would happen. Hera began to plant ideas in Semele's mind. "How can you know if he loves you like he loves Hera? He shows himself to her," she mused. After continuous prodding, Semele agreed that she would beg Zeus to reveal himself to prove his love for her.

Later that evening, Zeus granted her wish and she was instantly consumed by divine fire and lightning. From her smoldering remains came a vine that encircled and protected her womb. Inside was the child of Zeus, who took the baby and instantly loved it. He feared for the infant's safety, for he knew that the situation was caused by Hera's jealous trickery. The infant would not be safe anywhere in its helpless state, so Zeus cut open his own thigh and placed his child in it for safe keeping. He stitched it closed and waited until the baby was stronger. Later he cut his thigh open and the child was brought into the world a second time. Therefore he was born two times: once born by a mortal woman, then born by an immortal father. This is how Dionysus got the name "twice-born."

The second story is a bit more complex than the first but really gives the reader a strong sense of the ties between Dionysus as a symbol and provider of life after death and man's ties to divinity. It was believed that early in the time of the gods, before humans were made, the goddess Persephone was impregnated by Zeus while he was in the form of a serpent. She gave birth to the baby god in a cave and it was believed that her son would be the successor to the throne of Zeus. Hera became extremely jealous of the growing boy that had been given the name Zagreus. She knew that neither she nor any other god could harm the boy, so she enlisted the Titans in a plot to surprise and kill the young boy while he played with his toys in the cave.

The Titans painted themselves white with chalk so they looked like spirits. They attacked the boy and he tried to escape by changing forms. Eventually he was captured while in the form of a bull and the Titans tore him apart. They roasted his parts and feasted on his flesh. Some of the parts they had burned so badly that all that was left was ashes. It is said that a goddess saved Zagreus' heart and placed it in a basket to hide it from the Titans.

Zeus heard the news and rushed to the cave. He found the Titans feasting on his son's remains and smote them all with lightning. All that was left of them was a pile of ashes, mingled with the ashes of Zagreus. Interestingly enough, it is from those very ashes that the Titan Prometheus was said to have created the first humans. In other words, the remains of a divine being were used as building blocks for mortals.

At this point Zeus had the heart of Zagreus and made a potion from it that he drank prior to impregnating Semele. The child taken from the burnt husk of Semele was actually Zagreus' second incarnation. Therefore Zeus named him Dionysus after his unusual births. Dionysus' birth is the first example of rebirth in the myths that surround him, but it appears again.

Dionysus began his life by traveling throughout the world. In these travels he began to realize that he faced a big problem among the thralls of mortal worshipers. Because Dionysus was born of a mortal, many people would not accept that he was a god. This same problem was experienced by Jesus Christ as he traveled the world preaching, and there are many other similarities between Christ and Dionysus. Keep in mind that the latest evidence of the cults of Dionysus places them 300 years before the birth of Christ. Other estimates claim that the myth of Dionysus is as old as the original Greek mythos.

The lack of faith in his divinity by humans bothered Dionysus very much. In an attempt to bring favor to himself, he created wine from grapes and gave it to humans. This gift had mixed effects. The first man to give it to his friends was killed by them because they thought they had been poisoned. Curiously, the men ripped him apart as the Titans had done to Dionysus. Once people realized the pleasurable aspect of wine, many were ready to pay homage to Dionysus, the god of wine and fertility.

Although his power was great, Dionysus still had many disbelievers. No matter how strong and fanatical his followers were, there were always those who denied his power as fervently. To those who believed in him, Dionysus brought ecstasy and a promise of rebirth; to those who refused to accept him, he brought madness and despair. Stories abound of his followers, who were primarily women. They kept their rites secret because they involved controversial activities such as tearing apart animals in an orgy of ecstasy and consuming their flesh. The flesh was ritually believed to be the body of Dionysus and the wine they drank was his blood. The parallel between this ritual and Christian communion is striking.

In another similarity between Dionysus and Christ, the Thebian King Pentheus actually captured, imprisoned, and tortured Dionysus for his preaching. Little did Pentheus know that his own mother and the women of his town were followers of Dionysus. When he found out he tried to follow the group to watch their mysterious rites in the woods. In a state of ecstasy, Pentheus' mother mistook her son for a wild animal and the group tore him to pieces.

This is a prime example of the paradoxical, or dual nature, of Dionysus. He is often described as an easy-going, friendly, and unassuming man. In fact, he is often described as being effeminate. This exterior belies his ability to unleash the destructive power of nature in plants, animals, and humans alike. This power is raw and unassailable by the conscious mind. Humans cannot understand it and are swept up by it. He becomes both man and nature at once, a man-god that gives his body and blood in a sacrificial action to prove that the man and the god aspects can, and do, coexist.

Perhaps it is the very fact that man was made from the ashes of the original Dionysus that sparks the followers of Dionysus into action. The connection of mankind to the divine that is a part of their very existence is made very real in the character of Dionysus. He is a flesh and blood embodiment of the union of god and man. The very act of consuming the wine and raw flesh is a physical symbol of acknowledging the god inside the man. It is also a reenactment of the original death of Dionysus, which inevitably leads to his rebirth. The similarities to the Christian stories and belief system are quite intriguing.

Dionysus is also credited with bringing a mortal back from the dead. He traveled to the underworld to find his mother Semele. Rather than bringing her to the world of mortals, he brought her to Olympus, the kingdom of the gods, and made her immortal. In doing so, he set an interesting precedent. He broke the natural laws of life and death for mortals as he had done for himself through his rebirth. Not only did he break the rules of death by bringing Semele back, but he also took it a step further by bringing her closer to the gods and providing life everlasting.

The word "bacchanal," an intense party, owes itself to the Latin derivation of Dionysus. The Romans referred to him as Bacchus and his followers engaged in raucous parties. The parties often turned into orgies. The word "orgy" is also derived from the Greek "orgia," which means secret rite. The followers of Dionysus practiced their rites in secret, typically in the woods on the outskirts of town, where nature and civilization met. Here they drank to excess and engaged in ecstatic behavior that was outside the bounds of civility. Orgy, as it is used today, denotes the unleashing of a more primal, nonthinking aspect of an action. This could be connected to drinking, eating, destruction, or any primal action including sex. Just visit the Mardi Gras or Carnivale celebrations to see that Dionysus is still alive and encouraging the pleasures of life as much as he did over 2000 years ago.

The story of Dionysus is so entwined in Western culture because of its similarity to the story of Christ. The influence of Christian thought and belief in Western culture cannot be denied or minimized. If one believes that some of the story of Christ was influenced by the myth of Dionysus, we can say that this little known myth has helped to shape much of our modern world and its religions.

Echo and Narcissus

~

Narcissus

The myth of Echo and Narcissus is a bittersweet tale of unrequited love and deception, and a moral lesson. The story begins with Zeus and his desire to have a tryst with a mortal woman. He used a nymph, Echo, to distract his jealous wife, Hera, from discovering the affair. He asked Echo, who was an engaging conversationalist, to meet with Hera and discuss an issue or two. While Echo preoccupied Hera, Zeus snuck off and had the affair.

Hera soon found out about the deception and became enraged by Zeus' act of infidelity and his accomplice. She cursed Echo: "From this day forth, you shall not speak except to repeat the last word that you hear!" From that moment on, Echo could only repeat the last word of any sentence she heard. Confused and distraught, Echo hid in the mountains.

Meanwhile, in a nearby village, a young man named Narcissus had come of age. He was extremely handsome and consistently rebuffed the women who fell madly in love with him upon sight. The constant amorous advances became so frequent and annoying that Narcissus found life to be easier if he spent most of his time alone in nature.

One day, while roaming through the valleys, Narcissus heard a noise. He called out, "Is anyone here?" Echo answered, "Here, Here!" Narcissus called the mysterious person out by saying, "Come!," and Echo answered, "Come!, Come!" as she stepped from the forests, her arms outstretched to embrace this handsome young man who had found her. Narcissus saw her and could not believe that it was another woman who wanted him. He told her he had no interest in her and that she should go away and stop bothering him. Echo was so devastated by this rejection that she fled to a mountain cave, where she wasted away until only her repeating voice could be heard.

The goddess Nemesis watched this whole story unfold and became angry about the heartless, selfish actions of Narcissus. Through her powers, she led Narcissus through the woods to a clear pool of water that reflected all that was near it. Narcissus looked into the pool and saw himself for the first time. He immediately fell in love with his reflection and stared at it. As he was transfixed by his own image and consumed by his own love of himself, he slowly wasted away. The goddess turned what was left of him into a beautiful flower, the narcissus, which bears his name to this day. The word "narcissist" is used to describe someone who loves oneself too much, and in psychology, "narcissicism" is the term used to describe an excessive degree of self-involvement.

Echo lends her name to words as well, with the most obvious example being the word "echo." An echo sounder uses sound waves to determine the depth of water or where an object is located below water. An echo chamber is a room that is used to make echoing sound effects. Also, the word echo is used in communications as the code word for the letter "e."

Narcissus' story of conceit and vanity has inspired countless storylines, like the fairy tale "Sleeping Beauty" and Oscar Wilde's novel *The Portrait of Dorian Gray*. In these stories, the Queen and Dorian Gray, respectively, are excessively self-involved in their own beauty. Even in today's American culture, teenage girls and young women are plagued with obsessive-compulsive disorders in their quest to look like fashion models. The vanity that was expressed by this ancient Greek story of Narcissus will always be a part of our society, a fact that makes this a timeless myth.

Excalibur

❧

Swords have played an integral role in a large number of mythologies. No sword has had the impact and universal appeal as that enjoyed by Excalibur, legendary sword of the Britons. As popular and accepted as this symbol is, Excalibur is also one of the most misunderstood swords in mythology.

Every great hero has a weapon to avenge, protect, or hunt with. Beowulf had his Hrunting, Luke Skywalker the light saber, Dirty Harry the .44 magnum. Excalibur is certainly at the level of these legendary weapons, but it is special. The sword itself stands for more than what it is. Excalibur has transcended the simple description of a gilded long sword and become a symbol of the strength, pride, and power of an age long passed, yet attainable once again.

Excalibur was the sword wielded by King Arthur of Camelot. It was said to possess a magical keenness that made it extremely sharp and thus, valuable in battle. Equally important was the sheath that housed Excalibur. It was magical as well. No blood could be lost by the person who wore the sheath. Many times Merlin counseled Arthur that the sheath was more valuable than the sword, yet Arthur lent the sheath out often, while only lending the actual sword once. Eventually, the sheath was stolen by Arthur's archenemy Morgan Le Fey. It was returned, but after that the sheath seems to have disappeared from the story line, a loss that will plague Arthur later in life.

Most people think of Excalibur as the magic sword that Arthur pulled from the stone when he was a boy. Arthur did pull a sword from a stone in his youth and that act proved that he was next in line in the succession of kings, but that sword was not Excalibur. According to Thomas Mallory's *Morte d'Arthur*, the sword Arthur pulled from the stone was a well-made, regular sword. The plainness of the sword became evident when, as Arthur and Merlin were traveling across Briton, they came into conflict with a series of knights that wished to see Arthur dead. Arthur battled each and got the best of them, however, in the last battle, the sword he pulled from the stone broke during combat. Although Arthur still managed to defeat the knight, Arthur was unsettled and worried that he had no weapon with which to defend himself. Merlin told him that he knew where to get a blade that was powerful enough for a king. With that, the two ventured to find the mysterious and powerful Lady of the Lake. Arthur rowed a boat to the middle of the secluded lake where the sword was held just above the water, presumably by the Lady of the Lake. After Arthur took the sword, the hand that had been holding it disappeared into the depths of the lake.

Arthur's reign as King of the Britons was marked by glorious battles and the formation of the Round Table, which was an alliance of the most noble and valiant knights in the land. Under his leadership, the united front was able to stave off the attacks of the barbarians from the North. Excalibur was in his hand the whole time. His reputation on the battlefield helped make the sword legendary; it became seen as the sword of kings. The sword then became a more powerful symbol for his reign than any crown.

In his last battle, Arthur's bastard son Mordred inflicted a fatal wound upon him. When Arthur realized that the wound would kill him, he asked Sir Bedivere to return the sword to the lake. Bedivere agreed, but could not bring himself to do the act the first two times. Excalibur was the symbol of kingship, which made it very hard to throw away. Finally, Bedivere threw the sword into the lake, and it is caught by the same arm that first gave it to Arthur. It then disappeared below the surface.

The origin of Excalibur is somewhat obscured by different authors, but consensus lies with the smith of the gods, Wayland, as the person who forged the sword. The concept of an exceptionally skilled craftsman is a common theme in mythology. Swords of such power are made so that only a few or one specific person can effectively wield them. Other sources claim that the sword was forged from a piece of iron that fell from the heavens. This seems to be a reference to a meteorite, which might explain the otherworldly powers and keenness of Excalibur.

The name Excalibur has a very interesting lineage. It is derived from "Caliburn," the name of the magical sword in the works of twelfth-century author Geoffrey of Monmouth. His writings popularized the legend of King Arthur. Caliburn is very similar to the Latin *chalybs*, which means "steel." Prior to Monmouth's derivation, the sword was present in Irish myths as Caladbolg, which means "hard lightning." The sword was believed to have been wielded by the legendary Irish hero Cuchulain. The practice of hurling a weapon into a lake after the death of its owner was popular among the Celtic people. Archaeologists have found numerous weapons and armor in lakes throughout England and the Isles.

History is ripe with attempts to find the legendary sword. Like the Holy Grail, many people have claimed to have seen Excalibur. Richard I, the Lionhearted, gave Tancred of Sicily a sword in 1191 that he claimed was Excalibur. This seems highly unlikely and was more a ruse than truth. Any king, especially one from England, would have known the symbolic power of such an artifact. To give away Excalibur would be to give away all of England.

Excalibur has served as in integral part of many movies, some of which are serious and adventurous while others are comedic, juvenile, or just plain silly. Only a few serious movies focus on Excalibur, the most notable of which is *Excalibur* (1981), which is a fairly faithful telling of King Arthur's legend.

The comedic film versions of Excalibur are numerous. A recent example is *Arthur's Quest* (1999), in which Arthur is transported to modern day America while he is still a boy. Merlin catches up to him ten years later and must convince the fifteen year old that he is King Arthur before his archenemy, Morgana, has a chance to steal Excalibur. *Kids of the Round Table* (1995) features an eleven-year-old boy named Alex who has to band together with his friends to prove himself worthy of Excalibur. In a bizarre twist on the Mark Twain classic, *A Connecticut Yankee in King Arthur's Court*, the movie *The Spaceman and King Arthur* (1979) tells the story of an astronaut and his android double who are transported to the time of King Arthur.

For children, there are two animated films about Excalibur. *The Sword in the Stone* (1963) focuses on a young boy named Arthur, who is mysteriously able to remove a sword that is embedded in a stone. Merlin then takes the boy under his wing and teaches him how to become a hero. In *Quest for Camelot* (1998), Arthur's daughter Kayley must defend her father's kingdom from the evil Ruber. Fortunately she has the help of Excalibur.

For many, Excalibur symbolizes everything that is noble and valiant from Arthurian England. Its mysterious origins and power only add to the allure of the myth. In reality, however, the myth surrounding the sword helped romanticize a period of turmoil and battles in ancient England.

The Furies

◡

Have you ever been furious? Well thank the Furies for giving you a word to describe your feelings. These three Roman goddesses were known as the Erinnyes, or "the Angry Ones," by the Greeks. Alecto, Tisiphone, and Megaera were not a friendly trio. These hideous, winged creatures avenged misdeeds. They personified guilt and served two purposes: to punish evil men in the afterlife and to carry out curses with brass-studded scourges.

Accounts of their origins differ. In most versions, the Furies are a product of the drops of blood from Uranus when his son, Cronus, severed his penis. Aphrodite, the goddess of love, originated from this same violent event. In another version, they are the daughters of Mother Earth, Gaia, and Darkness. In yet another depiction, their parents are the Titans Cronus and Eurynome, which would make them sisters to the Fates.

While their origins were shrouded in mystery, the ruthless torment and vengeance of the Furies was well known among the ancient Greeks and Romans. No amount of begging and pleading could stop their persecution or protect the object of their harassment. If the Furies needed some help in ensnaring one of their unfortunate victims, they would call upon the goddess of justice, Dike.

Although the concept of three Furies is the modern notion of the myth, there were not always three. In Athens, statues of only two of the three have been found. Oftentimes the three Furies were depicted as the leaders of an avenging mob of Harpies, which were ugly female birdlike monsters. The Harpies would assist the Furies by capturing and hassling people.

The Harpies were not comely, but neither were their leaders. Alecto, Tisiphone, and Megaera were often depicted with bat wings, blood dripping from their eyes, and snakes entangled in their hair. In many images, especially modern ones, the trio's appearance has been tempered. They appear as relatively normal, albeit extremely angry women without the wings or blood dripping from their eyes.

Regardless of their appearance, the Furies were dreaded. People feared them so much that they seldom referred to them by name. Instead, they were called Eumenides, meaning the "Kindly Ones" or the "Solemn Ones." One of their victims, Orestes began this practice.

Orestes caught the attention of the Furies when he murdered his mother. While certainly a terrible crime, he was following the moral code of the time because his mother had collaborated in murdering his father. Unfortunately, the Furies did not agree with the moral code. Serving as Orestes' guilty conscience, the Furies hounded him mercilessly. Driven to the edge, he went to Athena and pleaded for her help. She brought his problem to the court of the Olympian gods, who judged him as innocent of the crime, but the judgment was not acceptable to the Furies. They threatened to destroy all of the crops and people of Athens.

Athena came up with a solution when she convinced the Furies to keep a sanctuary in Athens where they were worshipped by the Athenians. With this placation, the Furies agreed to leave Orestes alone, but the Harpies continued to torment him. Ultimately, he ended their harassment by offering a sacrifice of a black sheep. Něphalia, a drink made of honey and water, along with black sheep became typical sacrifices to the Furies.

The Furies were both revered and feared by the ancient peoples. Because the Furies lived in Athens, the Athenians held an annual festival called the "Eumenida" in their honor. In the city of Colonus, there was a grove that was one of their sanctuaries. To avoid arousing the wrath of the Furies, no one would enter the grove. In another city, Megalopolis, they were worshipped, but they were known by the name Maniai.

Although the Furies had their sanctuaries, they lived at the entrance to Tartarus. This gloomy place was deep inside the underworld. Damned souls were condemned to this infernal place where the Furies tormented them for all of their past misdeeds. In some accounts, the trio lived in Erebus, which was the darkest abyss of the underworld. There they would judge whether souls would be damned or not. They would unremittingly torment those who had sinned.

Mythology is littered with other individuals who incurred the wrath of the Furies. They played a crucial role in the story of Oedipus, who killed his father in self-defense and did not even know that the man was his father. After Alcmaeon killed his mother, the trio tormented him so mercilessly that he was driven mad. Even the Queen of the Amazons was not immune from their harassment. When she accidentally killed her sister, the Furies tormented her relentlessly.

These vengeful spirits personified vindication and retribution for the ancients. The concept of the Furies helped people explain the psychology of a guilty conscience. Over time, the Furies became primarily known for avenging offenses of family members. They specialized in punishing children who disrespected their parents and lack of hospitality to guests. Today, psychologists study the concept of guilt and rude people are berated on television talk shows, but the Furies live on in our expression of anger.

Galahad and the Holy Grail

The Holy Grail

The prevalent theme of impossible quests does not distinguish Celtic mythology from its cultural peers, but the symbolic use of a cauldron or vessel seems to be a defining aspect of many of their myths. The story of the Holy Grail combines these two themes into a highly charged and moving story that has impacted a great deal of Western cultural ideals of purity, faithfulness, and redemption. A direct descendent of the Celtic myths of old, Arthurian mythology blends the old pagan mythology with the ideology and symbols of the growing Christian communities that spread throughout the West during the Middle Ages. This blend may have been the reason for, or result of, many of the conversions to Christianity in the Celtic corner of Europe. In any event, it is the centerpiece of a great and timeless set of works that are collectively known as the Grail Quests.

The Grail, or Sangreal, was believed to be the cup from which Christ and his apostles shared the wine at the Last Supper. Additionally, it is believed that the cup was used to collect the blood that poured from the side of the crucified Christ after he was stabbed with a spear. As such, the cup was believed to have wondrous powers. There have been numerous descriptions and depictions of the Grail over time, ranging from ornate chalices of precious metals and ornate craftsmanship to simple, fired clay cups. A particularly interesting theory holds that because Christ was believed to be a carpenter, the Grail may have been a very ordinary looking cup carved from wood and stained red by wine and his blood. Whatever the description, the Grail holds a superior position in the field of symbolic imagery, and no mindset was more willing to accept that symbol than the people of Celtic descent.

Celtic mythology is brimming with magical cauldrons and liquid-bearing vessels. In the Welsh otherworld of Annwn, there was supposedly a giant cauldron of rebirth from which the dead would rise, restored but somewhat less than human. The great Celtic god Dagda had in his possession a cauldron of plenty that provided sustenance unending. Celtic heroes were sent on quests to gain the magical cauldrons of great kings. The list goes on and on. In the Grail, each of these cauldrons finds expression, although changed to reflect a particularly Christian flavor.

After the death of Christ, Joseph of Arimethaea, who held the cup and collected the blood of Christ, gave up his own tomb so that Christ could be laid to rest in it. It was believed that he kept the cup and the spear used to stab Christ and fled from Golgotha. Arthurian legend holds that he came to the isle of Briton to preach and brought the artifacts with him. Apparently the cup bestowed an extremely long life to Joseph, but eventually he died and the cup and spear were lost. It was believed that both were still within the limits of Briton.

This is the point in the story where Arthur and the Knights of the Round Table become involved. There are many texts that tell the Arthurian story of the Grail and they unfailingly contradict each other on important points. Each version stems from the oral tradition that is the myth's origin, therefore their inconsistencies are derived from their storytellers. Each storyteller would emphasize certain parts, omit some details, invent new elements, and sometimes misunderstand portions. The result is a set of tales that often have few similarities to each other.

The common elements to the Arthurian story involve a knight who comes upon a castle that is the home to the Fisher King. While staying in the castle, the knight sees a sword and a lance dripping with blood. While he feasts, he sees the Grail, and after the meal he is allowed to ask a question. If he asks the right question, he has the ability to heal the crippled Fisher King. If he asks the wrong question, disaster follows.

In one popular version of the story, Camelot and the Round Table were firmly established when the Grail was introduced into the story. As the tale goes, the Round Table had convened when a mysterious woman appeared and told the king and his knights that the Grail would appear to them that evening. During the meal, a vision appeared at the center of the table. It was the Grail, but it was covered by a piece of white cloth so none of the knights could see it. They did, however, feel its effects. That evening the food seemed more delicious and gave them great strength. They also saw each other in a different light. Each knight could see only the good in his fellows and a great sense of companionship and fellowship overtook the hall.

In many ways, this scene models itself after the Last Supper. When the meal ended the Grail disappeared and the knights were filled with a great longing for the return of the cup. They spoke of finding the vessel and actually looking upon it. Arthur somehow knew that this quest was full of danger and would ultimately lead to the destruction of the Round Table, but the knights were fervent. They decided always to leave a seat empty for the one who would come back with at least the sight of the Grail. So began the great quest for the Holy Grail.

The quest is intertwined with many of the other Arthurian tales. Other entries in this text tell of the stories that are not directly influenced by the Grail, but all are somehow connected to the great quest to get the Grail. Sir Gawain was the first to leave on the quest against the advice of King Arthur. Each knight that went on the quest was sidetracked at one time or another. Some came close to reaching their goal, others fell short, but each tale is a lesson in the virtues and failures of being human. The tales do not seem to be an attempt to show the evil that is in man; rather, they seem to be an exercise in demonstrating the complexity of human nature and the frailty of the human experience. Although all of the knights are great in their own right and possess many of the qualities that we, with our modern perspective, would consider noble, each has a flaw that becomes evident to the reader and themselves as they attempt to set eyes upon the Grail.

Arthurian legends are filled with knights who have sought the Grail and failed due to some personal fault. For example, after a long and arduous journey,

Gawain found that it was his patience and lack of discipline that made the goal unattainable. The great knight Tristan fell in love with Iseult, a woman who was forbidden to him, while on the quest. His love for her led to his death, which is told in a story that has a remarkable resemblance to Shakespeare's Romeo and Juliet. Even the king's champion, Lancelot, fell short due to his illicit yet true love for the queen. Many a knight learned their faults or died trying to attain that which was unattainable. This is very important because, as we have seen in many myths, heroes and gods are often sent on impossible quests only to come back victorious. These knights were great men, but still only human. They were destined to fail, with a few exceptions.

Of the knights that actually saw the Grail, only two are known: Percival and Galahad. Percival was not the greatest of the knights; in fact, he was considered to lack many of the qualities of the Knights of the Round Table. He was often characterized as naïve and of lesser skill in the art of warfare. As it turns out, it was his innocent nature that allowed him a glance of the Grail. He got to see part of it but was still considered not pure enough to view the vessel in all its glory.

Back in Camelot, Percival told his tale to an ever-diminishing Round Table. Arthur's kingdom was falling to pieces and his knights were lost, dead, or stricken by their own sense of self-loathing. The Round Table was crumbling in the face of this quest, not to mention the other problems that plagued Camelot. Arthur needed more knights, but the remaining knights had become quite picky because they recognized their own faults.

One young squire was often brought forward but turned away from the table due to his lineage. That squire was Galahad, who was the son of Lancelot by a woman who had tricked him into believing she was Guinevere. By the time he appeared to try for a position at the Round Table, rumors were already flying about the illicit love affair of Lancelot and Guinevere. Thus, Galahad was overlooked by the king and his knights.

This was a most unfortunate mistake, because despite his lineage, Galahad had the purity of spirit necessary for the quest. He had been raised by nuns and was believed to be without blemish, either physical or spiritual. He was pure, even more so than his father. Strong, handsome, generous, and benevolent, Galahad was the epitome of knighthood and a symbol of all that was good in man. After he had been turned away from the Round Table, Galahad opted to find the Grail anyway. He would be the only one to succeed.

Galahad's journey was no less arduous than any other knights, but his attitude was different. Although he was determined to find the Grail, he was willing to right any wrong he encountered along the way. His actions were selfless and he took little or no credit for what he did. All he asked was that he be pointed in the right direction.

Along the way he was given a shield as a present from a well-wisher. The shield was marked with the blood of Joseph of Arimethaea, the same person who had collected Christ's blood in the Grail. The gift was a clear omen.

Eventually Galahad found himself at the place where only Percival had come by mistake. He stood at the walls of Carbunek, the Grail Castle. Carbunek stood in the middle of a dying land. Its livestock were dead, its grain stores were empty, and its people were starving. The despair was almost too much for Galahad to bear.

Galahad found that the king of Carbunek, Pelles, was doing no better than his land. It was then that it dawned upon him that the land and its king were inseparable. Arthur's kingdom was in turmoil because Arthur was at odds with himself. He found that the king of Carbunek was suffering from a wound in the leg that would not heal. He had done some great wrong in the eyes of God and was suffering both physically and spiritually. The king informed him that the only way he could be healed and let Galahad glimpse the Grail was to have the Spear of Destiny—the spear that had wounded Christ on the Cross—touched to his own wound. Galahad immediately began the quest to find the weapon. His quest took a great deal of time, but Galahad eventually returned to Carbunek and healed the king, thereby healing the land. For this deed, the king accepted Galahad as the Redeemer and fit to set his eyes upon the Grail. It appeared to Galahad in a vision so great that he could only ask that he be allowed to leave this world. Then a voice came to him and told him that after this life he would be with Christ in heaven.

Various miracles followed this event and Galahad took his place at the Round Table. He sat in the special chair set aside for the one who saw the Grail. In true medieval Christian fashion, he found no great happiness from that time forth, as his mind was set on the greatness to come in his next life. Finally, Joseph of Arimethaea returned from the dead and visited Galahad. He placed the cup in Galahad's hands and the knight's spirit left his body with a great rejoicing in the heavens. Once Galahad the Redeemer had been released from the mortal world, the Round Table was forever lost.

The Grail continues to capture our imagination in movies and literature. For example, the 1991 movie *The Fisher King*, starring Robin Williams and Jeff Bridges is inspired by the basic plot of the tale. In the movie Williams plays the crazy street person who is obsessed with medieval history and has set out to find the Holy Grail. The movie sets the Arthurian legend in modern New York and equates madness with enlightenment. *Monty Python and the Holy Grail*, spoofs the Arthurian legend, complete with a very dangerous rabbit and knights that ride invisible horses mimicked by banging two coconuts together. In another example, T. S. Eliot's poem "The Waste Land" was inspired by the assertion that Grail legends are connected with the restoration of life.

One cannot read the story of the Holy Grail without noticing the strong resemblance of Galahad to Christ—noble, yet humble; powerful and true, yet unwanted. Selfless and determined, Galahad was what all knights wished to be, but could not attain because of their positions as knights. This paradox is central to the myth and ultimately central to all people: we wish to be more than human and that wish is part of what it means to be human.

The Giants Trick Thor

∽

On a fine day in Asgard, Thor, the Norse god of thunder, decided to journey to Jotunheim. Jotunheim was a wild land inhabited by a race of giants. Thor was not particularly fond of the giants, but he was extremely competitive. Being the strongest of the gods, Thor rarely found an equal to test his strength. Giants were the best competition be could find but taking a trip to Jotunheim was very dangerous, even for a god. The giants were a crafty bunch who loved using their magic to trick the unwary. Thor decided that the best defense against the giants would be to bring along Loki, the god of trickery and fire. As an added measure, he also invited his right hand man Thialfi to come along with them. Although a mortal, Thialfi was known among the gods as the fastest runner of all mankind. Thor decided that Thialfi would make the perfect porter to carry their possessions. After packing up their provisions they began the journey to Jotunheim.

They traveled all day and into the night until they found themselves in the middle of a massive forest. The sun was nearing the edge of the world and light was becoming scarce. They began to search for a place to spend the night and were quite surprised to find a large hall in the middle of the forest, next to a great mountain. They could barely see by that point, so they quickly entered the large open doorway to the hall and settled down for a quiet night of rest. But their sleep did not last long.

At the moons height a great earthquake shook the hall and woke them. Thor sprang to his feet and directed the others to search the back of the hall for a safer place to spend the rest of the night. Along the side wall they found another chamber and moved there to sleep. Thor, however, stood guard at the front of the hall, holding his powerful hammer Mjolnir. All night a fierce groaning and sounds of thunder could be heard. Thor looked forward to dawn.

When the sun finally rose, Thor ventured outside to find that the nearby mountain was not a mountain at all, but a great sleeping giant. This was no ordinary giant, for it was bigger than any Thor had ever met. Some accounts of the myth say that Thor was afraid. Just then, the giant woke up. "Hello, most grand of giants," said Thor. "By what name should I address thee?" The giant looked down in surprise and smiled. "I am Skrymir, and you, you are Thor, very great are your deeds, and well known to my people." The giant rubbed the sleep from his eyes and asked Thor "Have you seen my glove? I seem to have misplaced it." Thor looked about and realized, to his astonishment, that the hall they had slept in was the giant's glove and his companions were still sleeping in the thumb of the massive gauntlet. He called to his companions and they emerged to find the awesome spectacle awaiting them. The giant put his glove back on and asked them to join him on his way through the forest, for he knew the shortest way and wished to have company.

The trio agreed, gave him their provisions to carry in his bag, and began to follow the immense strides of the giant. Throughout the day they found themselves running to keep up with the giant's gait. When night fell again, they were more than happy to stop and rest. "Take your provisions from my bag to make supper. I am tired and would like to go to sleep," said the giant, as he drifted off to a deep slumber.

Soon Skrymir began to snore. The sound shook the trees and made it impossible for the trio to hear one another. Thor tried to get the provisions from the giant's bag, but he found that the knot was so tight that even his great strength could not undo it. He tried and tried, but it was no use. He became furious. He grabbed his hammer with both hands and struck a mighty blow to the head of the sleeping giant. The giant stirred and woke up, asking, "Did a twig or leaf fall from a tree onto my head?" Thor stood amazed and answered that he did not know.

Skrymir told them to eat supper and go to bed, as he fell into his awful snoring once again. Resolving themselves to a supperless evening, the trio lay down to sleep. Thialfi and Loki drifted off to the land of dreams, but the snores of the giant would not let Thor rest. Again he became angry and hoisted his hammer. This time he struck a blow twice as furious as the first. The giant merely stirred in his sleep and muttered something about the amount of leaves that were falling on him. Thor grew even angrier. He waited through the night and saved up all of his strength. Just before dawn he lifted his hammer a third time and, with all his strength, landed a blow upon the forehead of the giant that would have felled a mountain. The giant awoke and said, "Now the trees drop acorns upon me. It must be a sign to continue my journey."

Thor could only stand there bewildered. Never before had he felt such embarrassment. Was he not the strongest god in Asgard? Tired and confused, Thor woke the others and they continued their travels with the giant. Soon the time came for them to part, for the giant would go north while they were traveling along the eastern road to the kingdom of Utgard. The giant said farewell and gave them a stern warning. "The city of Utgard has many giants, some smaller, and others larger than me. It would do you well to be careful of your boasting and relying on your reputations, for they do not take kindly to smaller folk such as yourselves. Farewell my friends." With that, the giant strode northward and disappeared.

By the time the sun had reached its height, they were at the walls of Utgard. They stood in awe of the size of its gates. Walking under them, they found a group of giants sitting on benches in the front hall. There sat the king of Utgard, a great and ugly giant. "Ho!" he boomed. "If it isn't the little god Loki and Thor the thunderer. Gods you may be, but to stay here you must still prove your worth. Do you care to test your worth in a competition?" Thor, ever proud and sometimes hasty in speech, agreed to his offer and then thought to ask what the competition would be. "I would ask that each of you tell me what you excel at, and I will find a competitor among those in my court to compete with you," answered the king with a wry smile. "What feat do you have to offer?" he asked Thialfi. Thialfi stepped forward and spoke quietly. "I am the fleetest of foot among men." The king smiled. "Then we shall have a race and Hugi the swift will run against you."

The giants cleared a path and the two competitors waited for the call to begin the race. The call came and Thialfi exploded from the starting line, but as fast as he was, Hugi was faster. In fact, the giant passed Thialfi on his way back to the starting line. Three times they raced and the outcome was the same. Thialfi was bested.

Turning to Loki, the king of Utgard asked what feat he would choose to compete in. "I can eat quicker than anyone. I may be wiry but my appetite is bigger than anyone else's in this hall." Amused, the king called for a trough of roasted meat to be brought forth and asked the giant Logi to compete. "Each of you will start at an opposite end of the trough. Whoever reaches the middle first will be victorious. Begin the feast!" With that, the two competitors began to gorge themselves in a frenzy. Loki and Logi seemed evenly matched and reached the middle at the same time. Loki looked up and smiled at his accomplishment. Looking down again, he saw that while he had left the bones of the roasted beast, Logi had eaten not only the bones but also half of the wooden trough. He had lost.

"Now, Mighty Thor, what feat do you wish to be bested in?" the king asked with a laugh. Angry and embarrassed at the defeat of his companions, Thor boasted, "I can drink more than anyone in this hall." It was true. Thor was a legendary drinker and had downed many horns of mead. The giants became excited and a great drinking horn was brought into the hall. The king of Utgard spoke. "This horn is full, and any good drinker can finish it in one drink, although some men need to take two. Those who are weak will need three, but if what you say is true, this should be easy for the great Thor." Thor took the horn and put it to his lips. He drank and drank until his breath had nearly left him. Finally he stopped and looked into the horn. The level of the liquor was barely lower than it had been to begin with. Angry and embarrassed, he tried a second time. This time he drank deeper and longer. Yet, when he looked into the horn, the level of liquor had only scarcely diminished. The third time he drank, he did so as he had never done before. Exhausted and out of breath, he found that the horn was still nearly full.

The king laughed and Thor's face became red with shame. "Perhaps you are not the drinker you think yourself to be. Would you care to try an easier feat?" asked the king. Thor angrily agreed, for he wished to prove himself. The king brought forth a great gray cat that was the size of a horse. "All you need to do is lift this cat from the ground. It is a simple task." Thor knew he had the strength to do it so he strode to the cat and stood under its belly. With a great heave he lifted, but the cat simply arched its back and stretched upward. Its paws were firmly planted on the ground. Thor tried and tried, but the higher he pushed, until he was on his tiptoes, the higher the cat arched its back. Only once did one of the cat's paws leave the ground.

Thor became even more ashamed and angry. He called out, "Stop these silly games and bring forth from your group one who would dare to wrestle with me. I will show you the strength of a god!" "Fair enough," answered the king. "Bring the old nurse maid Elli to wrestle with Thor. She should prove enough for him." With that, an aged, toothless woman entered the hall to face Thor. They grappled with one another and it seemed that the harder Thor struggled, the stronger the old nurse became. Finally, Thor was forced down to one knee and the match was over. The competition was over and none of the trio from Asgard had won a match.

The giants felt sorry for the trio and asked them to stay and dine anyway. The night passed and Thor's anger disappeared. After a fine breakfast, the king showed the trio out of the front gate. Thor turned to him in sadness and spoke. "I am sad, for now you believe me to be weak and of little worth." Seeing the sadness in Thor's eyes, the king could no longer keep silent. "It is I who should be ashamed, for had I known your greatness before last night, I would have feared letting you into my hall in the first place. You are not weak or of little worth. The tests devised for you were all illusions. I was the giant Skrymir and the blows you rained upon me I narrowly escaped. If you go to those places now, you will find mountains shattered by your hammer. I would have been killed by the first hit had I not been as quick. Thialfi did not race with Hugi, he raced against Thought itself. No man or god can hope to outpace Thought. As for the eating contest, Loki contended not with Logi, but with the element of Fire, which consumes all. Neither he nor any other could have won that, but he came quite close. As for you, Thor, the horn you drank from was connected to the ocean itself. I was amazed by your feat, as you will be when next you visit the shore and see how low the ocean is. As for the cat, your feat astounded and struck me with great terror, for that was no cat at all. It was the great Midgard serpent whose length encompasses the entire world. No giant could ever move him, yet you did. Finally, you thought you wrestled Elli the nurse maid, but you wrestled Old Age, and you did not lie down. No one can defeat her, yet you would not go down easy. That was the most astonishing feat of all. Now that I have told you these things and certainly eased your fears, ease mine and promise me that you and your kind will stay away from here, for we fear you greatly and wish to be left in peace. If not, I will be forced to defend myself with illusions."

Now that he knew the truth, Thor was relieved and angry all at once. He had lifted the World Serpent, battled Old Age to a standstill, and drank a great deal of the ocean. He would make the giants tell others of his feats. It was his honor that was at stake. He raised his hammer to strike the king. At that moment the king, his men, and the city disappeared. Thor and his companions were left standing in a green field with no proof of the great feats they had performed and no hope of convincing anyone that any of the events had ever taken place.

As one of the most well known of the Norse gods, Thor and his mighty hammer have played important roles in movies. In *Erik the Viking* (1998), the title character journeys to Vallhalla and asks the gods, including Thor, to end Ragnarok, the apocalypse of Norse mythology. Thor also appears in the 1987 animated film *Vallhalla*, and, oddly enough, in the television series *Hercules*, which is about the Greek hero.

The comic book *The Mighty Thor* depicts the contemporary adventures of the Norse god, and in 1967 it was made into a television series. The premise of the comic centers on Don Blake, a doctor who finds an old walking stick. When he strikes it, he transforms into his true form, Thor, and the stick becomes his hammer, Mjolnir. One of his enemies in the series is his half-brother, Loki.

Thor's name symbolizes his awe-inspiring power, and he is one of the most colorful and well-known of the Norse gods. In ancient times, people often wore small hammers as tokens of loyalty and symbols of strength and power. He continues to be a symbol of power, in modern movies and comic books.

Gilgamesh and Enkidu

~

Gilgamesh

The story of Gilgamesh and Enkidu is a tragic tale of enemies who forge a friendship, and the sorrow brought on by death. The story centers on Gilgamesh, the king of Uruk, which was an ancient city in Babylonia. Many stories were written about Gilgamesh and the compilation of them survives today as the epic of *Gilgamesh*.

In the story, Gilgamesh was a super human being who was part god and part man. He was depicted as a cruel tyrant who mistreated his subjects and raped women. His subjects begged the gods to force Gilgamesh to change his ways, and because the gods were also displeased with Gilgamesh's behavior, they created Enkidu to destroy him.

Enkidu was a man who was the equal of Gilgamesh in nearly every way except that he was primitive. He loved the natural world and lived with the animals. He treated them as his friends. As a "wild" man, he seemed to be the perfect foil for the civilized Gilgamesh. Aware that the people and gods were conspiring against him, Gilgamesh sent a woman to weaken Enkidu. She seduced him and after sleeping with her, Enkidu found that the animals would no longer accept him. Not wanting to be alone, Enkidu learned the ways of society and how to live among people from the woman who had seduced him. Soon he won the acceptance of the country people, and he became their protector.

Enkidu championed for the people of Uruk by challenging Gilgamesh to a battle. The fight lasted for hours and shook the foundation of the city. When the conflict ended, neither man could claim victory, but somehow the battle created an intense bond between the two. They became the best of friends, and their opposing personalities balanced each other out. Gilgamesh brought culture and refinement to crude Enkidu, while Enkidu brought humanity and respect to the corrupt Gilgamesh. Thus, they tamed one another and learned to love and respect themselves.

With the strength of their new friendship, the duo assumed the role of protectors of Uruk. They easily solved problems and defeated enemies. The heroes traveled away from the city to the cedar forest to battle the beast, Huwatha, because Gilgamesh was convinced that he could attain glory by defeating the monster. While the pair overcame Huwatha, Ishtar, the goddess of sexual love and war, watched the young hero and fell in love with him. She attempted to seduce him with a golden chariot, tributes from kings, and fertile flocks of sheep, but despite, these enticements, Gilgamesh turned her down.

Ishtar did not take his rejection lightly. She begged her father, Anu, to send the Bull of Heaven to slay Gilgamesh. In defense of his daughter's reputation, Anu dispatched the bull. The wild beast wreaked havoc on the city of Uruk, but the two heroes easily defeated the bull. Amazed and angered, Ishtar appeared and cursed Gilgamesh. In response, Enkidu ripped the bull's leg off and hurled it at Ishtar. Turning her anger to Enkidu, she tormented him with dreams of his own death. The dreams consumed Enkidu, and after twelve days the formerly robust protector withered away from exhaustion.

Enkidu's death devastated Gilgamesh. He became obsessed with his own mortality. His fear of death caused him to leave his kingdom to search for the key to immortality. The former glory seeker set out to find Utnapishtim, who was given immortality as the sole survivor of the Great Flood. Utnapishtim suggested that Gilgamesh prove that he had the strength of a god by staying awake for seven nights and six days, but Gilgamesh failed the challenge.

Utnapishtim encouraged the disappointed Gilgamesh by reminding him not to complain about his lack of immortality, but to celebrate that which he possessed: his superhuman strength, kingdom, wisdom, and heroism. Then Utnapishtim gave him a magic plant that would give him everlasting youth. On his return home, Gilgamesh stopped to take a swim. He left the plant on the shore and a snake stole it. As the snake slithered away with its prize, it shed its skin, unveiling a youthful skin underneath. Obviously, this part of the myth is an ancient explanation for snakes shedding their skin. After losing his source of perpetual youth, Gilgamesh resigned himself to his mortality and enjoyed what remained of his life.

Gilgamesh's story is a reminder of the timelessness of the search for immortality and youth. The great explorer Juan Ponce de Leon was searching for the fountain of youth when he discovered Florida in 1513. Men and women have slathered beauty creams on their faces for centuries in hopes of attaining a youthful complexion. With cryogenics, people can even have themselves frozen upon death in hopes that they can be revived in the future.

Gilgamesh's story goes beyond describing the human quest for immortality. This ancient tale identifies the dual nature of man. While Enkidu symbolizes the animalistic and primitive nature of man, he also retains a love for all things and a gentle protective naïveté. Gilgamesh represents the culture and refinement brought about by the rise of civilization. He also acts as a prime example of the depravity and egotistical pitfalls that come with a growing society. Together they balance each other out and seem to be capable of anything.

As the story progresses, Enkidu becomes increasingly similar to Gilgamesh and vice versa. By throwing the leg of the bull at Ishtar, Enkidu proves that he has become too much like Gilgamesh, and the two of them together are unbalanced. Their power has become too great and threatens to upset the balance of the universe. One of them has to die to restore the balance. Perhaps Gilgamesh endures because he is the one who personified society and justified continued civilization.

The storyline of the epic of Gilgamesh can be seen in many movies, television shows, and other myths. One character sent to destroy another partners with him instead and then the two set out to defeat an enemy. For example, in the movie *Trading Places* Eddie Murphy plays Billy Ray Valentine, a bum who is enlisted by the Duke brothers to destroy the life of Louis Winthorpe III, a wealthy commodities broker played by Dan Aykroyd. The two eventually team up and destroy the scheming brothers.

In the movie *Donnie Brasco*, Johnny Depp plays the title character, an FBI agent who goes undercover to infiltrate and destroy the mob. He becomes friends with his enemy Lefty Ruggiero, played by Robert DeNiro, and he must wrestle with conscience at turning in his newfound friend.

Another example exists in the plot of the television show *The X-Files*. Gillian Anderson plays FBI Agent Dana Scully, who is enlisted to undermine the work of Agent Fox Mulder (David Duchovny). Eventually, the two become friends and they work together to defeat those who try to hide the truth about aliens.

The epic of *Gilgamesh* is important to our history. It is the only myth that has been proven to exist before the Greeks, and it is considered the oldest work of literature in the world. Undoubtedly it was part of the Sumerian oral tradition before it was first recorded. The story was not written down all at once. The first portions were written down in 2100 B.C. and the most recent parts date to 627 B.C. Although the story was based on the real king, Gilgamesh, who ruled Uruk, history did not record any information about the real king.

The epic of *Gilgamesh* is one of our few insights into our origins as a civilization. It also serves as a foundation for our culture's ideas of glory, friendship, and immortality. At a more simple level, it is an engaging tale.

The Greek Division of the World

❧

In Greek mythology, the world was divided into three parts: heaven, water, and the underworld. The split occurred when the gods defeated their parents, the Titans, under the leadership of Zeus. Once the gods obtained leadership of the world, they needed to create a new world order.

Cronus' three sons divided the world among themselves. The three brothers, Zeus, Poseidon, and Hades, agreed to draw lots to decide who would rule over each division. Zeus drew the sky, Poseidon seized the sea, and Hades became lord of the underworld. They left the earth as open territory, a common ground with no specific ruler.

Zeus was elected leader by the rest of the gods and immediately granted each god and goddess a domain of control. Deus, the Latin version of Zeus, is the origin of the word "deity." Additionally, Zeus was made protector and judge of the gods. He acted as a king would, with all of existence as his realm. By creating laws and the concept of the oath, Zeus established order and punishment.

According to the ancient Greeks, Zeus organized the entire universe. He placed all of the stars and planets into the sky, and he created and commanded all of the activity in the sky. He was responsible for rain, snow, thunder, and lightning. Supposedly, Zeus kept a quiver of deadly lightning bolts as weapons.

Few gods were foolhardy enough to challenge Zeus' power, but Hera, Poseidon, and Apollo once teamed together to try to overthrow him. They quickly gained the support of all of the other gods except Hestia. Their plot was simple: as Zeus was sleeping, they tied him to his couch. When he awoke, he could not move. The gods then mocked Zeus as he threatened to destroy them.

Fortunately for Zeus, he found an ally in the ancient goddess of the sea, Thetis. While the rest of the gods were arguing over who would take Zeus' place, Thetis fetched Briareus, a giant who had one hundred hands. In an instant, he was able to untie all of the knots that had bound Zeus. The vengeful god punished Hera by hanging her from the sky, and he did not release her until the rest of the gods promised never to betray him again.

Along with his anger, Zeus had quite a libido. In today's terms, we might call him a sex addict. He had affairs with mortals and immortals alike, and often slept with women by pretending to be their husbands. His numerous affairs resulted in abundant offspring, including eleven children by ten different mortal women. In one case, he did not need to have sex with someone to have a child. His daughter Athena supposedly sprang from his head.

The Roman version of Zeus was Jupiter, who leant his name to the largest planet in our solar system. The phrase "by Jove" comes from the Latin "pro Juppiter." Jove was a shortened version of Jupiter. The first appearance of the phrase was in the play *Appius and Virginia* in 1575, but it did not become popular until William Shakespeare used it in his comedy *Love's Labour's Lost*.

The second brother was Hades. As Lord of the underworld, he was responsible for the care and protection of the souls of the dead. Today, the word Hades refers to the underworld as well as the god. The Roman counterpart of Hades was Pluto, who leant his name to the eighth planet in our solar system.

The dead existed in Hades as shades, which were much like shadows of living people. Every shade was forced to cross the River Styx in order to enter the underworld. This crossing required the ferryman Charon to take each shade across at the price of his own choosing. Hades also placed his guard dog Cerberus on the opposite side of the River Styx. The three-headed beast was as ferocious as it was powerful. Any shade that tried to escape Hades was devoured by the guardian.

This dismal setting was created to help man learn how to lead better lives while they were alive. Hades was a punishment of sorts. It seems that it was not as scary and pain-ridden as the Christian concept of Hell. Most myths depict Hades as much more boring than painful. Hades made sure that the punishments prescribed by other gods were carried out, which was usually done by the Furies. He was also responsible for teaching mankind the rules and respect for treatment of the departed. Under his rule, numerous funeral ceremonies and proper burial rites were created and enforced.

Hades was an extremely private god, and he stayed out of touch with events on earth. He did not like visitors, and if anyone came to the underworld, they were not likely to leave. Even today, we use the phrase "go to Hades" if we want someone to leave and never come back. To move about unseen, he wore the "cap of Hades," which rendered the wearer invisible.

The third brother, Poseidon, took great pleasure in his control of the seas. He was responsible for all water and became the father and grandfather of numerous gods, goddesses, water nymphs, and others of this kind. Each was given dominion over a lake, river, or stream, depending on their loyalty. Poseidon's Roman counterpart, Neptune, is the inspiration for the name of the ninth planet in our solar system. The name was chosen because the blue color of the planet was reminiscent of the sea.

As lord of the sea, Poseidon also had a great measure of control over the land. He frequently exacted revenge for harmful deeds by creating tidal waves and sending monstrous sea creatures to destroy cities and temples. For this reason, he became the god of earthquakes as well. Poseidon seems to be as unpredictable a force as the sea itself. His fickle nature and quick temper made him both a friend and an enemy to most.

In one story about Poseidon, he wanted to marry Amphitrite, who was a Nereid, a nymph of the sea. To protect her virtue, she fled from his advances and hid out in the mountains, but Poseidon refused to give up on her. He sent messengers out to find her, and the dolphin Delphinus was able to find her and bring her back to the sea god. Poseidon was so overwhelmed with joy that he placed Delphinius' image in the stars as a constellation.

In modern society Poseidon has became associated with anything to do with the sea. According to myth, Poseidon lived in a grand underwater palace off the eastern coast of Greece, much like the mythical underwater city of Atlantis. *The Little Mermaid* and other movies that depict an underwater city usually feature a Poseidonlike character. *The Poseidon Adventure* (1972) is a disaster movie set in the ocean, which is what inspired its title. In another example of Poseidon's connection to the sea, his trademark trident is a common symbol for the ocean.

Zeus, Hades, and Poseidon were not alone as the gods of the Greeks. Zeus established a council of gods that was composed of the twelve major gods. These gods were called the Olympians because they lived on Mount Olympus, a mountain with a peak that was obscured by clouds. Ancient Greeks believed that the gods lived in a palace in the clouds. Supposedly it was always spring on Olympus; it was a paradise. The idea of living in the clouds has been used in many science fiction movies and television shows. In *The Empire Strikes Back*, Lando Calrissian lives in Cloud City, an oasis away from the turmoil of the empire. In the *Star Trek* episode "The Cloud Minders" the Troglytes are menial laborers who work underground while the elite rulers live a life of luxury in the cloud city of Stratos.

The Olympians included: Zeus; Poseidon; Hera, goddess of family and fidelity; Demeter, goddess of the earth; Apollo, god of the sun; Artemis, goddess of nature and hunting; Hermes, the messenger and patron of invention; Ares, god of war; Athena, goddess of wisdom and war; Aphrodite, goddess of love; Hephaestus, the craftsman's patron; and Dionysus, the god of wine and fertility. Today, the word "olympian" is used to describe anything godlike or majestic. The choice of a council of twelve is also rather common and seen in the Norse and Roman pantheons as well. Interestingly, the modern American legal system requires twelve jurors to make an informed and fair decision.

The concept of dividing the world into three parts, which are ruled by three gods or people, is a common concept in myth. It occurs in the Norse myths with the three brothers, Vili, Ve, and Odin. In Hindu mythology, the Trimurti of Brahma, Vishnu, and Shiva rule the universe and Christianity believes in the Trinity of the Father, the Son, and the Holy Spirit.

Hercules

Hercules versus the Hydra

Hercules may be the most well-known figure in mythology. He has appeared in almost every form of media, from artwork to movies, television shows, video games, and comic books. Kevin Sorbo, Lou Ferrigno, Steve Reeves, and Tate Donovan are among those who have portrayed the hero. He represents man and what man can achieve. The myth of Hercules has a violent, vivid, and emotional value that produces an intimate connection between the hero and his audience.

Hercules, the illegitimate son of Zeus and a mortal woman, had been driven mad by Zeus' jealous wife, Hera. In his fit of insanity, he murdered his own wife and children. To ease his conscience, he struck a bargain with King Eurystheus to perform twelve labors. Hercules accepted the deal only to find that each labor was a seemingly impossible task. The phrase "Herculean task" is drawn from this idea. When a job seems too large, overwhelming, or unattainable, it is often referred to as a Herculean task.

The theme of taking on a number of jobs or performing feats in order to gain something permeates our society, as evidenced in movies, television, and even our culture. One might argue that the American work ethic is a derivation of this mythical premise. The idea that hard work reaps reward is an integral part of American culture.

In looking at nearly any video game, one sees the seeds of Herculean myth. The typical adventure video game involves a series of specific tasks that must be accomplished to achieve a predetermined goal. Whether it is saving Princess Zelda in *The Legend of Zelda* or freeing the forest in *Sonic the Hedgehog*, the player completes one Herculean task after another in quest of the goal.

On television, game shows enrapture audiences with their Herculean-style challenges. Players move from level to level after successfully answering questions, bidding against opponents, or completing tests of endurance, all in an effort to win a vacation, money, or a new car. As the audience members cheer the contestant, they imagine their own success at the challenge.

In movies, characters are frequently charged with tasks to attain their desires. For example, in the classic movie *The Wizard of Oz*, Dorothy must protect her friends, endure the field of poppies, find the Emerald City, speak to the Wizard, and kill the Wicked Witch of the West before she can go home. In *Saving Private Ryan* Tom Hanks' character, Captain John H. Miller, and his troop must navigate the landscape, escape enemy fire, find Private Ryan, and defend a town so that they may go home.

The first of Hercules' tasks was to kill the Nemean Lion, a beast whose hide was impervious to any weapon. He traveled into the desert for thirty days to find the lion. After unsuccessful attempts to kill the lion with his club, Hercules strangled it, using brute strength alone. After defeating the lion, he took its pelt as a symbol of his victory and for its protective quality as a suit of armor.

For the second labor, Hercules had to defeat the Hydra of Lerna. As proof of his victory, Eurystheus ordered him to bring back the Hydra's teeth. Upon meeting the immense, reptilian monster, Hercules attempted to kill it with a sword. Each time he severed a head, two more sprang up in its place. After he began to give up hope, he got his friend Iolaüs to help him by cauterizing the necks after he cut the heads off. This ingenious use of fire helped Hercules conquer the Hydra.

"Hydra" is used in modern English to express a diverse evil that is not overcome by a single effort. Hydra-headed describes an organization that has many branches.

The goal of Hercules' third labor was to capture and bring the Erymanthian Boar to Eurystheus. According to the myth, the boar was extremely fast and had the endurance to outrun any foe. To reach the boar, Hercules had to travel far from home into the snowy mountains.

Along the way, tired and cold, Hercules found a cave inhabited by a friendly centaur named Pholus. He fed Hercules and gave him some particularly potent wine that was a gift from the god Dionysus. Other centaurs smelled this wine and became angered because they had not been offered any. This offense led to a bloody fight between Hercules and the centaurs. Hercules killed all of the centaurs and accidentally wounded Pholus with one of his poisoned arrows.

Pholus was the inspiration for the zodiacal sign of Sagittarius. As a centaur—half-man, half-horse—he symbolized the humanity and bestial nature that we all possess. The half-man, half-animal has been used in numerous movies, including *The Fly*, *Beauty and the Beast*, and *Werewolf.*

Hercules continued on to find the boar. He outwitted it by chasing it up into the snowy peaks of the mountains, where its short legs could not move through the snow. After capturing it, Hercules presented it to the king.

For the fourth labor, the king instructed Hercules to deliver the Ceryneian stag to the king. The stag was unusual because the goddess Artemis considered it one of her favorites. Its sharp golden antlers and fantastic speed made it nearly impossible to capture. It took Hercules a year to catch the stag and when he did, it was in the sacred grove of Artemis. He was about to kill the beast when Artemis and her brother, Apollo, appeared. Hercules explained his situation, and Artemis gave him permission to bring the stag to the king only if he returned it unharmed. Hercules respected her graciousness, despite the king's wish to keep the stag for himself.

For his next labor, Hercules was told to disperse a flock of razor-winged birds in the region of Stymphalus. These birds killed by attacking in groups and flinging their feathers like daggers. Because Stymphalus was a valley, hunters could not get above the birds without them seeing. This made the birds very hard to kill. Hunters couldn't get the upper hand. Hercules used his wits and a common bell to solve the problem. Finding a spot on high ground, Hercules rang the bell from a peak above the valley and startled the flock. As the birds looked for their enemy in the valley, Hercules shot them one by one with his arrows until the remaining birds flew to another roost far away.

In the sixth labor, Hercules "enemy" was manure. Augeas, a powerful prince, was in possession of one of the largest stables in the world. It is said that the stables had become so crowded with animals that no one had been able to clean them for years. The stables had become so full of dung that the animals were stuck and no human could get in. The king charged Hercules with cleaning the stables in just one day. Upon hearing that Hercules was going to try this feat, Augeas offered him the payment of one tenth of his herd.

Rather than attempting to shovel his way out of the predicament, Hercules diverted a nearby river so that it rushed through the stables and washed them clean in no time. When he returned to Augeas and asked for payment, his request was denied because Hercules used his wits instead of his strength to perform the labor. Hercules would take his payment later, in another myth.

Hercules' housework has brought two words into modern English. First, the word "Augean" has come to mean extremely formidable and difficult. Second, Augean stable is used to describe a place that is marked by great filth or corruption.

Years before the labors began, Zeus, the greatest of all of the gods, gave a mighty bull to Minos, the king of Crete. Minos' wife partnered with the bull to produce the dreaded Minotaur, a man-eating beast with the body of a man and the head of a bull. Eurystheus wanted to sacrifice the Cretan bull to his patron goddess Hera, the wife of Zeus, so he ordered Hercules to capture the bull and bring it to him as the seventh labor. Hera hated Hercules, so she made the task more difficult. Hercules succeeded, but the king did not sacrifice the man-beast. Because of the insult to divine order, Hercules set it free and it ravaged the countryside for years.

For the eighth labor, Eurystheus charged Hercules with the capture and delivery of Diomedes' herd of horses. These were no ordinary horses; Diomedes, the king of the warlike people of Thrace, owned and trained the herd of horses to eat the flesh of humans. Hercules stormed the stables and captured the horses with iron chains. As he attempted to leave, Diomedes and the people of Thrace attacked him. Hercules defeated his assailants and afterwards Hercules fed the body of Diomedes to the ferocious horses. Soon after he delivered the horses to Eurystheus, they mysteriously escaped into the woods where they were devoured by the wolves of Zeus.

Hercules's ninth labor involved obtaining the girdle of Hippolyte, the queen of the Amazons. The Amazons were a group of warlike women who were suspicious of men. Hercules met with Hippolyte and explained his need for the girdle, and she gave it to him without question. Unfortunately, Hera was not happy with the ease of this labor, so she provoked the Amazons by telling them that Hercules' men were going to kill Hippolyte. When the Amazons attacked to protect their queen, Hercules thought it was a trap set for him. Fearing he might die at the hands of the Amazons, Hercules slew Hippolyte and escaped by ship.

Amazons, as a mythical race, have been popularized in movies, television, and in comic books. They epitomize the strong, independent woman, and they are often portrayed in a role reversal with men. Wonder Woman, one of the few female superheroes, was an Amazon, albeit a twentieth-century, glamorous, crime-fighting Amazon.

The tenth labor took Hercules around the world. He set out to capture the cattle of Geryon, who was a mysterious man-beast with three arms, three heads, and wings. Geryon hid his cattle in a cave at night, but Hercules found them and herded them to his ship. Along the way, he battled giants, a two-headed dog, and many other perilous beasts. Although Hera made numerous attempts to thwart Hercules throughout his trip, none of them succeeded. Eventually, Hercules brought the herd to the king, only to find that they were sacrificed to Hera.

The eleventh labor was comprised of many adventures that culminated in obtaining the apples of the Hesperides. These apples were made of pure gold, but no one knew where to find them. Hercules traveled far and wide to learn of their location. Along his travels, he met Nereus, a shape-changing sea god who knew of their location. Nereus tried to withhold the information from Hercules, but the hero grabbed him and held tight as Nereus changed shape from a lion, to a boar, and so on. Finally, Nereus divulged the location and Hercules resumed his search for the apples.

On the way he encountered Antaeus, a giant who was the child of an earth god. No matter how hard he wrestled, Hercules could not beat the giant. In his struggle, he realized that as long as the giant's feet touched the earth, he could not be beaten. Hercules then lifted the giant from the ground and squeezed the life from him.

When Hercules finally reached the bottom of the earth, he met Atlas, who was the Titan who held the earth upon his shoulders. Titans were an earlier race of cruel gods that Zeus defeated and enslaved. Atlas also knew the secret location of the apples and he made a deal with Hercules. He agreed to bring Hercules the apples if the hero would hold up the earth. Hercules took the earth upon his shoulders, and Atlas set off to fetch the apples. Upon returning, Atlas was reluctant to resume his arduous task. Hercules sensed this and asked Atlas to hold the earth for him while he got a pad for his shoulders. Atlas, who was not the smartest of Titans, agreed. Hercules grabbed the apples and returned to the king, ready for his final task.

Hercules' final labor would prove to be the most difficult. Eurystheus asked Hercules to bring Cerberus, the three-headed guardian dog of Hades, to the upper world. Hercules entered the dark gloom of Hades and saw the shades of the dead. Along the way, his long-dead friends called to him. He attempted to free them and succeeded at freeing his dead friend Theseus, but the earth trembled at his attempts to violate the finality of death. Unable to help his friends, he resumed his task of capturing Cerberus. Pluto, the god of the underworld, agreed to let him take the dog if he could capture it without using weapons. He succeeded by wrestling the dog into submission and led Cerberus to the upper world.

After completing the labors, Hercules married a woman from a political family and was encouraged to enter into politics. When he became the leader of a city, he was murdered when someone poisoned his robe. He died almost instantly and Zeus took him to Olympus to join the gods.

Scholars have found many symbolic meanings behind the labors of Hercules. Some equate the twelve labors to the twelve months of the calendar. Others see Hercules as a symbol for the sun and his enemies as symbols for winter and snow.

The twelve labors have even found their way into the constellations. Hercules appears in the Northern Hemisphere from April to October, and can be seen in the north of the Southern Hemisphere. Four of the brighter stars in the constellation form a square called the "Keystone," and the stars that represent his arms and legs extend from it. Other Hercules-inspired constellations include: Leo, the Lion; Draco, the Dragon; and Hydra.

Hercules' story is timeless. It has served as the inspiration for over fifty movies. In films, Hercules has been to New York, conquered Atlantis, encountered the Three Stooges, fought against moon men, battled vampires, sparred with Popeye, and clashed with Kung Fu. He has also challenged more traditional enemies, like the Amazons and the Hydra. Producers in France, Great Britain, Italy, West Germany, Finland, and Spain have created movies about Hercules.

This hero has also inspired at least four television series. During the late 1990s three popular series were based on the Herculean myth. Disney created a popular animated version and Kevin Sorbo starred in the cult favorite, *Hercules: The Legendary Journeys*. This live-action version was so popular that it spawned *Young Hercules*, a series that was aimed at the teen audience.

Hercules' tale is a story of overcoming seemingly insurmountable odds. It also captures the imagination of its audience with its fantastic and otherworldly opponents. Despite his eventual downfall in the myth, Hercules remains the archetype of the hero to audiences around the world.

Icarus and Daedalus

Icarus

The myth of Daedalus and Icarus is a story of the sobering consequences of jealousy, disloyalty, and greed. Daedalus was an amazing problem-solver, artist, architect, and inventor. Although he was talented, he was also deceitful, untrustworthy, and immoral. While living in Athens, Daedalus earned a reputation through his lifelike sculptures and inventions like the sail, level, axe, and glue. However, his accomplishments and renown did not alleviate the jealousy that he felt for other talented inventors, and this jealousy would be his first downfall.

Daedalus' nephew, Talos, inflamed the inventor's jealously. The youth came to apprentice in Daedalus' workshop and he showed great promise. Talos invented a saw, although Daedalus claimed his nephew's invention as his own. The potter's wheel and drafter's compass were among the youth's other inventions. Fearing that Talos' skill would surpass his own, Daedalus lured him to the top of Athena's temple and pushed him off. His depraved deed was discovered while he was trying to dispose of the body. He either fled or was banished from Athens, and he had to find another place to call home.

On the island of Crete, Daedalus found receptive hosts in King Minos and Queen Pasiphaë. The queen had fallen in love with a beautiful white bull that had been given to the king by Poseidon. She engaged Daedalus to help her consummate her lustful feelings toward the bull. He complied by devising a cow device into which he put the queen. Using the device, the queen was able to mate with the bull, and the union produced a half-man, half-bull called a Minotaur.

Humiliated and angry at the bizarre bastard child, Minos employed Daedalus to develop a labyrinth in which to keep the Minotaur. The labyrinth was a chamber consisting of winding hallways. The ingenious design quickly confused those who entered and they became trapped inside. After the labyrinth was completed, Minos called upon the Athenians to offer humans as a sacrifice. Upon entering the labyrinth, the unfortunate sacrifices would become lost and eventually eaten by the Minotaur.

Clearly Daedalus did not have a conscience about his inventions. His lack of conscience and loyalty became clear to Minos when he divulged the solution to the Labyrinth to Minos' daughter, Ariadne. In turn, Ariadne revealed the secret to her love, Theseus, to save him from the Minotaur. When Minos found out, he punished Daedalus by subjecting the inventor and his son, Icarus, to the Labyrinth.

To escape from the labyrinth, Daedalus cleverly crafted two pairs of wings from feathers and wax. As he attached a pair to the back of Icarus, he warned him not to fly too low or the mist from the sea would dampen the wings and cause him to fall. He also cautioned Icarus against flying too high for the sun would melt the wax. The father and son took flight and the wings worked beautifully.

Despite his father's wise advice, Icarus quickly became enamored with the thrill of flying. As he soared up to the sun, the wax of his wings began to melt and he plummeted into the sea. Devastated, Daedalus pulled Icarus' lifeless body to the shore. The island onto which he carried the body became known as Icaria and the sea into which Icarus fell is called the Icarian Sea.

A broken man, Daedalus fled to Sicily. He found refuge in King Cocalus' palace. Earning his keep by making inventive toys for the king's daughters, Daedalus was able to maintain a low profile. In the meantime, Minos continued to search for his traitorous inventor. Finally, he arrived in Sicily and ran into Cocalus. The crafty Minos bet Cocalus that he could not thread a string though a spiral shell. Cocalus took up the bet. He ran back to the palace to have Daedalus complete the task. When Cocalus returned with the threaded shell, Minos knew he had found Daedalus. Minos demanded the surrender of the outlaw and Cocalus reluctantly agreed to do so but only after a feast that evening. When Minos arrived for the feast, Cocalus invited him to take a bath. As the king's daughters were tending to the guest, they poured bucket after bucket of scalding water over Minos until he was dead.

Daedalus could live without fear of reprisal, but he would never return to his homeland or see his son again. His uncontrollable jealousy and lack of loyalty cost Daedalus his happiness. Despite his unfortunate personal weaknesses, today Daedalus' name is more commonly associated with creative inventiveness as can be seen in the numerous consulting, software, and service companies that have adopted his name. In addition, his name inspired the adjective "daedal," which refers to something skillful or intricate.

Jason and the Argonauts

The myth of Jason and the Argonauts is one of the great tales of the Greek heroes. These seemingly godlike figures overcame insurmountable odds and monstrous enemies to achieve their missions. In the case of Jason, his mission was to fetch the Golden Fleece.

The story behind the Golden Fleece is fantastical in itself. It begins with the Thessalian king, Athamas, and his wife Nephele. They had a son and daughter, Phrixus and Helle. When Athamas married his second wife, Ino, she plotted against the kids. After sabotaging the country's crops, she falsified an oracle to say that the drought would cease after Phrixus and Helle had been sacrificed. When Nephele learned of the plot, she arranged for the children's escape on the back of the ram with the Golden Fleece, which she had received from Hermes, the messenger of the gods. As the children flew over the sea on the ram's back, Helle fell into the sea and drowned. When Phrixus landed at Colchis, he sacrificed the ram and gave its fleece to Aeëtes, the king of the land. Aeëtes then nailed the fleece to a tree, where it was guarded by a fearsome, sleepless dragon.

Jason entered the story soon after King Pelias of Iolcus received an oracle about his kingdom. The oracle told the king to beware of a man with one sandal who would bring the downfall of the king. When Jason arrived in Iolcus to help Pelias offer a sacrifice to Poseidon, the king recognized him as the man in the oracle—Jason had lost one of his sandals while crossing a river. Pelias asked Jason what he would do if he were in the king's situation and had received the oracle. Jason replied that he would require the potential murderer to bring the Golden Fleece to the king. After hearing this solution, Pelias charged Jason with the seemingly impossible task.

In need of a ship and crew, Jason set about preparing for the mission. He assembled a noble and valiant crew, including many men known from other myths. Not all versions of the myth agree about who was a member of the crew, known as the Argonauts. Some of those who are generally regarded as crew members include:

- Acastus, the son of King Pelias, who joined against his will
- Actor, the son of Deion
- Admetus, the prince of Pherae
- Argus the Thespian, builder of the *Argo* and the son of Phrixus
- Ascalaphus the Orchomenan, the son of Ares
- Asterius, the son of Cometes, a Pelopian
- Atalanta of Calydon, the virgin huntress
- Augeas, the man whose filthy stables were cleaned by Hercules
- Butes of Athens, the bee master who fathered some of Aphrodite's children
- Calais, the son of Boreas (the North Wind), who had wings on his head and feet
- Canthus the Euboean, who may have been the son of Poseidon
- Castor, the Spartan wrestler
- Coronus the Lapith, the son of a man named Caenus who was a woman before Poseidon turned him into a man
- Echion, the son of Hermes and Antianira
- Erginus of Miletus, the son of Poseidon
- Euphemus of Taenarum
- Euryalus, the son of Mecisteus
- Eurydamas the Dolopian, from Lake Xynias
- Hercules of Tiryns, the son of Zeus
- Hylas the Dryopian, the squire to Heracles and one of Helen of Troy's suitors
- Idas, the son of Aphareus of Messene
- Idmon the Argive, who was Apollo's son
- Iphicles, the son of Thestius the Aetolian
- Iphitus, the brother of King Eurystheus
- Laertes, son of Acrisius the Argive and father of Odysseus
- Lynceus, who had very keen sight and could supposedly see things underground
- Meleager of Calydon
- Mopsus the Lapith
- Nauplius the Argive, navigator and the son of Poseidon
- Oileus the Locrian, father of Ajax
- Orpheus, Thracian poet and musician
- Peleus the Myrmidon
- Peneleos, the son of Hippalcimus

- Periclymenus of Pylus, the son of Poseidon who could change his shape
- Phalerus, the Athenian archer
- Phanus, the son of Dionysus
- Poeas, son of Thaumacus
- Polydeuces, the Spartan boxer
- Polyphemus, the son of Elatus
- Staphylus, the brother of Phanus
- Tiphys, the helmsman
- Zetes, brother of Calais.

Jason and his men crafted a ship with fifty oars and christened it the *Argo*. Following the instructions of Athena, they attached a piece of oak from Zeus' sacred tree in Dodona to the prow of the ship. The wood spoke in a human voice and told the future. When the crew launched the ship, it appeared among the stars as the constellation Argo in the Southern Hemisphere.

The Argonauts stopped several times on their trip to Colchis. Early on, they freed the blind King Phineus from the torment of the Harpies, frightening, winged monsters with birdlike bodies and women's heads. Whenever Phineus was about to eat, the despicable Harpies would swoop down and snatch his food. To make matters worse, the remaining food and the air itself would reek of their foul stench.

King Phineus offered to help the Argonauts if they would help him escape the Harpies. In honor of his guests, the king served an immense feast. No sooner was the dinner on the table when the Harpies dove down from the sky and devoured everything, leaving their disgusting odor in their wake. Two of the Argonauts, Calais and Zetes, set out after the Harpies. They were the sons of the North Wind, Boreas, so they could fly, and they were very fast. They quickly caught up to the monsters and were about to kill them when Iris, Hera's messenger, stopped them. She promised that the Harpies would leave King Phineus alone if Calais and Zetes would spare their lives.

In addition to being Hera's messenger, Iris was the goddess of the rainbow. It is no wonder that her name means rainbow. She also lends her name to our modern term for the round, pigmented, contractile diaphragm portion of the eye.

The two Argonauts returned to their group with the news that the Harpies would no longer bother the king. Phineus, who happened to be a seer, instructed Jason how to navigate through the Symplegades, which were frightening rocks that crashed together whenever anything passed between them. He advised him to release a dove. If the bird made it through the Symplegades, then the *Argo* would be able to pass.

As the *Argo* approached the rocks, Jason released the dove. It flew through and came out safely, with only its tail feathers harmlessly torn off near the end of the passage. When the rocks opened again, the Argonauts rushed through.

Only their stern ornament was lost as the rocks snapped shut behind them. From that time forward, the Symplegades stood still because it was fated that they would never move again after a ship had made the passage.

The Argonauts stopped on an island to rest and four castaways approached them. They identified themselves as the sons of Phrixus and Chalciope. Jason thought they might be helpful in convincing their grandfather to give up the Golden Fleece, so he invited them to join his crew.

When Jason arrived at Colchis, he decided to try the straightforward approach: he would go to King Aeëtes and explain his situation. Unfortunately the king was unimpressed. He demanded that Jason complete a series of impossible tasks to get the Golden Fleece. Luckily, Jason had the help of Hera and Athena, who sent Eros to make Aeëtes' daughter Medea fall in love with Jason. Her love for the hero would cause her to betray her father's loyalty and help Jason get the fleece with her witchcraft.

Jason was charged with two tasks. First he had to yoke a team of ferocious, fire-breathing oxen and plow a field with them. Before he took on the oxen, he sprinkled a charm from Medea over himself and his weapons. The charm would make him invincible for the day. Because the charm protected him from the oxen's fiery breath, he was easily able to harness them, plow the field, and move onto his next task.

For his second task, Jason had to sow the teeth of a dragon in the field and then destroy the armored warriors that sprung up from the teeth. As the warriors emerged, Jason began dispatching them with his sword and then threw a stone into the middle of the melee, which caused the warriors to turn on each other.

Aeëtes was not a good loser. He did not immediately turn over the fleece. That night Medea snuck off to join the Argonauts' celebration, where Jason vowed to marry her. She helped Jason get the fleece by using her powers to cause the sleepless dragon to sleep. Jason grabbed the fleece and the lovers set sail as soon as they reached the *Argo*.

As the Argonauts fled Colchis, Aeëtes' men, including his son Apsyrtus, were not far behind. Apsyrtus trapped the *Argo*, so the Argonauts found refuge on an island that was sacred to Artemis. Medea then lured her brother to the island, where Jason ambushed and killed him. Then they killed everyone aboard Apsyrtus' ship and escaped.

Zeus was outraged over the betrayal and murder of Apsyrtus, so he brewed up a storm and ordered the Argonauts to seek purification from Medea's aunt, Circe. She was a witch, the one who would later trap Odysseus and his men and turn them into swine. To appease Zeus, the Argonauts set out on the long trip to Circe's island Aeaea.

Circe purified them, but when she learned of their misdeeds, she chased them off the island. As they passed the island of the Sirens, these evil women tried to seduce the sailors with their song. Orpheus countered the song by singing and playing his lyre as loud as he could. Because of Orpheus' efforts, all of the Argonauts were able to resist the Sirens, except Butes. He was so overcome by their enchanting song that he jumped over and swam off to be with them. Today the word siren describes a seductive woman or a device that produces a warning noise.

Next, the Argonauts had to navigate a narrow strait that consisted of the cliff of the six-headed monster Scylla on one side and the whirlpool of the beast Charybdis on the other. Thetis, the ancient goddess of the sea, secretly navigated them safely through the perils. The phrase "Scylla and Charybdis" is the origin of our saying, "between a rock and a hard place."

When the Argonauts finally reached home, Jason discovered that his parents and brother had been killed by King Pelias. He then plotted with Medea to seek revenge. Medea disguised herself as an old woman and visited Pelias with promises to restore his youth. She required his daughters to participate and she gave them proof of the spell. She chopped a lamb into pieces, cooked it into a stew, and then lifted out a lively little lamb. The daughters killed Pelias and cooked up his body parts and then hopelessly waited for their father's return.

Jason and Medea quickly fled to Corinth, where they had children and spent many happy years together. Medea was not popular among the people of Corinth. She frightened and disgusted them and Jason began to feel the same way about her. He divorced her and set out to marry the king's daughter, Glauce. Medea did not take the news well. She killed the children that she and Jason had together and sent a wedding gift to Glauce. The gift was a robe that burst into flames when Glauce tried it on. The fire not only consumed Jason's bride, but also her family and their palace. The grieving Jason went to visit the wreckage of the *Argo* to find consolation in his glory days, and a beam from the ship fell on his head and killed him.

The story of Jason and the Golden Fleece contains enough action and adventure to fill dozens of movies. The silent movie *The Golden Fleece*, released in 1918, was the earliest film to feature the story. In 1963, the epic *Jason and the Argonauts* featured spectacular special effects. The 1970 film, *Medea*, based on Euripides' drama by the same name, starred the opera diva Maria Callas as the title character. In the realm of television, *Jason and the Argonauts* (2000) featured Jason London as Jason, Jolene Blalock as Medea, and Dennis Hopper as Pelias in a retelling of the epic adventure.

Jason's challenges, fortunes, and misfortunes produced an engaging tale that has endured for centuries. It has brought a few colorful monsters, like the Harpies and the Sirens, into our modern common culture. The myth provides us with a moral as well: winning isn't everything; it's how you play the game.

Lancelot

❧

The story of the love triangle between Lancelot, Guinevere, and Arthur contains some of the most powerful themes in mythology. Friendship gained and lost, forbidden love, and the loss of innocence all come to the forefront in this complex tale. Unlike Greek and Roman myths about love affairs, this British myth represents infidelity as a sin and a moral flaw in the lovers.

Lancelot du Lac is the central figure in this story. He was born to a noble couple but was separated from his parents as an infant. The Lady of the Lake cared for the infant Lancelot and he grew strong and learned the ways of the fairies and mankind. She was a benevolent caregiver, a mystically powerful woman, and she was the keeper of Excalibur until she gave it to Arthur. She had a court of fairies and lived in a secluded wooded lake. Lancelot became a champion of great strength, honor, and beauty through protecting the lake, the lady, and the fairies. Eventually he left the seclusion of the lake to find a group of equals, but there were few knights who were as well trained and honorable as him.

On his search, he met Arthur, a king whose code of chivalry met Lancelot's high standards. Loyalty was very important in medieval times because a king depended on his loyal knights to defend his castle from attackers. This idea of loyalty evolved into a complex code of chivalry, which governed the appropriate behavior of honorable men. Lancelot pledged his loyalty to Arthur and became one of his knights. Eventually, it was these similarities that would drive the friendship apart.

One of the first missions that Lancelot performed for Arthur was to escort the King's wife-to-be, Guinevere, from her home to the kingdom of Camelot. It is believed that Lancelot and Guinevere fell in love during that journey, but Lancelot forswore that love for his pledge to King Arthur.

Historians have tried to pinpoint the actual site of Camelot. Some argue that it was Colchester, while others describe it as being near Tintagel, where Arthur was supposedly born. The most likely place is Cadbury Castle in Somerset. This castle today consists of an earthen hill with an enclosure at the top.

Guinevere and Arthur married and Lancelot became a member of the king's elite Round Table of knights. From that day forth, he busied himself with any and all assignments that he could, in order to distract himself from the queen. These adventures only helped to bolster his growing fame and make him dearer to Arthur. As champion of the Round Table, his job was to defend the honor of the king and the queen. He was also selected to carry out special missions of mercy, diplomacy, and combat. But even being dubbed a champion of the famed Round Table could not extinguish the longing he felt for Guinevere.

The queen loved him dearly, as did many women. Many times Lancelot was captured and tricked by women in their efforts to become his wife. In one act of trickery, Elaine pretended to be Guinevere and seduced Lancelot. Their night of passion resulted in a son who would grow up to be Sir Galahad, and, in a twist of fate, the only knight pure enough to see the Holy Grail.

Eventually, Lancelot and Guinevere gave in to their passion and destroyed the trust and loyalty that was at the foundation of Camelot. Fellow knights became suspicious and accused the queen and Lancelot. To preserve the honor of the queen and Arthur, Lancelot was forced to fight and defeat the knights. The Round Table became fractured and wars ensued. Eventually Arthur became aware of the affair and, in a rage, declared war on Lancelot's castle. The war was bitter, but it stopped when Guinevere was captured by Arthur's enemy, Melagaunt, an evil knight who wished to weaken the kingdom of Camelot so that he could take it for himself. Lancelot preserved the kingdom by saving the queen and killing Melagaunt.

After defeating Melagaunt, Lancelot cloistered himself and lived as a hermit. He traveled the world trying to do penance for his misdeeds. He would have died a hermit if news had not come to him of the growing war between Camelot and Mordred, the evil bastard son of Arthur. Mordred wished to take the throne prematurely and to take Guinevere as his wife. Mordred's actions were so offensive that Lancelot, regardless of the peril to himself, came back to Camelot to wage war upon Arthur's enemy. He returned to find the battle underway and proved that he was still a champion of the Round Table. Arthur forgave Lancelot just before Lancelot fell on the battlefield. Arthur also lost his life that day, a victim of Mordred's weapon. Mordred died in the battle as well when he fell upon Arthur's famed sword, Excalibur. With the death of Lancelot and Arthur, the power and glory of Camelot began to fade.

Lancelot's chivalrous personality and forbidden love for his best friend's wife has made him an engaging character in films. Nearly all of them focus on the love affair between Lancelot and Guinevere. In *Knights of the Round Table* (1953), starring Robert Taylor, Lancelot battles with Morgana and falls in love with Guinevere, who is played by Ava Gardner. *Lancelot du Lac* (1974) depicts the Knights of the Round Table as greedy and conniving, and the affair with Guinevere ends with disastrous results. In the 1995 movie *First Knight*, Richard Gere stars as the unfortunate knight who betrays the king's (Sean Connery) trust.

The affair of Guinevere and Lancelot has inspired television shows as well. William Russell starred in the title role of the series *The Adventures of Sir Lancelot* from 1956–1957. A 2002 series called *Guinevere Jones* featured a teenage reincarnation of the queen who is trained by Merlin to defend the innocent.

Lancelot's betrayal of the king was shocking and condemned in the medieval world. On the other hand, the forbidden love of Guinevere and Lancelot, coupled with the chivalry of the Middle Ages, is interpreted as romantic by modern audiences. For this reason, the myth surrounding them will continue to be popular and inspire modern works of art, literature, and cinema.

Leprechauns

L eprechauns have become synonymous with anything Irish or lucky. These little fairies are such an accepted part of our culture that people often forget they are mythical creatures. Leprechauns are most frequently depicted as short, old men adorned in old-fashioned hats, green pants, green jackets, and buckled shoes. The University of Notre Dame's mascot may come to mind when one imagines a leprechaun.

According to Irish myth, these unfriendly beings lived alone making shoes. The name "leprechaun" is derived from a combination of *leith brogan* meaning "shoemaker" and *luacharma'n* meaning "pygmy." Luporpan, Lubrican, and Lubberkin were other variations on the name. The leprechaun could be tracked down by the sound of his tapping shoemaker's hammer. They often lived in cellars and were known to help people by performing tasks for them or giving them lucky charms. At the end of the day, leprechauns got together for wild drunken feasts.

The leprechaun's treasure is one of the enduring parts of the leprechaun myth. This treasure usually takes the form of a pot of gold located at the end of a rainbow. Some versions of the myth describe the leprechaun's treasure as left by the marauding Danes. According to the myth, a leprechaun could be coerced into giving up his treasure, but the crafty creature could always trick his captors into looking away, at which point the leprechaun would disappear, with the treasure.

One memorable tale involves a man who managed to capture a wily leprechaun. After forcing the leprechaun to reveal which tree he had buried his pot of gold beneath, the man tied his red handkerchief around the tree to mark it. Then he left to find a shovel, but when he returned, he found every tree in the forest had been marked with identical red handkerchiefs.

Leprechauns are mainly found in Irish folklore, but the folklores of other countries have similar counterparts. In Holland, there are friendly little people called Kabouter, while the Scandinavian counterpart is a troll. The Manx version is called Phynnodderee, who possessed great strength and would help people complete tasks like driving home sheep and harvesting crops.

In the United States and the United Kingdom, the leprechaun has become a symbol of Irishness and luck, which is why leprechauns are so frequently used in marketing campaigns. For example, Lucky Charms cereal features Lucky the Leprechaun, who proclaims the cereal is "magically delicious." While Lucky Charms cereal may be one of the most recognizable marketing campaigns using leprechauns, there have been many more. Among the leprechaun-related terms that have been trademarked, there are "Toys of the Leprechaun," "Leprechaun's Gold," "Lucky Lime Leprechaun," "Leprechaun Tree," "What Leprechauns drink when they're not drinking beer," Leprechaun Software International, Ltd. and "Leprechaun Lawns 'For a Magically Green Lawn'."

Leprechauns have played central roles in several movies. In *Darby O'Gill and the Little People* (1959) Albert Sharpe played Darby, an old man who spins outlandish tales about banshees and leprechauns. When he captured a leprechaun, no one would believe him. Warwick Davis starred as an evil leprechaun in a series of movies called *Leprechaun*. In the first movie (1993), Jennifer Aniston played Tory Reding, who teams up with her friends in a battle against the leprechaun who is out to destroy anyone who gets in the way of his quest to regain his stolen treasure. The original movie led to five sequels including *Leprechaun 4: In Space* (1996) and *Leprechaun in the Hood* (2000).

Perhaps because of the simplicity of the leprechaun myth, modern companies have latched on to this mythical creature. Its popularity in modern society ensures that the legend of the leprechaun will hardly be forgotten.

Loki's Children

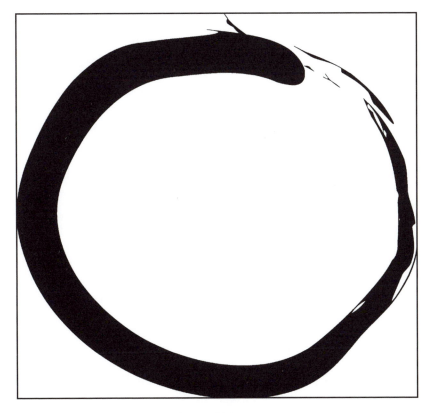

The World Serpent

Procrastination seems to be part of human nature. We have the propensity to put things off that we don't want to deal with and say "I'll do that later." Soon, later has passed and we have forgotten about the situation completely. The Norse people were aware of this particularly human trait and composed stories that explained the danger we face when we ignore and procrastinate. Once again, the motive character behind this lesson is Loki, the god of fire and mischief who seems perfectly happy to point out the flaws of his godlike peers, while giving us a glimpse of our own human frailties.

Loki was not overly happy with the way the other gods treated him. He was, after all, not really one of them, but a transplant or step-god. He was more related to the giants than he was to the gods. The giants treated him with respect and he often found himself in their company.

Like many of the gods, Loki had lovers other than his wife. Also like the gods, he had children by his concubine. The other gods took warrior maiden giants as lovers, but Loki chose a powerful user of magic for his lover. Loki was a powerful magic user in his own right, so he chose a lover that shared his interests. Her name was Angrboda, and she had no special love for the gods because they feared her magic and shunned her just as they shunned Loki's gifts.

Unfortunately, when Loki and Angrboda got together, their offspring were far from what anyone would have expected. Their first child was Fenrir, a powerful wolf cub who was playful and very, very hungry. The second child was a large and sinuous serpent. Third and most hideous was their daughter, Hel. From her head to her waist, Hel was as normal looking as any girl, but from the waist down, she was nothing but decay and filth. Rotten flesh and maggots fell from her legs, only to be renewed by more of the same. This trio of offspring lived in a cave with their mother among the great mountainous region known as Jotunheim.

Word reached the halls of Asgard that Loki and his mistress had produced offspring. When the messengers described the children, the gods became revolted and remarked that the evil of Loki and Angrboda had been made manifest in their children. They decided to pay a visit upon the couple and their kids. They stormed the cave and kidnapped the children against the will of their parents. It was against all laws of the gods to kill a child born of a god, so they could not rid the world of these beastly children.

Odin looked at the serpent and decided to hurl it into the ocean where it could not come close to any who lived in Asgard. The serpent landed and sank to the bottom of the ocean where it began to swim, eat, and grow. Soon the serpent grew so large that it circled the entire world. It could bite its own tail and make a loop about all of Midgard. It became know as Jormungand, the World Serpent.

Odin looked at Hel and was so appalled that he tossed her from Asgard, into Niflheim, the Land of the Dead. There he cursed her to stay forever and look after those who died of illness and old age. Hel, at first angered at the decree, was confused. Once she tasted the power she had over the dead, she began to enjoy her reign. She built a great hall from which she could watch the deaths of all people in the world. She took pleasure in spreading illness and starvation. Her power slowly grew, just as her brother the serpent continued to grow.

Finally, Odin looked upon the wolf pup, Fenrir. He and the gods agreed to let him roam freely among the fields because he seemed to be no different than any other wolf, except that he was a bit larger than normal. Soon, he was much larger than a normal wolf. He was huge and strong. He continued to run through the field and hunt the largest stags with ease. Fenrir took pleasure in being near the gods and spoke to them of his adventures and hunts. The gods, initially pleased with the growth of the wolf, began to become nervous as the growth continued unabated. The wolf was becoming far too powerful and strong minded. They asked the fates about the wolf and were told that Fenrir would cause the death of Odin, the all-father.

Because the gods could not kill the wolf, they decided to capture and chain the beast so he could not cause mischief or strife. They fashioned a great chain with strong links to put around Fenrir's neck. They named the collar Laeding. They showed the chain to the wolf and goaded him by saying he was not stronger than it. Fenrir laughed and allowed them to wrap the chain around his neck and chest. Once it had been wrapped around him tightly, Fenrir pulled and strained against it. To the gods surprise, the links popped and the chain fell to the ground in pieces. "Now you see how strong I am!" howled Fenrir. The gods regrouped and began fashioning another great chain. This time they made it double the thickness of Laeding and tested each link. Those that were found wanting were reinforced or replaced. When it was finished they named it Dromi. They brought the chain to Fenrir, and it took all the gods to carry it. The gods played to Fenrir's need for praise: "If you can break this chain, then songs will be sung about your strength throughout the world."

Fenrir looked at the mighty chain. It was obviously strong and he questioned whether he would be able to break it. Then, as he watched the eyes of the gods, a thought occurred to him—"What if this is some sort of trick? Will they let me go if my strength fails to snap this great chain?" He had grown since the last test and decided that the risk was worth it. The gods draped the chain around him and tightened it so that it was snug around his neck and chest. With a great growl the giant wolf began to pull against the chains, his breath became quick, and his fur bristled. He pushed and pulled with all his might and heard the first link pop. This gave him encouragement and he pulled with the last of his strength and broke the greatest chain ever made by the gods. "Now you know that I am stronger by far than any of you!" growled the great wolf as be bounded off after a herd of elk.

The gods conspired once more, for their fear had now risen at the wolf's tremendous show of strength. "We must get the dwarves to make an enchanted chain; one that cannot be snapped by this beast. Only the dwarves possess that kind of magic," said the all-father. They sent a messenger to the land of the dwarves telling them what they needed and offered great amounts of gold for the work. Dwarves, who were greedy by nature, were more than happy to make the commissioned cord. They fashioned the chain so that it was no thicker than a ribbon and smooth to the touch. It looked flimsy but was stronger than any cord or chain ever fashioned by god or man. They named it Gleipnir. The gods were fascinated by it and called Fenrir to test it. "It is not strong enough to hold you . . ." said the gods, "but try it anyway." Fenrir looked at their faces and saw a shadow of untruth in their eyes. He knew that something was truly amiss for he smelled the faint aroma of magic about the thin cord they wished him to put around his neck.

Sensing a trap, he offered the gods an exchange. "If I try on this cord, then I want one of you to place your hand in my mouth. This way I will be assured of my freedom if the cord holds. I would not wish to be trapped here." The gods looked at each other in surprise. None of them wished to place their hand in the wolf's mouth, for they knew the cord could not be broken. The dilemma was that if no one did it, Fenrir would be allowed to roam freely and fulfill his destiny of killing the all-father. With this in mind, the god Tyr, the most trustworthy and noble of the gods, placed his hand in the great wolf's mouth. The cord was placed around the beast's neck and tightened. Fenrir pulled upon it with all his strength, but it held. He tried again and again but the cord would not snap. The gods had found a way to bind him.

"Congratulations," he said. "Now free me." The gods all backed away except for Tyr, whose hand was still in Fenrir's mouth. Knowing now that he had been tricked, the wolf bit down and crushed through the gods wrist, separating hand from arm and gulping it down. Tyr jumped back and the gods bound his stump to stop the bleeding. Fenrir howled and pulled upon the cord in a rage, but he could not escape. There he would have to sit and wait until the final battle of Ragnarok, the end of time. At that point, he would fulfill his destiny, regardless of the gods' attempts to stop him. Tyr would go on to be the most respected of the gods. He would be asked to judge disputes, for he was obviously willing to give up personal needs for the group.

Out of the three children of Loki and Angrboda, Fenrir makes the most appearances in modern culture. Many companies use his name, such as Fenrir Industries, Inc., which offers forced-entry equipment for law enforcement and has a wolf as its logo. In the 1990 movie *Runestone*, a Norse runestone is found in Pennsylvania and a prophecy tells that Fenrir will be released from the stone and bring about Ragnarok. Many video games, like *Final Fantasy*, often include him as an element in the game.

The age-old idea that if you ignore something, it will go away obviously did not work for the gods. It only got them into bigger and bigger trouble, literally. Our culture is rife with situations that illustrate this point. Governments destroy other regimes and leave a small faction in place, thinking that they are too small to cause a problem. Years later, they find out that the little group they ignored has grown into a bigger and more dangerous threat than they could have imagined in the first place.

Popular children's stories focus on the forgotten child who is ignored by everyone only to become greater than the others. Usually, these stories are told from the point of view of the forgotten one, like Cinderella. In another example, Superman, a powerful and heroic figure, chose the disguise of Clark Kent, a mild-mannered and utterly forgettable figure, to escape notice and keep his enemies wondering. Inevitably, that which is ignored by the populace will eventually be seen as an enemy if it grows too large. This idea was not lost on the ancient Norse people. Their mythology reflects the idea in a graphic and colorful way.

Loki's Gift to Odin

Some lessons in life are learned through hindsight. One looks back on a series of events and says "If only I had or hadn't done . . . then I wouldn't be in the predicament I am in today." Each of us, in one way or another, has probably had this experience and learned a valuable lesson from it. In mythology, where a story most often serves a higher purpose, the lessons learned by the protagonists may take a bit longer to make themselves clear. Such is the case with the offspring of Loki.

Loki is the Norse god of fire. Like most fire gods, he is seen as a magician, capable of changing shape and controlling his surroundings. This is a great power to have and can be used to benefit those who see you as a friend. It can also prove quite dangerous to those who become your enemies. In the mythologies of the Norse people, Loki uses his powers to help the gods become great and, in turn, to aid in their downfall. But his character is more complex than a mere "bad" guy. He has reasons for turning against his own.

The high gods of the Norse lived in a fantastic city in the sky called Asgard. The all-father and leader of their group was Odin. He and the other twelve high gods were constantly at war with the giants. These giants were not the dumb giants that are often depicted in children's stories. They were brave warriors, with cunning minds and magic. The gods fought with them, but sometimes took them as wives as well. One giant who was brought to Asgard and lived among the gods for quite a while was Loki. Originally a child of the giants, he was made a member of the family of the gods by Odin. Whether he was Odin's stepbrother or a kind of adopted son is still debated, but he was considered a part of the family. Family or not, Loki was very different. He was skilled in the art of strategy and capable of solving dilemmas that left the other gods perplexed. Perhaps this is why he was never treated like the rest of the gods.

To keep their city safe, the gods decided to build a huge wall around Asgard. This would take an enormous amount of work and time. The gods had decided to begin the tremendous task when a stranger appeared. This stranger was a massive giant leading a strong black horse. The stranger told the gods that he could build the wall in a day and a night. The gods laughed at the stranger and told him to be on his way. The giant answered, "If you don't believe me, then let me try. If I do it, I can have whatever price I wish." The gods, not thinking ahead, agreed to the terms before asking what his price would be. The giant then explained that if he finished the wall by the next morning, he would take Freya, the most beautiful of the goddesses, as his wife. Initially shocked by this price, the gods decided to wait. Surely the giant could not do what he proposed.

The giant began to build the wall. He sent his horse off and drew his plans. Not much later the horse returned, pulling hundreds of huge rocks behind him. Clearly this was no ordinary horse. The rocks were put into place and the horse went to get more. Meanwhile, the giant plugged the holes with mud. Before the sun had set, the horse brought many loads to the giant and the wall was already half finished. The gods began to panic. The wall was going to be done on time and they would have to give Freya to the giant. Odin was the most displeased because he had made the agreement. He asked Loki to find a way to get them out of the situation and Loki did just that. He went to the quarry where the horse was and changed himself into a female horse. Apparently he did a convincing job of it because the horse chased him. Loki led the horse away from the worksite and coupled with it. The horse relaxed and fell asleep.

Meanwhile, the giant had been working away. The wall was almost finished except for the last load of rocks. He waited and waited, but the horse never came. He began to panic and searched high and low for the horse. His faithful workhorse was nowhere to be found. This had never happened before; he had always been able to count on the horse. The sun would be coming up soon and the work was not going to get done. He had failed. The gods saw what was happening and were relieved that their most prized goddess would remain with them in Asgard. As the giant stormed about and vented his frustration, the gods celebrated in the great feasting hall. "We have kept our precious Freya and we have but a few rocks to place in order to finish the wall," Thor said. "What great wisdom you showed in this situation, Odin," claimed Freya.

Odin did not answer. He continued to watch the giant, who was beside himself with anger. When the horse returned, he saw it being scolded by its master. Something in his heart bothered Odin. He felt guilty, but he could not give up Freya. The deal would have to stand as it was made. He gathered up the gods and they made their way to meet with the giant. They reached the wall and the giant began to hurl insults. "You have won this wall by deceit. Let it be known that you are all liars and cheats," he yelled. Turning to Odin he asked, "Where is your honor all-father? You make deals knowing that you cannot pay the price." He stepped forward in anger saying, "Then I will destroy the wall. For it is not yours to keep!" The gods rushed upon him and threw him out of Asgard, telling him never to return for fear of death. Then they returned to Odin's great hall to celebrate.

The gods sang and ate while Odin sat upon his throne in deep thought. This duplicity bothered him. The gods had gotten their wall by trickery and this unjust act was against the way of Asgardians. It was just plain wrong. His anger began to turn toward Loki for having tricked the horse. He spoke of it to the gods and slowly each of them shared his anger with Loki. They shared the guilt and anger for a season while Loki was mysteriously absent.

As the gods were still stewing in their own guilt and their anger at Loki, the great trickster appeared at the throne room. Loki had returned. The gods immediately began to scold him and Odin asked, "Why did you bring shame upon our realm? You used trickery and cheated the giant." Loki stood there, stunned. "Why? Because you asked me to. You got yourselves into a mess that you could not get out of and you asked me to solve it. Do not be angry with me. I did what I had to. I suffered for a season bearing the offspring of the stranger's great horse. I brought it with me as a gift to you, all-Father. Please, forget your anger as I present you with this gift." He left the hall and came back with a magnificent stallion, black as coal and standing upon eight powerful legs! The steed neighed and trotted toward Odin and the all-father could not contain his happiness. This was the fastest and most powerful horse in all the realms. He forgot his anger as he pet the muzzle of the horse. He welcomed Loki into the hall and bade him to drink and be merry. Loki did as he was told, but he could not be merry. He felt betrayed by his own family. He had saved them heartache, only to be chastised. He would never be the same again, and so began the slow fall of the glory of Asgard.

This story is about making choices and living with them. Each of us has the ability to choose our destiny in ways both large and small. Simple decisions can affect the outcome of a situation quite far removed from the present. We can also affect other people by the decisions we make. Odin and the gods chose to gamble without really knowing what was wagered. They failed to recognize the real outcome of their actions. Although Odin seemed to understand that he had made a mistake in judgment, he failed truly to learn from it. His use of Loki as a scapegoat proved to be a most disastrous decision because he lost Loki's loyalty and turned him against the gods. Just as Odin and the other gods failed to learn from their mistakes, we, too, are often blind to our own poor decision-making processes.

Movies and television shows tend to use this framework for many stories. The "your past mistakes will come back to haunt you" theme seems to be the easiest route for horror films such as *I Know What You Did Last Summer*. The central characters of the movie all pay the price for a decision they made concerning the supposed death of a stranger. The leaders make poor decisions and use those who are in lower positions as scapegoats, only to find those scapegoats trying to usurp power.

The movie *Star Wars: Attack of the Clones* shows a young Anakin Skywalker being consistently scolded for his attempts to do things that are right but not in line with the beliefs of his teacher. Although he has been told to think about his choices, he chooses to ignore the teachings and go with his baser instincts. Unfortunately, he turns increasingly evil as a result of those decisions, finally becoming Darth Vader, a Sith lord who wields the power of the Dark Side of the Force. In the final movie of the *Star Wars* story, *Return of the Jedi*, Darth Vader realizes the consequences of his choices and makes amends with the help of his son, Luke Skywalker.

Loki's crafty ways make him an intriguing character who appears in many movies, such as *Wizards of the Lost Kingdom II* (1988). Matt Damon plays Loki, a mischievous angel who falls from heaven, in the 1999 movie *Dogma*. One of the henchmen in *Power Rangers: Lightspeed Rescue* is named Loki. One of the most popular movies involving Loki was the 1994 film *The Mask* starring Jim Carrey. In the movie, Carrey plays shy Stanley Ipkiss, who finds a mask that depicts Loki. Whenever Stanley puts it on, he transforms into a wild green-faced superhero.

We do not get a chance to go back and erase the choices we have made, but we can help repair the damage those decisions have on others by looking at ourselves and accepting responsibility. Odin did not do that and the gods wound up paying for it. We are just as easily fooled into believing that our decisions will have no large-scale effects. In this case, Odin serves as an example of what not to do when you are in a position of authority.

Man the Animal

Ra

Mythology is filled with bizarre creatures and powerful heroes. Among these characters are a group of hybrids, half-human–half-animal amalgams who range from antagonists to protectors of protagonists in the myths. They deserve mention because they serve a very important purpose in humankind's definition of itself as well as the coinhabitants of our world.

The most notable of the animal-man hybrids is the god Pan and his followers. Pan, the half-man–half-goat, is a symbol of man's undeniable connection to nature. He was a lustful and unrestrained god, and he was associated with bountiful harvests.

Another group of hybrids that had quite a bit of interaction with heroes was the centaurs. Centaurs were a half-man–half-horse mixture. From the head to the waist they were men, but the bottom half was a horse. They were powerful warriors who were particularly skilled with the bow and arrow. Chiron, the most famous of the centaurs, served as a teacher to Hercules. He is the model for the zodiacal symbol Sagittarius. Although powerful, the centaurs were also prone to petty bickering and infighting. This particularly human trait is what led them to their downfall. Centaurs have appeared in movies such as the animated Disney film *Hercules* (1998), *Monkeybone* (2001), and *It's a Greek Life* (1936). There are also centaurs in *Harry Potter and the Sorcerer's Stone* movie and the popular book series.

Hybridization was just as common for females in Greek myth. Medusa, a once-beautiful woman, was transformed into a ghastly beast due to her vanity. Still beautiful in face and figure, the Medusa had a head of poisonous asps instead of hair. This writhing mass of snakes made her so terrible to behold that anyone who looked into her eyes was instantly turned to stone. This myth is fascinating because it can be interpreted many ways. One interpretation is that vanity has a way of destroying any hope for having a real relationship. The other is the danger that beauty holds for the one who falls for it. Either way, it is certainly meant to showcase a very human propensity for the superficial. Medusa's fantastic appearance is well-suited for movies, and she is a character in *3Ninjas: High Noon at Mega Mountain* (1998), *Clash of the Titans* (1981), *The Night Life of the Gods* (1935), and *Medusa* (1997).

The Harpies were a hybridization of birds and women. Initially, they were pictured as beautiful and beneficial spirits, but they turned out to be malign beasts who robbed battlefields and defiled the dead and wounded. They were also known to steal children and eat them. They are pictured as having huge bird bodies with the breasts, arms, and heads of women. The faces of the women are typically bloodstained and their hair is a mess.

The Sphinx, half-woman–half-lion, kept the entire city of Thebes in fear. She ate many of the town's citizens who could not answer her riddle. Only Oedipus was cleaver enough to do so. When he unraveled her riddle, the sphinx hurled herself to her own death in anger and shame, but her riddle has inspired many filmmakers. The 1981 suspense film *Sphinx* is set in Egypt, with the

Sphinx in the backdrop. She even plays a role in the Pink Panther movie, *The Pink Sphinx* (1968). In addition, her memorable figure is synonymous with Egypt.

Man-animal hybridization reached its apex in the Egyptian pantheon. When depicting their gods, the Egyptians chose to anthropomorphize the animal kingdom. Giving human traits to animals seemed to be the best way to lend specific natural qualities to the gods and goddesses. It was easier to understand that a god was a sky god if he had the qualities of a bird. Hence, Ra, the sun god, was pictured as a muscular man with a hawk's head. Thoth, the wise god and a symbol of patience, was illustrated as a man in robes with the head of an ibis, a heronlike bird that wades in rivers to feed on fish. The ibis stands very still for long periods of time in order to catch its aquatic prey. This patient behavior was reflected in the head of the wise god. The Egyptians even had a goddess of cats. Bastet had the body of a beautiful woman, topped with the head of a cat. It is interesting that the Egyptian cat deity was female, as most westerners typically associate cats with femininity.

Certain gods and goddesses were not given animal heads because their sphere of influence was a particularly human area. Isis, the goddess of magic, remained human, as did her lover Osiris, lord of the dead. Animals may die, but humans are the only species that seems to fear death and picture it in the future.

One of the most famous hybrids in our culture is Satan. Much of the information on Satan seems to be derived from tales much younger than the Bible itself. According to the story, Lucifer, God's most trusted angel, led a rebellion against God and was cast out of heaven. Rather than having the beautiful white wings of an angel, Lucifer was transformed into a horrible beast. Dante's *Inferno* depicts Satan as a huge three-headed man with the bottom half of a goat and six batlike wings. Most people describe Satan as a red devil who resembles Pan.

Whether they served as friends or foes, these hybrids allowed people to see the very animalistic tendencies to which humans are prone. Western culture uses this motif in many ways, such as the numerous Wolfman movies Hollywood has produced. Movies like *The Little Mermaid*, *The Shaggy D.A.*, and *Spiderman* illustrate the complex relationship of human and animal and the fascination with the connection between the two worlds. These movies range from happy and light-hearted to tales of horror that unleash the bestial nature of humanity.

Medusa

Medusa

When the name Medusa is mentioned, one imagines a terrifying image of a hideous woman with a writhing mass of snakes in place of hair. But Medusa was not always so grotesque. She was one of three daughters of the sea gods, Ceto and Phorcys. Medusa was extremely beautiful, and her silky ringlets were her crowning glory.

Unfortunately, this mortal enchantress caught the attention of Poseidon, the god who ruled the sea. He raped her in the temple of Athena, the goddess of war. The virgin goddess did not take kindly to this desecration of her sacred home, and she made certain that men would not court Medusa again by transforming her into a repulsive Gorgon with snakes for hair and a gaze that would turn men to stone. She had sharp teeth, brass claws, and wings, and her body was covered in scales. In other versions of the myth, Medusa warranted the curse because she boasted that she was more beautiful than Athena.

As a Gorgon, Medusa lived with her two immortal Gorgon sisters at the end of the earth, where there was no light from the sun or the moon. The word "Gorgon" was derived from the Greek word for "terrible," and terrible the Gorgons were. Surrounding their lair were stone figures of people and animals that had foolishly glimpsed into the Gorgons' eyes. The sisters seemed invincible; any competitor would need to slay Medusa without looking at her or her sisters, and then quickly flee to escape the wrath of the immortal sisters. Only the most foolish would even attempt such a risky task.

Medusa's challenger, Perseus, was not foolish, but he was desperate. King Polydectes had fallen in love with his mother, Danaë. She refused his offer of marriage and Perseus supported her decision, but this did not stop the king from scheming to get her. Polydectes devised a plan to get rid of Perseus so that he could take Danaë by force. His plot was relatively simple: he announced his intent to marry the daughter of another king and arranged a banquet in honor of the event. In accordance with the code of honor at the time, everyone in the kingdom had to bring the king a gift for the banquet, and in this case Polydectes demanded that everyone bring him a horse. Perseus was the son of a slave and there was no way that he could meet the king's demand. Rather than flee the kingdom in shame, he offered the king the head of Medusa. Polydectes took him up on the offer because it would certainly result in Perseus' death.

Fortunately Perseus had some help from Athena, who still did not care for Medusa. Athena brought him to the Naiads, who were nymphs. They lent him three items that he needed to defeat Medusa: winged sandals to allow him to approach and flee swiftly, the cap of Hades to make him invisible, and a pouch in which he could carry Medusa's head. Hermes, the messenger of the gods, helped Perseus as well by giving him an unbreakable sword.

Armed with these gifts from the gods, Perseus set off to the visit the Graeae to find out where the Gorgons lived. These three sisters had one eye and one tooth that they shared among themselves. When he arrived at their cave, he hid and waited until one of the sisters removed the eye to pass it to her sister. While they were temporarily blind, Perseus swooped in and snatched the eye. As he held their eye captive, he was able to force the Graeae to tell him how to find the Gorgons. Once he had the information he wanted, he threw the eye into Lake Tritonis and set off to the Gorgons' hideout at the edge of the earth.

Perseus donned the cap of Hades, invisibly crept up to the Gorgons' lair while they were sleeping, and used reflections in his brightly polished shield to guide his attack. The reflections allowed him to see Medusa without looking directly at her and becoming a stone figure. He swiftly lopped off her head with the sword, stuffed the head into his pouch, and flew off with the winged shoes before the Gorgon sisters realized what happened. From Medusa's lifeless body sprang Pegasus, the winged horse, and Chrysaor, who later became the king of Iberia. Supposedly these offspring were fathered by Poseidon.

The hero began his journey home, but he made several stops along the way, including one in which he acquired a wife and son. When he arrived home, he discovered that Polydectes had attempted to rape his mother and that she had found a safe haven at the altar of the gods. Outraged, Perseus went to the king's palace and announced that he had completed the king's request. In disbelief, Polydectes called upon Perseus to prove his claim. The youth gladly complied by turning his head away and pulling Medusa's head out of the pouch, which turned the king and his guests to stone. With his mother safe from Polydectes, Perseus returned the weapons to Hermes and the Naiads. To show his appreciation to Athena, he gave her Medusa's head, which the goddess mounted to her shield.

Medusa has been an enduring subject of artwork since ancient times. In early artwork, she is depicted as a hideous creature with scales and claws, but in later images she often has a beautiful face surrounded by snakes. Sometimes she is illustrated alone and other times she is depicted with Perseus, as in Paul Klee's *L'esprit a combattu le mal* (1904).

Ancient Greeks believed that Gorgons had magic powers. Above their doors they placed plaques of Gorgons to ward off evil. In a similar vein, they placed an image of Medusa's head on their shields for extra protection, just as Athena did. Athena's Medusa-decorated shield was called an aegis and today we use the expression "under the aegis" to mean "under the protection or sponsorship."

According to the ancient Greeks, the power of Medusa was not limited to her image, but it existed in her blood as well. It had healing powers that could reanimate the dead and could be a deadly poison, depending on the side of the body from which it was taken. Many scholars connect the blood of Medusa to menstruation, which had negative connotations of its own. Ancient Greek men had difficulty understanding women's menstrual cycles, which caused them to bleed without a wound or pain. To them, menstruation was clearly associated with something mystical and evil.

To the ancient Greeks, Medusa personified the mystic qualities of women. She is one of the most vivid characters in Greek myth. Her powers and attributes are well remembered today. One only needs to look to the Electric Light Orchestra song "Turned to Stone" to see how well-known the story is today.

Merlin

Merlin

In all of Arthurian legend, Merlin is one of the most powerful and enigmatic figures. The character of Merlin appears in almost every version of the tales of King Arthur and his knights. While Merlin acted as a teacher, vizier, court magician, and seer, he also played the part of surrogate father to Arthur.

As the archetypal magician, Merlin has been depicted in many ways, from a wise old sage to a youthful spirit with a fondness for trickery. Throughout the numerous tales of King Arthur, he called upon the powers of nature and controlled the elements. He was also capable of changing his appearance, often transforming into animals. Merlin did not always give away his services; many times he bargained with both friends and enemies to get what he wanted. The most famous example involves a deal he made with Arthur's father, Uther Pendragon.

Uther wanted to sleep with the wife of one of his enemies, so he asked for Merlin's help. Merlin agreed under the condition that any children produced from this affair would be given to him. Uther agreed and Merlin put a "glamour" on him, making him look like the woman's husband. The fruit of this union was Arthur. Uther was compelled by the law of chivalry to stay true to his word. Although he loved the child, he gave him to Merlin.

One can only speculate about Merlin's motives, but they do not necessarily seem good-hearted or well-intentioned. The story of Arthur's conception is characteristic of Merlin's mysterious nature. It is difficult to decide whose side he was on as he carefully wove stories and situations that led to the fortune or demise of others. One of his powers was a blurry vision of the future, and he used it to his advantage. He embodied the chaotic, playful, and sometimes dangerous aspects of humanity.

Although Merlin may not have been one of the nicest people, he chose the Knights of the Round Table as cohorts. Merlin acted as advisor and mediator to this opinionated bunch to balance them out. These were noble men with even nobler ambitions. Unfortunately, this one-sidedness left them extremely open to idealistic fantasies. Merlin was there to keep them on track and to provide honest opinions.

One of the most interesting aspects of the legend of Merlin is that it was based on a real person. According to a few stories, he was a man named Myrddin who studied the ancient rites of the druids and kept council with the spirits of nature. Druids revered nature, believed in reincarnation, and were the most learned people in Celtic society.

In all likelihood, Myrddin was an astronomer and healer as well as a counselor to rulers. With so much knowledge, this man was probably considered quite valuable and would have had a great deal of influence. In fact, some accounts describe him as an advisor to chieftains of the British tribes. From the remaining fragments of poetry left from those earlier times, scholars believe that Myrddin created quite a bit of unrest between these tribes in order to get them to battle each other, but his motives for causing the unrest are unknown. Tales say that

Myrddin was punished by some supernatural force and driven mad. Most of the accounts say that he wandered off into the countyside, never to be seen again.

Other stories say that Merlin was actually a man named Lailoken, who was from a high ranking tribe from the lowlands of Scotland. It was believed that he lived in the sixth century. The stories say that Lailoken went on a search for meaning. He deserted his family and lived in the woods, learning to survive the harshness of nature. It is said that it was in nature that he found wisdom and power. He was most likely a druid as well. Apparently, Lailoken offered a great deal of wisdom and advice to chieftains and commoners alike. There is no mention of magic or demonic influence in these stories.

In other stories, Merlin was described as the offspring of a nun who was raped by a demon. This union of opposites certainly gives credence to the chaotic, trickster nature that Merlin exhibited. In any event, it is fitting that his background remains shrouded in mystery while the bloodlines of all the characters that surround him are meticulously spelled out. Since he is shrouded by mystical forces and powers, we can only guess as to his true nature.

Geoffrey of Monmouth's depiction of Merlin has lent the most to our modern notions about prophet and sorcerer. He told of the demon and nun union in his *Vita Merlini* (Life of Merlin). In his *Historia Regum Britanniae* (History of the Kings of Britain), which he wrote around 1135, he described how Merlin used his magic to help King Aurelius transport Stonehenge to Salisbury Plain, from where it supposedly originally resided in Ireland.

In one of the enduring stories about Merlin, the trickster became the victim of an adversary's trick. According to the legend, Merlin fell in love with Nimue, who was also known as Viviane. Nimue was a sorceress who wished to learn from Merlin. The wise sorcerer foresaw that this tutelage would lead to something bad for him, but he decided to go ahead with it anyway. Perhaps he was looking for some companionship, for he soon fell in love with Nimue and showed her some of his most powerful magic.

Nimue learned quickly and soon became almost as powerful as Merlin. One day, while Merlin was showing her a powerful spell, she turned the spell back onto Merlin and trapped him. The stories vary as to the vessel of entrapment. Some say he was trapped in a tree or a bush, while others say it was a standing stone, like the ones at Stonehenge. Whatever the vessel, it was a natural object. Since Merlin was a force of nature, it is fitting that his spirit was locked in a natural object and not a man-made tomb.

In some versions of the story, Merlin died within the trap, but in others he devised a method of escape, descended into madness, or pined for the love of Nimue. In a later Welsh version of the story, he voluntarily retreated into an underground lair, where he watched over the Thirteen Treasures of Britain and the True Throne of the Realm, on which Arthur would sit when he returned.

Merlin's enigmatic and entrancing persona has served as the basis for engaging film characters since the early days of cinematic history. In 1899, he served as the title character in a black-and-white silent film called *Merlin the Magician*. One hundred years later, Rik Mayall starred as the magician in the movie *Merlin: The Return*, in which Merlin's archenemy Mordred and his mother Morgana, played by Craig Sheffer and Julie Hartley respectively, escape from their imprisonment in another world. Merlin and a reawakened King Arthur team up to prevent the dastardly pair from entering into twentieth-century life.

Merlin's appearance in movies about King Arthur illustrates the comical way that he has often been characterized. For instance, in the animated film *The Sword and the Stone*, Merlin follows the archetype of fool instead of magician. Although he serves as Arthur's father, teacher, and friend, his forgetfulness and clumsiness provide comic relief. When he helps Arthur, his bumbling nature causes accidents that wind up benefiting the situation. Likewise, in the live-action movie, *Excalibur*, Merlin is a very wise, yet comical character.

As a wise, magical advisor, Merlin has become a prototype for modern characters such as Obi-wan Kenobi from *Star Wars* and Gandalf from *The Lord of the Rings*. Obi-wan takes Luke Skywalker under his wing and his magic takes the form of the Force. In a similar sense, Gandalf leads a fellowship of men, hobbits, an elf, and a dwarf on a quest to destroy the One Ring of the Dark Lord Sauran before he can reclaim it to destroy Middle-earth. Not even a human, but sent to protect the peoples of Middle-earth, he was capable of many magical feats such as the creation of and wielding of fire.

The mysterious nature of Merlin is as powerful as the magic he was said to have used. The readers of his stories are attracted to his character as he was attracted to the powers of the elements. At once, he is a tender spirit who seeks to help and a raw force of nature that can destroy anything in its path. Much can be seen of his character in the fantasy literature currenty written, so it is not surprising that Merlin remains present in the minds and hearts of westerners.

Midas

Midas

King Midas was both the subject of myths and a real person. According to myth, he loved his life of leisure and pleasures, planted one of the first rose gardens, and spent his days listening to music and enjoying sumptuous feasts. His mother was the goddess Rhea and either his father or stepfather was Gordius. When Gordius died, Midas became the ruler of Macedonia. From that day forward, the kings of the land were alternately named Gordius and Midas.

Some versions of the myth surrounding Midas tell about the future leader when he was a baby. Supposedly a line of ants carried grains of wheat to the baby's mouth while he slept. The oracles decided that the event was an omen of Midas's future wealth and power.

The most well-known myth about Midas is his "golden touch." When Midas was king, an old drunk satyr found his way to Midas' rose garden. Satyrs were half-man–half-goats who lived in the woods and were fond of lechery and frivolity. It was not uncommon for satyrs to overindulge in everything, including alcohol. Today, the word "satyr" is synonymous with a lecherous or lustful man. Midas, who was a devotee of Dionysus, recognized the old satyr as Silenos, Dionysus' beloved mentor. He treated the visitor as an honored guest and entertained him for ten days and nights. The satyr regaled his host with tales of his travels and adventures. After wining and dining Silenos, Midas brought him back to Dionysus.

Eternally grateful to be reunited with his lost friend, Dionysus offered to grant Midas a wish. Unfortunately for Midas, he didn't think very long before selecting. The foolish ruler figured that more wealth would bring him more happiness, so he asked for everything that he touched to be turned to gold.

This wish was granted and Midas went on his merry way to test his newfound power. He reached out and plucked an oak twig from a tree, and it instantly turned to gold. Delighted, he touched rocks, roses, and dirt, which all transformed into pure gold replicas of their previous forms. He could have barely imagined a power so wonderful, until he sat down for his evening feast. Every morsel of the delectable food hardened into gold in his hands. Even the wine could not quench his thirst for it turned to gold in his throat. He began to panic, and in some versions of the myth his daughter went to comfort him. As he embraced his dear daughter, she too changed into a gold statue.

The heartbroken and hungry king realized the error of his ways; wealth was not what brought him happiness. He begged Dionysus to relieve him of his power. The god directed him to the source of the River Pactolus, where he was to submerge himself in the water. Midas did as he was told and the river washed his "golden touch" into the sand, where the gold could be found in ancient times, but it has long since been removed. In the versions that include Midas' daughter, she is restored to her living form when he washes her in the river.

This was not Midas' only episode of foolishness. One day a large hole opened in the ground and no one knew how to close it up. The pit caused consternation and problems for the people who lived near it. An oracle informed Midas that if he threw his most valuable possession into the hole, it would close. The king acted foolishly once again and threw gold and silver into the abyss, but it did not close. His son, who was seemingly far wiser than his father, realized that human life was the most valuable possession. The brave young man jumped into the pit, which immediately closed, taking him with it.

In another myth about Midas, he got himself into trouble again when he served as a judge in a music contest between Apollo and a satyr named Marsyas, who had been bragging that his music skills were better than Apollo's. In some versions of the myth, the contest is between Apollo and Pan. In either version, Midas took the unwise stance against Apollo. The offended god retaliated by transforming the king's ears into those of an ass. As unfortunate as Midas' predicament, Marsyas' was worse. Apollo sentenced the braggart to death for his vanity.

Ashamed by his hideous ears, Midas hid them under a hat, but his barber knew of the deformity. The king swore the barber to secrecy, but the burden was too much for him. He went to the bank of the River Pactolus, dug a hole, whispered the secret into the hole, and covered it up. A bed of reed grew where the hole had been, and when the wind blew the reeds whispered the secret. Soon everyone knew of the king's embarrassing secret.

Although the myths present a foolish and colorful character, much less is known about the real Midas. The historical King Midas ruled over Phrygia, which is located in what is now western Turkey. He lived between the 740s and 696 B.C. Like the myth, he owned beautiful gardens in Macedonia. History also recorded his marriage to the Greek princess Hermodike as well as his political relationship with Greek cities and Asian neighbors.

In 1957, archeologists excavated what is believed to be Midas' tomb in Turkey. Inside the tomb, evidence of a funeral banquet was discovered. The mournful meal was also celebratory and attended by about one hundred people including priests, priestesses, and members of the king's family. Recent analysis of the food left in the drinking bowls reveals that the mourners dined on a spicy stew of lentils and barbecued lamb or goat meat and they drank a mixture of beer, wine, and mead. While today the name Midas is used to refer to a rich man, the tomb of the man with the mythical "golden touch" did not contain anything made of gold.

Minotaur

Minotaur

The myth of the Minotaur takes place in the very early days of ancient Greece on the island of Crete. King Minos ruled Crete, and the culture that flourished there in the early second century B.C. is referred to as the Minoan period after him. The myth revolves around Minos' failure to respect properly the gods and the fallout that followed.

When Minos began his reign, he prayed to Poseidon to deliver an animal to him to prove that the gods approved of his right to govern. If his request was granted, he promised to sacrifice the bull to show his subservience to the god of the sea. Poseidon complied and gave him a beautiful snow-white bull, but when Minos saw the creature he decided that it was too handsome to sacrifice and he kept it. Poseidon wanted revenge for the broken promise and got it by making Minos' wife, Pasiphaë, fall in love with the bull.

As odd as it sounds, Pasiphaë could not stop thinking about the bull; she simply had to have sex with it. The bull, however, was not the least bit interested in the queen. Daedalus, the ingenious inventor, happened to be staying at the royal palace, so Pasiphaë convinced him to help her. His solution involved a wooden cow contraption that included a compartment in which the queen could hide. She climbed in and proceeded to have intercourse with the bull. The bizarre union resulted in a hideous beast called a Minotaur that had the body of a man and the head of a bull.

Shamed by the product of his wife's peculiar affair, Minos wanted to hide the beast. Unaware of Daedalus' role in the debacle, the king employed the inventor to create a labyrinth to house the Minotaur. The labyrinth was an elaborate structure with winding passages that confused everyone who entered. Soon after entering the maze, entrants became lost and eaten by the Minotaur. Today we use the word "labyrinth" to describe any perplexing arrangement.

Every year, Minos demanded fourteen young men and women from Athens to serve as sacrifices to the Minotaur. The unfortunate victims would be sent into the labyrinth and devoured by the Minotaur. The situation seemed hopeless for the Athenians until the king's long lost son, Theseus, came back home. He set off to Crete as one of the sacrifices, but his real purpose was to defeat the Minotaur. When he arrived on the island, he met Minos' daughter, Ariadne, who fell in love with the heroic young man. Ariadne had learned the secret of labyrinth from Daedalus. In turn, she tried using her knowledge to gain Theseus' affections. Once she had secured a promise of marriage from him, she disclosed the secret.

The secret of the labyrinth was quite simple: it was a ball of thread. Theseus attached one end to the beginning of the maze, and was able to follow it to find his way out after he killed the Minotaur with the sword that Ariadne had provided. At the time, a ball was called a "clew" or "clue." Over time, the word came to describe anything that helps solve a mystery or problem.

When Theseus emerged from the labyrinth he escaped with Ariadne in tow, but he abandoned her on an island on his way home. Eventually she found love and a husband in Dionysus, the god of wine and revelry. Theseus continued home victorious, but he forgot to switch the black sail on his boat to a white one to signal his father that he was alive. When Minos saw the black sail, he assumed that his son was dead and threw himself into the sea.

The Muses

~

In the early stories of the Greeks, the Muses were merely beautiful nymphs who danced and sang, but today their legacy permeates our language. When these maidens weren't singing and delivering epic poetry to the gods during mealtimes, they sang and danced around the sacred springs of Mount Helicon and Mount Parnassus. Over time, the Greeks' beliefs about the Muses changed; there were nine Muses, and they were elevated to minor goddesses who presided over the arts. Their ability to inspire artists led to our modern use of the word "muse" to describe someone who does just that: inspires an artist.

Until later myths, the Muses' parents varied. Sometimes they were Uranus and Gaia, other times they were Pierus and Antiope, and still other times, Zeus and the nymph Neda. In the later accounts of the Muses, they are described as daughters of Zeus and Mnemosyne, who was the Titaness synonymous with memory. Mnemosyne is the origin of our word "mnemonic," which is used to describe a trick that helps stimulate memory. According to the myth, Zeus slept with Mnemosyne nine nights in a row to create divinities who could entertain the gods during their celebratory feasts. In turn, Mnemosyne delivered the nine Muses.

In early versions of the myths, there were sets of Muses in different locations. On Mount Helicon, there were three named Aoede, Melete, and Mneme who represented song, meditation, and memory respectively. At Delphi, there were another three named Hypate, Mese, and Nete who represented the strings of the lyre, a popular instrument in ancient Greece.

Once the nine Muses of later myths had been established, they were named Calliope, Clio, Erato, Euterpe, Melpomene, Polyhymnia, Terpsichore, Thalia, and Urania. Each muse had a specialty. Calliope was the leader of the bunch and she was the muse of epic poetry. Her name meant "beautiful voice" and depictions portray her graceful beauty, often with a tablet or book. Her relationship with Apollo resulted in two children, Hymenaeus and Ialemus, who grew up to be poets and musicians. With her husband Oeagrus, she gave birth to Orpheus, the great poet and musician who saved the Argonauts from the Sirens. Once Zeus called on her to mediate a dispute between Aphrodite and Persephone. Both goddesses wanted beautiful Adonis for themselves. It isn't surprising that "adonis" is one of our modern words for a physically perfect man. Calliope appeased all parties in the dispute by equally dividing Adonis' time between the two goddesses, while allowing Adonis some time for himself.

Clio was the muse of history. Her name meant "famegiver" and she is usually illustrated wearing a laurel wreath on her head and carrying a book. In some accounts, she is attributed with the introduction of the Phoenician alphabet to the Greeks. Like Calliope, she is involved in a myth with Aphrodite. After she teased the goddess about her love for Adonis, the goddess made Clio fall in love with Pierus, who was the king of Macedonia. The union produced a daughter named Hyacinthus, who lends her name to the hyacinth flower.

The remaining seven Muses were not as colorful. Erato was the muse of love poetry, so it was fitting that her name meant "awakener of desire." Melpomene was the muse of tragedies. By some accounts, she is the mother of the Sirens. Euterpe, whose name means "joygiver," was the muse of lyric poetry. Polyhymnia was the muse of heroic hymns and mimic art. Interestingly, she is often depicted in a solemn pose with her finger on her mouth. Terpsichore was the muse of dancing and choral song, and her sister, Thalia was the muse of comedy. Urania was the last of the Muses and she governed over astronomy. Artists often depict her with a globe and compass.

The 1980 movie *Xanadu* is one of the most memorable popular culture appearances by the Muses. In the movie, Olivia Newton-John plays Kira, a muse who helps a disillusioned artist out of a rut by getting him to build a roller disco nightclub. It's an odd concept, but she serves the classic muse role: inspiration to artists. Although her name differs from the Greek Muses, she is one of nine sisters and her parents are Zeus and Hera.

The Muses appear in several Greek myths, sometimes as collaborators, other times as competitors. As collaborators, they gave the Sphinx her riddle and taught Echo to play music. Aristaeus learned healing and prophecy from the talented goddesses. However, the Muses were not always charitable.

In several myths, the Muses display vindictive qualities when their talents were challenged. For example, Thamyris, a famous bard from Thrace, foolishly challenged the Muses to a musical contest. If his music outshined theirs, Thamyris would get to sleep with all of the Muses. Unfortunately for the hapless challenger, he lost and they struck him blind and dumb. The Muses accepted a poetry challenge from the nine daughters of a king. When the daughters lost, the Muses transformed them into birds. In yet another challenge, the Muses took on the Sirens. When the Sirens lost, the Muses plucked the half-women, half-birds and made crowns from their feathers.

Not all of the myths about the Muses dealt with contests. In an account by Plato, song appeared when the Muses were born. Some men were so taken with the music that they sang constantly. They forgot to eat and drink and they eventually starved to death. The Muses transformed the dead men into locusts, allowing them to sing continuously through their lives.

The Muses were revered by the ancient Greeks, especially the artists, musicians, and poets. In the sixth century B.C., the Greeks began "Mouseai" festivals honoring the Muses. Oftentimes, philosophy schools would house muse-cults because the scholars looked to the Muses for inspiration. These places of research and learning were called *mouseions*, which is the origin of our modern word "museum."

The word "music" is derived from the Muses as well. A person who danced, wrote, painted, sang, or practiced any of the Muses' arts was called a *mousikos* and the arts were called *mousike*. Music was considered the highest of the Muses' arts and soon the word mousike became associated solely with music.

A few of the individual Muses have inspired modern words as well. For example, John C. Stoddard named his shrilly pitched steam-whistle organ calliope. Its unique sound is synonymous with showboats, circuses, and merry-go-rounds. The quantitative analysis of history is known as "cliometrics" after the muse of history, and "terpsichorean" refers to dancing.

Our world today would seem dull without the music and art inspired by the Muses of ancient Greek mythology. These fictional beauties danced, sang, and entertained to earn the respect of the ancient Greeks. While the Muses did not actually exist, the concept of someone who inspires artistic greatness is an important element of our culture.

Odysseus

Cyclops

Odysseus is probably the most famous of all characters in mythology. One of the most well-known adventure tales is the story of Odysseus' travels as they are told in the epic poem, *The Odyssey*. This tale of heroism, hardship, and determination has contributed words into our modern vocabulary and impressed images of fantastic creatures like the Cyclops and the Siren into our minds.

The Odyssey begins after Odysseus met and married Penelope. They moved to Ithaca, where Odysseus became king. When the Trojan War began, an oracle warned Odysseus that if he went to Troy, it would be twenty years before he saw his home and his beloved Penelope. Despite this omen, he set off to fight in the war and eventually arrived in Troy.

To gain entry into the city, he and his men created a giant horse with a secret compartment inside. The men hid inside the compartment and left the horse at the gates of the city. During the night after the Trojans brought the gift into the city, Odysseus and his men jumped out of the horse and attacked the Trojans. The slaughter of the Trojans angered the half of the gods who sided with the Trojans, and they punished Odysseus and his men by making it nearly impossible for them to get home. Odysseus boarded his ship after ten years of war, and he would spend the next ten years trying to reach the shores of Ithaca.

To punish him, Poseidon, the god of the sea subjected Odysseus and his men to violent storms that threw them off course. After being tossed about, they landed the ship on a strange island inhabited by the Lotus Eaters. Some of the men ate the fruit of the lotus, and they fell into a deep sleep or forgot everything about their former lives. Realizing the danger, Odysseus rounded up the rest of his men and left before he lost them all. The deep sleep of the men was similar to a drug addiction and might have been symbolic of the sailors who became addicted to opium in foreign ports. In *The Wizard of Oz*, Dorothy and her friends encounter a similar situation when they fall asleep in the poppy field on the way to the Emerald City.

Next, Odysseus and his men landed on an island that seemed to offer a safe haven. The hungry men began to search for food, and they soon found a cave that contained lambs, goats, pails of milk, and huge baskets of cheese. Assuming the owners would understand their predicament, they helped themselves. The owner, however, was a Cyclops name Polyphemus. Cyclopses were foul-tempered giants with a single eye on their foreheads and a fondness for the taste of human flesh.

When Polyphemus returned, he rolled a huge boulder in front of the entrance, trapping the men inside the cave with him. He began eating the men, but Odysseus convinced Polyphemus to drink wine until he passed out. He then plunged the end of the Cyclops' staff into his eye, blinding him. The Cyclops screamed and scrambled to the entrance. When he moved the boulder aside, Odysseus and his men escaped from the cave using the sheep as camouflage. They ran back to their ship and set sail.

The one-eyed Cyclops figure appears in many stories, like the Cyclops in the comic book *X-men* who is a mutant with laser beams that shoot from his eyes. In another example, the Cylons in the television series *Battlestar Galactica* are one-eyed robotic enemies. The concept of the regular man being able to defeat a giant enemy appears in many stories, from David and Goliath to Jack and the Beanstalk.

Odysseus and his crew reached the floating island of Aeolus, the ruler of the winds. Aeolus sided with the Greeks and wished to help Odysseus return home. He welcomed them into his palace and presented them with a sack full of winds. Aeolus cautioned them to open the sack on a calm area of the ocean where the vengeful Poseidon was not watching. After they set sail, a few of the more impatient and less faithful men put a sleeping drug into Odysseus' wine so they could open the sack and speed their journey. Unfortunately, the sea was too rough and the winds blew them farther away from home.

The sack full of winds is very similar to the story of Pandora's box. In that story, Pandora receives a box from the gods, who warn her not to open it. She cannot contain her curiosity and opens the box, releasing a mass of evils upon mankind. She manages to close the box in time, leaving only hope inside. So despite the troubles Pandora unleashes, mankind still has hope. Today the term "Pandora's box" refers to an abundant source of problems.

When they reached the island of Aeaea, Odysseus sent some of his men to explore. They came upon the palace of Circe, a witch who cast a spell upon the men, turning them into swine. One of the men, Eurylochus, had stayed behind and watched as she transformed the other men, and he ran back to tell Odysseus what had transpired. As Odysseus headed for the palace to rescue his men, the god Hermes gave him a charm that would protect him from Circe's magic. She transformed the swine back to men after Odysseus agreed to stay with her. Odysseus and his men stayed there for many years, and he fathered three of her children: Agrius, Telegonus, and Latinus. Although he honored his agreement with Circe, Odysseus could never bring himself to love anyone but his wife, Penelope. Eventually, Circe let him go and sent him to Tartarus, the underworld of the dead, to visit the ghost Teiresias, who was a seer.

The crew traveled through the hellish landscape of Tartarus and dealt with Charon, the ferryman of the River Styx, to reach Teiresias. He warned Odysseus that he would pass an island where Helios keeps his cattle and if any were harmed, he would never reach home. Teiresias also told him of the trouble back in Ithaca. Men were trying to seduce his wife Penelope and steal his kingdom. Armed with this knowledge, Odysseus and his men headed back east toward Greece.

Soon they passed the island of the Sirens, beautiful maidens who sang so sweetly that no man could resist their charms. Odysseus had his crew members put wax in their ears, but he wanted to hear the song of the Sirens, so he had his men tie him to the mast so he could hear the Sirens but not be tempted away. The word "siren" soon came to mean an alluring woman who seduced men. In 1819, Charles Cagniard de la Tour adopted the name for his device that produced sound at a constant pitch. From there, siren has come to mean any warning device that produces sound.

As they headed through a narrow strait between two islands, the ship encountered Scylla and Charybdis. Scylla was a beast with many mouths that lived in a rocky outcropping. Charybdis was a whirlpool that would destroy the ship if it came too close. In essence, the men had to choose between the monster in the rocks and the whirlpool. They decided to sail right between the two dangers, which resulted in Scylla devouring six men; the situation proved impossible to solve without some loss. This is where the saying "between a rock and a hard place" comes from.

Eventually the men reached the grazing land of Helios' cattle. When they landed, Odysseus made his men promise not to touch the cattle, but stormy seas trapped the men for a month. Desperate and consumed by hunger, the men finally ate one of the cattle while Odysseus was away. Odysseus tried to make amends by promising Helios he would punish the offenders, but this was not enough for Helios. He complained to Zeus, and Zeus sent a storm that killed the entire crew except Odysseus.

Left floating on the remains of his ship, Odysseus drifted for days until he reached the island of Ogygia, home of Calypso, the beautiful goddess of the island. She imprisoned him on the island for seven long years. He declined her offers of eternal youth and immortality if he would stay forever because his love for Penelope was too strong. Eventually, Zeus ordered Calypso to free Odysseus and she gave him some supplies and the materials he needed to construct a raft. Today Calypso lends her name to a style of West Indian music, an orchid, and the boat of underwater explorer Jacques Cousteau.

Despite incurring another of Poseidon's rages, Odysseus managed to float to the island of the Phoenicians. With help from the king, he returned to Ithaca, disguised himself as an old beggar, and met with his son, Telemachus. While Odysseus had been away, Mentor tutored and guided Telemachus. Today "mentor" means counselor or tutor. Together Telemachus and Odysseus worked to get rid of the suitors who were staying in his home. Having learned patience and trickery through his journeys, Odysseus concocted a plan and made Telemachus swear not to reveal his identity. They went to the palace and Telemachus introduced Odysseus to the suitors and his mother, explaining that he had met the beggar only recently. Penelope instantly recognized a scar on Odysseus' thigh, but she kept quiet to protect him from harm.

Odysseus and Telemachus gathered the suitors' swords, shields, spears, and helmets and locked them away. The following day, Penelope announced that she would marry the suitor who could bend Odysseus' bow, string it, and shoot an arrow through the loops of twelve axe handles as Odysseus had once done. Each of the suitors took a turn, but none could bend the bow far enough to fit its bowstring. Finally, Odysseus strung the bow, fired the arrow through the axe handles, and, together with his son, killed every suitor in the house. He was finally reunited with Penelope and his travels were over.

Although *The Odyssey* is a long and winding story, it has served as an outline for several other stories. James Joyce's *Ulysses* is the Odyssey told through one man and his actions on one day. Mark Twain's *Huckleberry Finn* is a story of one boy's trials and tribulations as he travels along the Mississippi River during the nineteenth century. The television show *Star Trek Voyager* depicts the story of a spaceship crew blown off course and trying to find its way home. Kirk Douglas starred in a 1954 big screen version of the story called *Ulysses*. And the film *O Brother, Where Art Thou?* is also based on *The Odyssey*. The main character Everett Ulysses McGill and his friends escape from jail and run into sirens, a Cyclops, and a blind prophet on their way back home.

Currently the word "odyssey" refers to a long and wandering voyage or a spiritual quest. The story of Odysseus has undergone its own long and wandering voyage, influencing our modern tales and lexicon along the way.

Oedipus

~

The story of Oedipus is loosely contained in the trilogy of plays written by Sophocles, which is comprised of *Oedipus Tyrannus* (The King), *Oedipus at Colonus*, and *Antigone*. Additionally, the play *Seven against Thebes*, by Ascychelus, is based on the aftereffects of *Oedipus Tyrannus*. These plays have been lauded for their keen and extremely ironic treatment of the concepts of fate and family. The stories were written with a passion and power that captured the pain and sorrow of regret, disobedience, hopelessness, and determination.

Each of the stories revolves around Oedipus, a misinformed individual who does his best to avert a fate he is destined to follow. Oedipus was born to King Laius and Queen Jocasta of Thebes. When he was born, an oracle told the couple that the child would grow up to kill his father and marry his mother. Obviously upset by this news, as oracles were nearly always right, the couple decided to dispose of the infant by having a servant leave the baby in the country to be devoured by wolves.

The servant was going to do as he was told but reconsidered at the last moment and left the infant where a shepherd would easily find him. The shepherd took the infant and brought it to Polybus and Merope, the king and queen of Corinth. They instantly loved him and adopted Oedipus as their own son and future ruler of Corinth. Oedipus grew up strong and wise and expected to become king one day. Unfortunately, he learned from the Delphic oracle that he was destined to kill his father and marry his mother. Believing that the king and queen of Corinth were his real parents, Oedipus decided to cheat fate and leave the kingdom of Corinth forever. This way he would bring no harm to his father.

Oedipus chose to travel to the famed city of Thebes, which had been experiencing some troubles. As he traveled along, he came to a crossroads where he got into an argument with a caravan. The argument escalated into a battle that left the members of the caravan dead, including their leader. Oedipus composed himself and continued his journey to Thebes. This journey took some time and as Oedipus neared the city, he began to hear tales of Jocasta, the widowed queen of Thebes who would give her hand in marriage to the one who solved the riddle of the dreaded Sphinx.

The Sphinx was a horrible, but intelligent monster. It had the head of a woman, the body of a lion, and the wings of a great bird. She would kill anyone who did not solve her riddle. She was very similar to the great sphinxes of Egypt. No one could solve the riddle and all who came before her were devoured. The cities greatest men were being consumed one by one, but Oedipus decided to give the riddle a try.

Eager to acquire a new victim, the Sphinx asked Oedipus to answer the following: What speaks with one voice and walks on four feet, then two feet, then three feet? Oedipus asked the Sphinx to promise that she would commit suicide if he answered the question correctly. Believing that no one would answer the riddle, the Sphinx agreed. With the promise secured, Oedipus answered, "The answer is man. Man lives but one life and speaks with one voice, yet crawls on all fours when an infant, walks on two feet when in middle age, and requires a cane, or third foot, when age begins to consume him." Aghast that this man had answered her question so deftly, the Sphinx was forced to end her own existence.

Through his defeat of the enigmatic and dangerous Sphinx, Oedipus proved that he was not only an able fighter, but also a clever man with a strategic bent. He was a perfect choice for taking the kingship of Thebes. He married Queen Jocasta and rebuilt Thebes. Jocasta bore him four children: two boys and two girls.

Life was idyllic and happy in the city of Thebes until a plague broke out and nothing could cure it. The Queen's brother Creon went to the oracle of Apollo and returned with the news that the plague could only be cured if the murderer of King Laius was found and punished. Oedipus declared that the murderer must pay for his sins by being banished from the city forever and he promised to root out the offender.

All attempts to figure out the identity of the murderer failed and Oedipus became impatient. He called upon the blind seer Teiresias to aid him. He was hesitant to help, but Oedipus forced him to answer. Teiresias said that Oedipus himself was the murderer. Oedipus became enraged because he believed this was a plot to dethrone him and that Creon was behind it. Jocasta soothed Oedipus by telling him that this could not be true because a seer had told her that her child would kill Laius and marry her. That had not happened because she and Laius had abandoned the child in the wild and Laius had been attacked at the crossroads by a robber. Oedipus remembered having killed a man at the crossroads but he put it aside as mere coincidence.

Soon a messenger arrived in Thebes to tell Oedipus that Polybus had died. Oedipus felt relief, believing he had escaped the fate of killing his father. He informed the messenger that he would only return to Corinth when his mother had passed away so that his fate could be completely evaded. The messenger listened to his story and told him that he had nothing to fear because Polybus and Merope were not his true parents. He explained that the couple had adopted Oedipus when he was brought to them by a shepherd from the house of Laius. The old shepherd concurred with the messenger and told of how he had brought them the baby instead of leaving it to die.

Together, Oedipus and Jocasta came to the realization that he was actually her son and that the fate assigned to him had come true. Jocasta ran to her room and hanged herself in horror because of the shame of her actions. Oedipus cursed himself for attempting to cheat fate. Tormented by the tragedy of his life and his action, he could no longer stand the sight of the city, or his dead wife and mother. He could not even bear to look upon his children. In a grand action of punishment, he gouged out his own eyes and imposed on himself the exile he had promised to impose on Laius' murderer. So ended the story of *Oedipus Tyrannus*, but the tale was far from over.

Oedipus' family members were tied inextricably to the fate of their father. Each member of the family responded in a different manner to their fate. His two sons, Etocles and Polynices, vied for the throne of Thebes and ultimately killed each other. The story of their rivalry is called *Seven against Thebes*.

The two daughters, Antigone and Ismene, tried to help their father and brothers as best they could. Antigone was the stronger and more persevering of the two, by far. After helping her father at Colonus, she was intent on saving the body of her brother from a cruel fate. Creon, seeing his chance to usurp the throne, ordered that the body of Eteocles be given a proper burial and thus be able to travel to the land of the dead and be given his proper glory. At the same time, he decreed that the body of Polynices was never to be buried and thus broke the divine laws set forth by the gods. Antigone would not allow her brother to be disgraced in this manner. She planned to allow Polynices the graces he was due, and thus broke Creon's decree and ritually buried him. For her rebellion, Creon sent her to her death.

Creon's youngest son had already been killed and Ismene, the lover of his oldest son Haemon, took her own life when she heard of Antigone's fate. Upon finding the body, Creon and Haemon argued over whether it was Creon's fault for trying to be in control of fate. Haemon struck out in anger at his father, then stabbed himself in order to join his beloved. Creon returned home with the body of his son, only to find that his wife had heard the news and killed herself as well. Left in his parlor, he accepted that he alone was responsible for the fate of his family. He pleaded with his servants to slay him, as he had no reason to live. The play ends with his being lead away from the terrible scene in sorrow.

The central theme of these plays is struggle. Each individual struggles against a power, motive, or force that is beyond his or her abilities or understanding. In the case of Oedipus, he runs from a fate he cannot escape. The irony of his situation only adds to the frustration that the reader or audience of the play must feel.

The theme of changing the future or rewriting the past in order to alter the fate of the world or one's own personal path is frequently used in many science fiction movies, television shows, and books. The television series *Star Trek* deals with the complex moral issues involving the altering of events in the past. The idea that history should unfold as it is intended is the correct moral imperative. This fatalistic view is due to the benefits of hindsight and time travel. The theories are intriguing, but the overall idea remains the same as the ideas presented in the Oedipus cycle: your personal fate cannot be escaped and attempts to outwit or change the future inevitably lead to the realization that all was for nothing and the pain and frustration level is usually greater.

The classic novel *The Time Machine*, by H. G. Wells, also provides an example of this kind of thinking. The 2002 movie adaptation adds to this fatalistic view as the main character travels back in time to save his beloved from a fatal accident, only to find that she is killed in another accident shortly thereafter.

Sigmund Freud had a great reverence for this play and used Oedipus to name a psychological aspect of growth in human males. He believed that many boys go through a stage in their early development wherein they attach to their mothers and actively show contempt for their fathers. This stage affects the dynamic of the family as the father and son grow. The father becomes weaker as the son grows in strength, and the father subconsciously or consciously competes with the son for fear of being eclipsed. According to Freud, the Oedipal Complex is quite natural and normal if taken with a grain of salt and not heightened to the level of actual aggression. A similar complex exists between mothers and daughters and is known as the Electra Complex, and refers to a Greek tragedy in which a daughter avenges the death of her father by the mother.

The plot of Oedipus has served as the basis for many plays and movies. *Oedipus Rex* has been adapted for the movie screen several times—in 1911, 1957, and 1968. The 1968 version featured Christopher Plummer and Orson Welles. In Steven Berkhoff's play *Greek*, he twists the concept and has the main character and his mother stay together despite the fact that they know about their mother–son relationship. In Woody Allen's *Mighty Aphrodite* (1995), the father of a brilliant adopted child searches for his son's biological parents. When he finds out that the birth mother is an unintelligent prostitute and porn star, he is disappointed. A Greek chorus intermittently links the plot to that of Oedipus.

The Greeks believed the Fates control the events that happen in a person's life. Clearly Oedipus was no exception. Destiny was a powerful concept to the ancient Greeks and, to an extent, in our modern society. Today many people visit psychics to learn about what the future holds for them.

Orpheus

◠

Orpheus appears in Greek myth more than a few times, which is unusual because he was not a king or powerful warrior. He was, however, a musician of unparalleled talent. As a Thracian, he came to Greece to find adventure, tell stories, and sing. He did all these and more.

Orpheus was an ardent follower of the god Dionysus. He was one of only a few men who were allowed to watch and participate in the rituals of the Maenads, female devotees of Dionysus who would be overcome with madness in the rituals. The music Orpheus played on his lyre soothed them and allowed him to remain safe. It is commonly believed that Orpheus introduced King Midas to the worship and rituals of Dionysus.

One of Orpheus' most famous exploits was as a member of the famous adventuring party, the Argonauts. Although prized as a musician, Orpheus could swing a sword as well. But it was not his swordsmanship that saved the Argonauts; it was his music. As the Argonauts searched for the Golden Fleece, they ran into the dreaded Sirens just like Odysseus and his company did. The singing of the Sirens was beautiful and powerful enough to enslave the mind of anyone, but Orpheus' song was even more powerful. His soothing voice and careful playing of the lyre not only broke the spell of the Sirens, but it also charmed them. Jason and his Argonauts escaped certain death solely by the talent of Orpheus.

Because Orpheus used his gifts for the benefit and enjoyment of others, he was revered. In fact, he became a rather important figure in the cult of Dionysus. He rose in the ranks of the clergy and held a very powerful position.

All was well with Orpheus. He met a beautiful river nymph named Eurydice and they fell in love. Orpheus seemed to be happier than ever before and, as such, was kinder and more patient with his followers. As far as he was concerned, Eurydice was the one thing he had longed for his entire life. In finding her, he believed his life was complete.

Just after the wedding, Eurydice and the other river nymphs were walking along the bank of the river. She was so overcome with happiness that she did not notice the snake at her heel. She stepped upon its head and was bitten. The snake's poison acted immediately and she dropped dead right there. Her spirit, now just a shade, traveled into the underworld and was gone. The nymphs wept and brought the tale to Orpheus and the rest of the wedding party.

Orpheus was so grief stricken that he refused to eat or sleep, which worried his friends terribly. No one heard even one note from his lyre and he had not spoken or sung since the day he found Eurydice along the bank of the river. His friends had reason to worry: Orpheus was planning a journey that all ancient Greeks supposedly took, but not until the end of their lives. He was planning to go to the underworld and he planned to come back with Eurydice.

This plan broke all the laws of the universe. No human was ever supposed to come back from the land of the dead. Nonetheless, Orpheus was committed to garnering the safe return of his beloved from the underworld, no matter the cost. He planned to seek out Hades and his queen, Persephone. He would plead his case to them and gain his wife's release. Anyone who has read Greek myth knows that getting an audience with the king and queen of the underworld was a bit more complicated than simply going down there and asking a few questions. Hercules and Odysseus had done it and barely escaped alive. And while Hercules was the greatest warrior ever and Odysseus was considered among the craftiest of men to have ever lived, Orpheus was neither.

Orpheus was met at the entrance to the underworld by the dreaded Cerberus, the three-headed dog of Hades. The beast snarled and paced as the musician approached. Just as Cerberus was about to pounce upon Orpheus, the musician plucked a few notes on his lyre. Cerberus stopped and cocked his heads to the side. The musician began to play a ballad of loss and sadness that was so powerful, even the beasts of the underworld could understand it. Cerberus sat there in silence with his jaws dropped.

Passing on to travel into the depths of the earth, Orpheus soon came upon the River Styx, which erased the memory of any who swam in it. The only way to cross the river safely was to procure the services of Charon the ferryman, who was very selective about his passengers. The only way to obtain his services was to pay the fee by putting a gold coin into the ferryman's skeletal hand. This is why the dead were buried with one coin in their possession. Charon arrived and immediately noticed that Orpheus was not dead. He refused to take the musician across the river and bade him to return to the natural life that he was destined to live. Orpheus began to tell his story and of the love he lost. The poem was so well performed that Charon was saddened and offered to bring the brokenhearted musician across the river.

Finally, Orpheus came to the palace of the dead and faced the twin thrones of Hades and Persephone. The royal couple was not happy with his presence, but they allowed him a moment. Orpheus began to play a song telling of his great love and his sorrow for her loss. It told of his trip to the underworld and the lengths to which he would go to save Eurydice. The final part of the song explained that if he could not get her back, he would remain there, among the dead of the underworld.

As he played, the shades and shadows of the dead began to weep. The power and sadness of his music were so strong and moving that Sisyphus stopped rolling his ball and Tantalus paid attention to the musician alone. Persephone and Hades told Orpheus that he could bring Eurydice back to the land of the living under one condition: he could not look at her until they entered the full daylight of the upper world. If he broke this oath, Eurydice would die once more and never return. Orpheus happily agreed to the contract and began the ascent to the world of the living.

As they continued their journey, the terrain became rough and hard to climb. Even though he wished to help his wife, Orpheus would not look behind him for fear of breaking the oath. That conviction became harder to sustain as they continued on. With each step they took to the surface, the desire to see his beloved grew in his heart. He struggled to contain the desire to turn around. Finally, they neared the opening to the cave and some light filtered in. Orpheus turned to look upon Eurydice in the half-light of the cave. He saw his beautiful wife and the underworld shook. Eurydice died and turned to shadow once more. She whispered good-bye to Orpheus for the second time as her shadow was pulled back to the realm of the dead. Had Orpheus only waited a few moments more to see her, she would have been allowed to stay with him. His mistake devastated him; his very love for her was the cause of her second death.

Unwilling to give up on Eurydice, Orpheus decided that he would return once again to get her back. He traveled downward and found himself at the River Styx again. This time Charon approached and Orpheus told his tale to an unwilling guide. Charon refused to give him passage a second time. He had lost his patience with the musician who had already made him feel sad. So Orpheus sat along the bank of the River Styx for seven months, grieving the loss of his wife and still believing that it was unfair. He neither ate nor slept while he kept vigil. He blamed the gods of the underworld for the unfairness of death and cursed the Fates themselves for the loss of his beloved. Finally, when his anger was somewhat subsided, he returned to the world of the living. He was not the same man anymore. He could not be in the company of women and refused to play his lyre or sing for anyone. One evening, the Maenads were performing their rituals and became whipped into a frenzy of violence. The music of Orpheus that once calmed them was not to be heard. In their frenzy, they rushed upon Orpheus and tore him apart, limb by limb. They scattered his pieces all over the earth as his shade sank into the underworld to meet his long lost Eurydice.

Orpheus can be seen as a hero or a failure. On the one hand, he defied the edict of the gods and was the epitome of bravery. On the other hand, he let his emotions rule all aspects of his life. For all the amazing deeds that he per-formed, he was still unable to accept that death is inevitable and fate cannot be altered. His was a classic case of denial, which is a natural response when a loved one is lost. The denial and desire to return the loved one's life are almost always experienced by the ones left behind. This, too, usually ends when the living friends and relatives finally accept the loss and grieve appropriately. The story of Orpheus is one of a journey that ends in a tragic inability to come to grips with loss. Although Orpheus grieved for seven months, he was still angry at the gods, fate, and the human condition. He could not let that go and he could not heal. He truly became dead himself.

Resistance of fate and death are common themes in literature, movies, and television. They play an important role in the defiant spirit of much of Western civilization. Dante's *Inferno* tells the story of a man who travels throughout the afterlife to find his true love. On the spookier side of literature, *Pet Sematary* by Stephen King tells the disastrous consequences of bringing someone back. The movie *Flatliners* allows the main characters to experience death so that they might see what is beyond and change the natural order of the cycle. This leads to disaster and unhappiness. Even the Mary Shelley classic, *Frankenstein*, reminds readers that the dead are to remain dead. Any attempt by the living to alter that edict will spell their own doom or visit an unhappiness upon them that makes them wish they were dead.

Our culture is obsessed with death and how to escape it. Take a look in any magazine or watch television commercials. A great number of advertisements promote some form of antiaging or life-changing product. The quest to defeat all disease and live forever is not going away. It seems that the myth of Orpheus is as true, if not more so, than it was in its day.

Pan

Pan

Pan, or Aegipan, was one of the most unusual and oldest of the Greek deities. He was also the most widely recognized member of the pantheon, the group of officially recognized Greek gods. Pan was depicted as a short god with the upper body of a man, the lower body of a goat, and a pair of small horns protruding from his forehead. His bestial look embodied his duty as god of nature and shepherds. Pan, which means "all" in Greek, was probably a significant god in the early mythology of the Greeks because he ruled over all of nature, including human nature. The myths portray Pan as a fun loving and lusty god who made no excuses for his behavior. He was nature personified after all.

As a god of nature, Pan was associated with fertility and fecundity. For this reason, shepherds wishing to increase the size of their flocks would worship him. He represented both humankind and the natural surroundings of the shepherds.

Pan was known for his ability to shout so fiercely that mortals and even monsters were terrified. Athenian citizens worshipped Pan because they believed that the Persians abandoned the battle of Marathon in fear of his horrifying cries. People who wandered into forests often became scared and overtaken by thoughts of harm and the unknown. This unfounded fear was associated with Pan and dubbed "panic fear," which gave us the modern word "panic."

As a lover of wine and women, Pan's behavior was seen as uncivilized and carnal. Farmers and rural people revered him, while the urbanites favored more "civilized" deities like Athena. As time passed, the people of the Roman cities began to call their rural neighbors pagans, after their avid worship of Pan. At the time, the word referred to a farmer or country person. During early Christian times, pagan evolved to signify a person who believed in the polytheistic religion of ancient Rome. Christianity grew and while the organized church espoused the values of Jesus, it also worked to gain converts. One method for acquiring converts involved trying to discredit the religion of ancient Rome. In its campaign against the old religion, the Christian church depicted the pagans as decadent, self-indulgent pleasure-seekers. Today, "pagan" refers to a hedonistic person who quests for material goods and sexual pleasures.

Pan was a pleasure-seeker and one day he fell hopelessly in love with a nymph named Syrinx. He began to chase her and she did all she could to evade him. He chased her through the woods until she was exhausted and, as a last resort, she transformed herself into a stand of reeds just as Pan was about to grab her. Pan grabbed the bunch of reeds in sorrow. Just then a wind blew and the reeds made a beautiful sound. Pan took the reeds and glued them together with wax, making the Pan flute, which he named Syrinx in memory of the nymph he loved. In modern English, Syrinx lent her name to the word "syringe."

Today, the Pan flute, which is also called a "syrinx," is a musical wind instrument that is made of a series of reeds in graduated lengths. It is rare to find an image of Pan where he is not carrying his trademark flute, and his musical talents were noted often. In one myth, King Midas was asked to judge a musical competition between Pan and Apollo. When Midas chose Pan's music over Apollo's, the younger god became angry and changed the king's ears into those of an ass.

Pan was as cunning as he was musical. When the gods were faced with the threat of a horrible monster named Typhon, Pan suggested that they all transform themselves into animals to escape Typhon's fury. The plan worked, but unfortunately, Pan attempted to turn himself into a fish, but only turned his bottom half into a fish while his upper half was transformed into a goat. The symbol for the zodiacal sign Capricorn is derived from this accidental transformation.

There is also speculation that this myth was created to connect the Egyptian gods with the Greek gods. The casual observer of the Egyptian pantheon will notice that a great number of the gods had the physical features of animals. Perhaps the Greeks were trying to make a connection between the two cultures by creating this myth.

A race of Pan-like beings, called Satyrs, emerged in mythology. They lived in forests and delighted in playing, drinking, feasting, and sexual exploits. As symbols of the old god Pan, they even show up in classic Disney movies like *Fantasia*.

In ancient Greece, Pan continued to be a popular and revered deity as the religions and myths of the Greeks were adopted and transformed by the Romans. Two Roman gods, Silvanus and Faunus, were inspired by Pan. Like Pan, they were gods of nature and Faunus even adopted much of the appearance of Pan.

With the growth of city-states and the widespread belief that humans were made to rule over the land, a rift began to grow between the worshippers of Pan and the followers of the more "dignified" gods and goddesses. Pan became a belief to avoid rather than embrace or accept. With the evolution of religion and myth and the continuing civilization of society, people shunned the decadent pleasures of carnal debauchery. With the popularity of virtuous and chaste lifestyles, Pan fell into obscurity.

He was all but forgotten, but Christians adopted his image to depict Satan. By changing Pan's skin color to red and replacing his pipes with a pitchfork, this Greek god of shepherds became the Christians' personification of the evils of humankind. Although Pan is rarely remembered today, his legacy remains strong in our modern vocabulary, music, and ideas of pleasure.

Pandora

⌒

Although the Greek myth of Pandora is a relatively simple one, it explains the origin of women as well as the evils in the world. According to the myth, Zeus created the first woman, Pandora. His motivation for creating Pandora was not altruistic, but to get revenge against Prometheus and man. Prometheus had offended Zeus by giving man the fire that he stole from the gods; man's crime was accepting the gift.

Zeus' revenge involved destroying mankind's ideal existence of leisure, health, and goodness. He swore that he would plague mankind with evil and his plan centered on the creation of a mortal woman. By pooling the resources of his fellow gods, he was able to create an enchanting creature. Hephaestus began the process by using earth and water to craft Pandora's seductive figure and bewitching face in the likeness of the most beautiful goddesses. Athena dressed her and taught her skills like weaving. Aphrodite's contribution was Pandora's elegance and sexual appetite. Her melodious voice was a gift from Hermes, who gave her a persuasive and deceitful nature as well. Her name means "all-gifted" and is a reflection of the collaborative effort of the gods.

Once his seductive gift was complete, Zeus offered Pandora to Epimetheus, Prometheus' brother. Knowing that Zeus was up to no good, Prometheus (whose name means "foresight") warned his brother against accepting the gift. Epimetheus (whose name means "hindsight") ignored his brother's advice, welcomed Pandora into his home, and by some accounts, married her.

Initially, Pandora's existence on earth went well, but her insatiable curiosity about a covered jar soon got the better of her and changed mankind. Some versions of the myth describe the jar as another gift from Zeus to Epimetheus, while others depict Pandora as its owner. Regardless, Pandora was not supposed to open the jar, but she could not resist. Upon her opening of the jar, the evils of mankind escaped and began to ravage mortal life. Illnesses, work, envy, revenge, death, and insanity transformed man's formerly idyllic existence. Realizing her error, Pandora scrambled to replace the lid, but only "hope" was left inside.

When this myth is related today, people refer to the container of evils as "Pandora's box." Hesiod's (eighth century B.C.) account, one of the earliest and most cited versions of the story, describes the container as a pithos, which is a storage jar. When an influential sixteenth-century humanist named Erasmus confused the word "pithos" with the word "pyxis," he transformed the jar of evils into Pandora's box. Today, we use Pandora's box to describe something that holds unknown or uncontrollable misfortunes or difficulties.

The story of Pandora's creation and role in humanity bears a strong resemblance to the story of Eve in Hebrew myth. Both Pandora and Eve were the first mortal women in their cultures and both of them succumbed to curiosity, which lead to the suffering and mortality of humans. Although these stories do not reflect these first women in a positive light, Pandora's story offered the ancient Greeks the prospect of hope.

Persephone and Hades

❧

The myths associated with the goddess Persephone are more than simple stories that can be used to explain the change of the seasons. The myths also tell the story of life for all things on earth and the waxing and waning of youth, beauty, responsibility, and more. For many readers, this myth can become quite personal as they connect with the conflicts, struggles, and acceptance that Persephone experiences.

Persephone's story begins with the Greek pantheon, which was ruled by Zeus, the king of the heavens. His brother, Hades, had the unenviable position of controller of the underworld. Although quite powerful in his own right, Hades was extremely lonely. No one wished to go to the underworld before their time, and once there, they were not exactly in a festive mood. Understandably, Hades was not thrilled with his situation and thought hard about how to remedy it.

Meanwhile, the other gods were enjoying themselves. Zeus and the goddess of plants and growth, Demeter, were having a fling and found themselves pregnant with a goddess. When the baby was born, it seemed that the sun shone just a bit brighter and the birds chirped a little more; the world changed somehow for the better. Demeter was instantly and irrevocably in love with her daughter. This baby, who she named Persephone, was the epitome of innocence and beauty.

Persephone's childhood was carefree and full of fun. She explored the world and seemed to bring a happiness and liveliness to all things and people with whom she came in contact. Everyone and everything loved her. As she grew into a young woman, she was given responsibilities to care for her mother's creations. She tended to the plants and animals of the earth as well as the crops of farmers. She was the babysitter for any new gods and the heroes who were born to gods. It was easy to see that she was a reliable and caring young lady who had gained the respect and admiration of her godly peers and the adoration of mortals. For all the love she garnered from mortals and gods, no one loved her as much as her mother.

This love for Persephone was soon rivaled by another godly influence. Hades had become too bored with life in the underworld. He asked Zeus, each time he saw him, to find a woman to be his wife. Zeus tried again and again to find someone who would be willing to become the queen of the underworld. Regardless of the royal title, no one wished to spend eternity in the underworld. Zeus could find no one who would willingly wed Hades. Saddened by this state of affairs, Zeus couldn't bring himself to tell his brother the news and continued to string him along. This tactic worked for a time, but Hades was a smart god and began to realize that his brother was keeping something from him.

Hades decided to pay Zeus a visit at Mount Olympus and ask him why he had not found a wife for his faithful brother. While in council with Zeus, Hades happened to notice the beautiful Persephone, now a woman, tending to the gardens of Olympus. He at once became enraptured with her. This would be his queen, for she was more innocent, beautiful, and alive than any being on Olympus. He told Zeus that he had found the one who would be his wife and pointed to Persephone. Zeus would have been overjoyed at the thought of this union, but he knew that Demeter would never allow it to happen. She prized the attention of Persephone too much and would not permit the separation from her daughter.

Knowing that his promise to Hades must not be broken, Zeus hatched a plan for Hades to kidnap the lovely Persephone and bring her to his underworld kingdom. From there, he could marry Persephone and Demeter could not do anything to Hades or retrieve her daughter. Zeus knew that once Persephone ate her meal at the wedding feast, she would be bound to the underworld and could be called back if she attempted escape. He had thought of the perfect plan. All parties involved would eventually accept the situation and be happy.

Unfortunately, Demeter was anything but happy about the situation. She became enraged that her daughter had been abducted by Hades and her rage was felt by all the beings of the earth. So angered by the situation, she threatened the utter destruction of all mankind by famine. If her daughter was withheld from her, then she would deny her gifts of grain and vegetation to the earth. Such was the power and conviction of her love for Persephone.

Zeus heard of her plans to starve the earth and realized that he must demand that Hades return Persephone to the world. Hades was angered and saddened by this request. He truly loved Persephone, even though he knew that the balance of the world and the orders of Zeus came before his needs. Besides, Persephone was actually beginning to settle in to the underworld. She seemed comfortable enough and was growing to understand Hades. If given enough time, Hades was sure that Persephone would come to love him. He just needed a way to ensure she would return to him someday. She had never actually eaten anything since she was abducted, so she was not under the curse of the underworld. Hades desperately needed that to ensure her return.

The truth is that Persephone did not dislike Hades. Instead, she felt a sweet sadness for his situation and admired his somewhat romantic aspirations. In many ways, she pitied the god. Hades was not so blinded by love that he did not realize her pity for him. In fact, he began to use it to his advantage.

When news came that Persephone must return to the world, Hades let his sadness flow forth. He begged Persephone to stay and she replied that it was the will of Zeus that she return. Undeterred, he pleaded with her to stay for a last meal with him, but she would not. Finally, he asked that she simply have one pomegranate seed to eat. This was the only gesture of love he asked for, just one morsel. Overcome by her emotions and a sense that she was abandoning the king of the underworld, Persephone accepted the seed and ate it, thereby setting in motion a series of events that would create a cycle of seasonal events.

During this time, Demeter had withheld her graces from the earth, and it had become cold and barren. Vegetation had died and the green of the earth had become brown and dead. Crops no longer grew and the people huddled in their homes to escape the cold, harsh weather. Life above ground had become somewhat similar to the underworld. When Persephone emerged from the Underworld, Demeter gleamed with happiness and let forth all of her graces once again. Immediately crops began to grow and flowers bloomed in uncountable colors. Birds began to sing and animals brought forth their young to warm themselves in the sun. The earth was as full of life as it had been when Persephone was born. The world was greener, livelier, and happier. Persephone's presence had brought life back to the world.

The happiness of mother and daughter seemed to grow stronger over the next few months and the world flourished, but below, in the underworld, Hades was becoming impatient. He would have his wife back, for Persephone had tasted the food of the dead and was bound by divine law to return to the underworld one way or another. He called a council of the gods and presented his case before the stunned audience. Zeus could say nothing to deny his rights, for Persephone had known that if she ate the seed, she would be bound. Finally, Persephone was brought before the council with Demeter.

The council agreed that it was unfair to keep Hades' wife from him, but that the sadness of her mother was not good for the mortals of earth. They decided that for one-third of a year, Persephone would live in the underworld with her husband, and the rest of the time she could spend with her mother and the rest of the gods. Hades agreed to this, as he understood the importance of balance. Demeter, however, was not happy with the situation. She felt that it was unfair to keep Persephone in the underworld at all, even though Persephone herself had agreed.

After the verdict, everyone returned to their activities and enjoyed each other's company, but soon the time for Persephone's return to the underworld would be upon them, and Demeter became depressed. The air became cooler and the vegetation drier. Persephone tried to make her mother understand, but she was immovable. Finally, Persephone left to join her husband and Demeter closed herself off from the world. According to the myth, Demeter's cycle of happiness and sadness governed the seasons. Thus, Winter always follows Fall. Each Spring, Persephone returns and the world is reborn. This cycle begins again each year, with Demeter plunging into depression each time her daughter leaves, only to celebrate her daughter's happy return.

As time passed and Persephone returned to her husband each year, she grew to love him. Although she was the queen of the underworld, she was worshipped for her role in the herald of Spring and as the symbol of rebirth and change. It is her ability to transform that become so important. She transformed the earth, she changed Hades for the better, and she even changed herself by accepting her responsibility.

The story of Persephone is more than a clever story to explain the seasons, although it succeeds quite well at that. The subtle myth is the story of the human life cycle and the growth of this carefree child into a woman who must make decisions based on more than just herself. She grows and must take responsibility for her choices as well. This story teaches the tough lesson that life and growing up are not always easy, not even for the most popular, beautiful, or gifted people. In fact, sometimes it is just that person who must make decisions that affect all of us. It becomes their responsibility and ultimately their success or failure.

The world of art, poetry, and music are rife with depictions of the abduction of Persephone. Such an example is the painting "The Rape of Persephone." In our language, seasonal change is used as a metaphor for the stages of life. For example, a marriage of an older individual to a much younger counterpart is often referred to as a "May–December Marriage."

The return of a loved one, like Persephone returning to her mother, is also used as a powerful emotive force in stories of growth. The idea that one must go away from the familiar and venture to the unknown, or dangerous, is part of the mythic story of growth. The return to one's roots and sharing of that experience is just as important a step in that process, for it changes the entire group for the better.

Prometheus

～

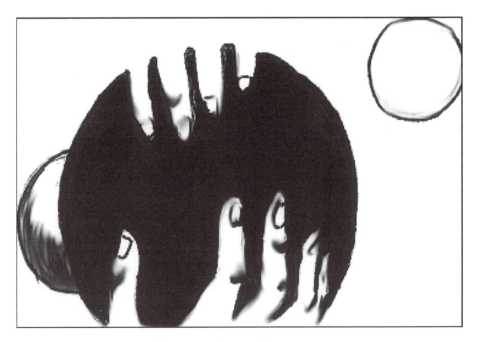

The World

When the story of Prometheus is told, it usually centers on his involvement with Pandora. This particular story, however, deals with the life and unfortunate decisions that Prometheus made in order to help humankind. Prometheus was the son of a Titan and an elder god. When Zeus and the younger gods battled against the Titans, Prometheus did not fight against Zeus, and for that reason, he was not punished when the younger gods emerged victorious. Because the gods determined that Prometheus was no threat to them, he was free to stay on earth instead of being banished to Tartarus.

When the earth was still young, Prometheus was given charge of humankind, and his brother Epimetheus was in charge of giving gifts and abilities to the animals. Epimetheus gave flight to birds and doled out claws, fangs, and all sorts of helpful abilities to the rest of the animal kingdom. Impressed by his brother's creativity in gifts, Prometheus wanted to give an original gift to humankind, but he was at a loss as to what he could give them. Not only did he want the gift to be unique, but he also wanted it to allow humankind to attain mastery over all of the other creatures on earth. With flight, fangs, poison, claws, night vision, and the rest already given, Prometheus could think of nothing original with which to equip humans. This left them in a pretty sorry state because they were rather simple animals. They had no defenses and seemed to be at a disadvantage compared to the animals. Night came and they huddled in caves in fear. Winter came and many died from the cold. Worse yet, when they happened to catch an animal for food, the raw meat was hard to eat and caused them stomach pains. Prometheus watched the plight of men and felt great sorrow. He vowed that he would find an original gift that would cure their problems.

In Olympus, Zeus was going about his duties as the all-father. He had a world to run and it was important that rules be established for the safety of all of its inhabitants. He sat with his council one evening and discussed the rules he wished to make, while they enjoyed roasted oxen and ambrosia. As he pulled a piece of roasted meat from the spit, he felt the intense heat of the flames. He thought to himself about the properties of fire and that although it was a great asset, it was also among the most dangerous things on earth. If not handled properly, fire could consume the entire earth and destroy all that he and his fellow gods had fought for and worked so hard to achieve. Thinking long and hard on this, Zeus proclaimed that fire was much too dangerous for anyone but the gods to handle. He decreed that fire would only be kept in Olympus and never be given to any beasts of the earth, especially humans. The gods agreed and made a special vessel to contain fire so only they could use it.

Zeus' decree on the prohibition of fire went out to all the gods. When Prometheus heard this, he didn't think much of it and went about trying to figure out what to give humankind. He watched humans forage for meager foodstuffs until winter came again. Night after night, he watched as the people huddled together in their caves, afraid, cold, and starving. Then the thought occurred to him: fire gives light in the dark. If humankind had fire, they could use it at night to see that there is nothing to fear. He realized that fire would bring warmth and ease the suffering that his people felt in winter. Fire could end much sickness and death, and it could also be used to roast the flesh of animals so they can be properly eaten. Additionally, people could burn some of the animals in sacrifice to Zeus. Certainly, that would make Zeus quite happy. He convinced himself that it was unfair for Zeus to keep fire from humans; it was the perfect gift. Prometheus made his decision: humankind would have the gift of fire and he would bring it to them. They would love him for bringing such a wondrous gift.

That night he crept into Olympus and opened the special vessel that contained fire. He plunged a thick tree branch into the flame until it caught fire. Quietly, he left Olympus with the torch and headed down to earth to present his gift to humans. When he reached the cave, he held forth the torch and the people cowered in fear. Prometheus assured them of their safety and showed them how this gift would make their lives simpler and ease their fears. He spent a great deal of time instructing humans in the proper use of fire.

Although they were afraid at first, humans soon learned that fire was helpful and kept it hidden and sacred. They shared it among each other so that soon all of the tribes had their own sacred fires and were able to multiply and find time for leisure. They also learned to use fire for other purposes. Sometimes they became lazy and inattentive and the fires would go out; or worse, they would blaze too fiercely and get out of control.

On one such occasion, a fire consumed an entire village and the flames could be seen from the height of Olympus. Zeus spied the fire and became enraged. He caused a great rain that quenched the flames and rid the area of fire. Upon closer inspection, he saw that there were multitudes of small fires everywhere and sitting around those fires were humans. He flew into a rage because he knew that someone had stolen from the sacred vessel against his orders. He knew that only one god would have been so closely attached to humans to break his law. He called for Prometheus to answer for his crime. When Prometheus came before the all-father, he was prepared to explain the benefits of his actions and the good qualities of his gift of fire.

Zeus listened to Prometheus' earnest defense, then rose and spoke. "Prometheus, what you say is true, but you underestimate mankind. This is your undoing, for they do not use fire only for the benefits that you describe. They are a wily lot and have found more uses for the fire you gave them. Let me show you."

With that, Zeus let Prometheus see far and wide across the earth with vision greater than any eagle. "See there. That tribe has learned to use fire to burn and destroy the homes and crops of another tribe. They conquer them and starve them out. And there . . ." he pointed to a small group of men surrounding a great fire. "Those humans mine ore and forge metals into bowls and precious rings." "That is good!" exclaimed Prometheus. Zeus shook his head. "Yes, that is good, but they also forge swords and spears to make war on each other and cause death." Prometheus stood wide eyed in disbelief. He hadn't imagined that humans would be so crafty and misuse the gift. "I will take it back Zeus. I will gather all the fire and find a different gift that humans cannot misuse."

Once again Zeus shook his head. "I have tried that already. Last night I sent rain and water to extinguish every fire that humankind had, but you see there?" He pointed to a human rubbing a stick against another. The sticks created smoke and eventually a flame. "We cannot take the gift back Prometheus, for they have learned to make fire for themselves. None of the gods can undo what you have done. Not even me."

Zeus rose again in anger and ordered Prometheus to be shackled and brought to a great mountain where he would be chained to a great rock. Naked and stretched across a massive rock, Prometheus was bound and exposed to the elements for eternity. This punishment would have been bad enough, but there was more in store for the half-titan–half-god.

Each day, a great eagle would descend upon Prometheus and tear open his side with its sharp talons. For the remainder of the day, the eagle would feast upon Prometheus' liver until it was gone. Then it would fly away at sunset. When morning came again, the liver would have grown back and the wound on his side was completely healed. The eagle would return and the process would repeat itself until the end of time. The pain that Prometheus experienced was never ending.

Over time, Prometheus began to focus on listening to the happenings on earth. His hearing became so strong that no sound or word escaped him. He heard the oracles speak of the beautiful river spirit, Thetis. He learned that she would have a son who would be greater than his father. This did not mean much to Prometheus at the time and years passed. Then he heard of the competition between Zeus and his brother Poseidon. They were both in love with Thetis and wished to have her. Each of them chased her about the earth and eventually she ran to hide near the rock upon which Prometheus was bound.

Zeus found her and was about to ravish her when Prometheus told him what he had heard about the son Zeus would make with Thetis. "The son will be greater in power than his father Zeus. This will be your undoing." Zeus stopped his advances and approached Prometheus. "After the punishment I have decreed for you, you still look to protect me?" Prometheus winced through his pain. "I think of you and the earth itself, for you rule justly and I cannot say if one greater than you would be so fair." Zeus was touched by this act and believed that Prometheus had made amends for his mistakes.

Prometheus had saved Zeus from making the biggest mistake of his life. Taking pity on Prometheus, Zeus unshackled him and bade him to join the gods again. Weeping, Prometheus declared, "I shall do so all-father, but I will also do my best to help humankind temper their hearts and use their gifts wisely. I know now that I cannot underestimate them and that I must also punish them for their misdeeds so they can see the error of their ways." Prometheus was forgiven.

Many poets choose to write about Prometheus and his punishment because it has such a deep effect on the human psyche. The romantic poets Byron and Shelly, in particular, focused on the endurance and plight of the Titan who served humans. In addition, Goethe wrote a poem titled "Prometheus."

Prometheus has added to our language as well. The adjective "Promethean" means life-bringing, creative, or original. In addition, celiac disease, which is a genetic disorder of the liver, is also known as "Prometheus disease," in reference to the god's horrible punishment.

Prometheus has become a symbol of endurance in the face of horrible suffering as well as the spirit of humankind. In many ways, Prometheus was like each of us. He learned by making mistakes, and that sometimes involved payment for the misdeeds. It was his acceptance and understanding of the mistakes that makes his story so meaningful. He was willing to look beyond himself and deal with the consequences of his misgivings. More importantly, he bore no ill will toward those who punished him. In fact, he wished to help them rather than take revenge. Had he let Zeus have a child with Thetis, the balance of power in the throne of Olympus would have been upset and world order would have been disrupted as well. He could have chosen to let it happen and watch Zeus suffer as he had, but he did not. At the height of his pain, he chose to do good rather than exact revenge. He redeemed himself and provided an example for humankind to follow in their worst situations.

Pygmalion

In today's society, we look for our perfect mate in bars, singles groups, personal ads, and the dreaded blind date. In ancient Greece, people had a far simpler and effective way to find their soul mate: ask Aphrodite, the goddess of love. The story of Pygmalion illustrates Aphrodite's matchmaking abilities.

As a talented sculptor, Pygmalion crafted amazingly beautiful and realistic statues of women, but real women did not live up to his ideal that he created from ivory. The town where he lived had a whorehouse and the prostitutes' behavior disgusted him and convinced him to renounce women altogether.

One day Pygmalion set to work on an immense block of ivory and formed the sculpture of a woman who was exquisitely beautiful and far more comely than his previous creations. He found the sculpture so enchanting that he named it Galatea, which meant "sleeping love." As the days passed, he found himself enamored with his lifeless creation. He bought polished pebbles for her and adorned her with jewelry.

In no time, Pygmalion obsession with his artwork reached a new level; he wanted to marry her. Fortunately for the lovelorn sculptor, his need for help occurred during a festival celebrating Aphrodite, the goddess of love and beauty. He went to her temple and prayed for the goddess to bring him a wife who was like his marble creation. When he returned home, he kissed his precious statue. Slowly, the cold stone turned to warm flesh and blood. Aphrodite had granted his request and transformed the object of his affection into a real woman.

Pygmalion and Galatea soon married and had two daughters, Paphos and Metharme. Realizing the generosity of Aphrodite, the couple brought gifts to her for the rest of their lives and in return the goddess gave them a marriage of happiness and love.

Although the story of Pygmalion is a simple one, its concept has influenced countless storylines. Movies, plays, and poetry have all been inspired by this simple story. For example, *Snow White* and *Sleeping Beauty* feature a kiss that animates someone. In addition, entire plots have been derived from the myth.

The most notable adaptation of the Pygmalion myth is George Bernard Shaw's 1912 comedy, *Pygmalion*. In the story, Professor Henry Higgins bets his friend Colonel Hugh Pickering that he can take a poor Cockney flower girl and pass her off as a member of high society by teaching her to talk and act properly. The duo settle on Eliza Doolittle and Professor Higgins begins teaching his pupil proper dictation. Doolittle learns quickly and soon convinces English society of her good breeding. Shaw's story does not end as blissfully for the Pygmalion character. Instead of living happily ever after, Higgins is abandoned by Doolittle when she discovers the bet. The musical *My Fair Lady* was adapted from Shaw's comedy and in 1964 Audrey Hepburn and Rex Harrison starred in the movie version of the musical.

The 1983 movie *Trading Places* has a similar plot in which Dan Aykroyd and Eddie Murphy's characters Louis Winthorpe III and Billy Ray Valentine are subject to a bet made by Don Ameche and Ralph Bellamy's characters, Mortimer and Randolph Duke. The Duke brothers' bet involved passing off down-and-out Valentine as a member of high society and forcing high-brow Akroyd to degenerate and embrace crime. In the end, Winthorpe and Valentine discover the bet and bankrupt the brothers as revenge.

Movies often depict stories of inanimate objects being transformed into living beings due to someone's love. For example, the 1987 movie *Mannequin* features Andrew McCarthy as a frustrated sculptor who cannot keep a job. He creates a beautiful mannequin that he names Emmy and then falls in love with her. When she comes to life, played by Kim Cattral, they are able to create beautiful window displays together. *Life-Size*, a Disney made-for-television movie, which aired in 2000, has a similar plot. A little girl attempts to resurrect her late mother by casting a spell, but she only succeeds in bringing her favorite doll to life.

Pygmalion's story of being unable to find the perfect mate and companion resonates with audiences. The idea of being able to create and shape a human being intrigues people as well. These qualities make the myth of Pygmalion endure and continue to be inspiration for our entertainment.

Pyramus and Thisbe

❧

Very often a television show or movie will focus on a pair of star-crossed lovers who are perfect for one another, but for some reason are not allowed or able to come together. This theme has been used so many times that it is almost a cliché and is often described as "just another retelling of Romeo and Juliet." Perhaps the most famous and best known of Shakespeare's works, *Romeo and Juliet* is usually treated as the "star-crossed romance" from which all forbidden love stories are modeled. This is a common misconception. *Romeo and Juliet* was, in fact, just a retelling of a far older and simpler tale of forbidden love and tragic death.

The story begins in the ancient city of Babylonia. Deep within the teeming city were two homes joined by a single wall. Although the families that inhabited the homes lived right next door to one another, they did not get along in the least. For years they had been civil to one another but they never came together as friends.

Both of the families had children. Among the children of the first family was a youth who was said to be the most handsome in all of Babylonia. Pyramus was his name and he was among the brightest and most athletic of the town's men. Next door lived the fair Thisbe, who was gentle, kind, and beautiful. Each had talents that promised a great amount of notoriety for their families.

It was only a matter of time before they met, even though their parents tried their hardest to make sure neither of them was aware of the other. When they finally saw one another, the attraction was immediate and they knew they could not fight it. They also knew that any attempt to be together could spell disaster for their families. So great were their feelings for one another that they decided to stay apart until they could think of a way to see one another without upsetting the already tenuous relationship between their families.

One day, by sheer chance, they discovered a crack in the adjoining walls of their houses. Through this crack they could hear one another. The wall that kept them apart was flawed, and their desire for one another allowed them to find a way to be together in words if not in the flesh. Each night, after their families had gone to bed and fallen asleep, the couple would lean against the wall with lips or ear against the crack and profess their love for one another.

Each night Pyramus cursed the wall for separating them from one another and then thanked it for having a flaw that at least allowed them to speak. Nightly, the vows of love and sweet poems of devotion flowed from the lips of one through the crack and to the heart of the other. They knew that they must come together no matter what the consequences, so they planned to sneak out of the house on a particular evening and make their way to a special grove. According to the myth, when they reached the grove they were to go to a tree that bore white berries. With the time and place set, they needed only to wait and dream of the night they could finally come together without fear.

The night came and they both snuck out of their homes at the appointed time. Thisbe headed to the grove and found the mulberry tree. She sat in this peaceful place and watched the stream as it flowed along nearby. Much to her surprise a movement by the stream caught her eye by the stream. It was not Pyramus, but a lion that had come to drink on the warm night. Scared and confused, Thisbe ran to a group of outlying rocks and hid within them. As she ran, she did not notice that her veil had fallen to the ground near the mulberry tree. The lion, who had come to sate his thirst after killing some game, still had it's victims blood covering it's paws and mouth. It loped about the area and soon found the veil. Playfully, it tore at the veil and chewed upon it until it became bored. Then it crept off into the night to find a place to rest.

Just after the lion left, Pyramus arrived. Looking about, he could not find Thisbe. He began to worry and question until he saw the veil. It lay there, torn and bloodied. Bloody lion prints were everywhere around the site. Pyramus was overcome with grief. He believed that his one true love had been murdered by a lion and was dragged off into the woods. He could not bear the thought of life without her. The wall between life and death had no cracks in it and he refused to be deprived of his one true love.

Unsheathing his sword and placing it to his breast, he thought only of joining her in death. He plunged the blade into his heart and fell to the ground. His blood flowed into the ground and seeped deeply into the soil until the roots of the mulberry tree drank it up. The blood flowed through the sap of the tree and changed the berries from white to the blood red they are today.

Thisbe had waited long enough for the lion to leave and was afraid that it might have encountered Pyramus, so she crawled from her hiding place to find her lover. On the way back, she became confused because the trees were some-how different. Their color was not the same. Pondering this, she stumbled across the corpse of her dead lover. The sight of this drove her to her own end. Knowing that life without Pyramus was no life at all, the devastated Thisbe fell upon his sword and died upon him, their blood mixing as one in the berries of the mulberry tree. So ended the lives of the forbidden lovers who would sacrifice everything, including life, to be together.

It is obvious to anyone who has read the stories of Pyramus and Thisbe and *Romeo and Juliet* that Shakespeare borrowed heavily from the ancient Greek myth. In fact, he mentions the myth in another of his famous plays, *A Midsummer Night's Dream*. In that play, he describes a band of very inadequate actors attempting to put on the play of *Pyramus and Thisbe*. The inability of the actors to understand the meaning of the wall as a symbol of forbiddance is quite entertaining. Perhaps Shakespeare was paying homage to the myth, or making fun of the fact that even in Shakespeare's day, star-crossed lovers was a theme that was overused.

The theme of lovers who are forbidden from one another is still alive and well in Hollywood and in romance novels. Recent adaptations of *Romeo and Juliet* that cater to a new generation ensure that the spirits of Pyramus and Thisbe will not fade away. Countless teen movies that focus on forbidden love are released each year and tend to use problems like racism, sexual orientation, class differences, and ideologies as reasons for the wall between the lovers. This tension is also commonly used in romantic comedies. Today's moviemakers borrow the initial idea, but the tragic ending is usually omitted in favor of a more upbeat and positive ending.

Ragnarok

∾

Fenrir

Humankind has a peculiar habit of thinking in a linear fashion. We exist in time that seems to flow from past into the present and on to an unforeseeable or hazy future. Our past experiences explain our personal present and inform our future. Because we think in a linear fashion, everything has a beginning and an end. We have countless creation stories and myths to describe the origins of our world. They range from the separation of light from dark to the Big Bang Theory. The real question is, How is it all going to end?

Just as there are numerous creation stories, there are a fair number of apocalyptic scenarios and myths. One interesting fact concerning these myths is that they rarely, if ever, involve the complete and utter annihilation of everything. For example, in Hindu myths, Shiva destroys everything so that Brahma can remake everything. Although everything is destroyed except the gods themselves, all things are actually renewed by the process and begin all over again.

Contrasting the Hindu myth is the Christian story of apocalypse, in which humankind is separated and some are left on a dying, corrupt planet while others spend eternity in heaven. One can assume that those left on the planet earth die out eventually and the folks in heaven remain in a state of bliss forever. In any event, vestiges of humankind remain in heaven with God being a god to them. Although the environment changes, the relationship between God and his people remains the same.

Apocalyptic stories may sound like the end of everything, but they are more like second drafts for the world. These are stories about rebirth instead of death. Unfortunately, that rebirth can be quite terrifying and painful.

The Norse myth of Ragnarok is a good example of the frightening side of renewal. The Norse believed strongly in the concept of fate, as did the Greeks and the Romans. Inherent in this belief system is the concept of a beginning and an end that are predestined. Fate is like a script that allows for the actors to ad-lib as much as they want, but the end result will always be the same. According to the Norse, your fate was already prescribed for you.

Interestingly, the Norse gods were not always aware of their fate. When they were, they seemed more interested in the fate of others and than in their own fate. In many cases, specific gods ignored the warnings given about their fates. The Norse visualized time and fate as three females acting as one. Urd (Fate), Skuld (Being), and Verdandi (Necessity) are a young girl, a fertile woman, and an old crone respectively. They also represent the past, present, and future. Together these three spin the yarn that creates the tapestry of time. They seem to be mimicked in Charles Dickens' *A Christmas Carol* by his ghosts of Christmas Past, Present, and Future.

In Norse mythology, the end of the world would occur at Ragnarok, a terrible battle waged by the gods. Odin, the all-father, learned the fate of the world from the Norns and was aware that he could not change it. Because of his powerlessness in this realm, he chose not to tell the rest of the gods. He remained silent as the gods followed a course to disaster, and he bore a painful burden.

Ragnarok was put in motion with the death of Balder, the son of Odin. According to the myth, from that point on the Norse world would begin to fall apart. The Norse people would begin warring with each other on a scale never seen before and humankind would slip into a barbaric state. The world would turn cold and wintry for three full years and starvation and strife would become commonplace. Families would fall into battles with one another, then tear themselves apart. The sun would become weak and finally fall prey to the great wolf Skoll, who had been chasing the sun forever. Once he had caught her, he would tear her to shreds and her droplets of her blood would fall upon the earth. The moon, too, would be torn to shreds by the great wolf Hati and all the stars in the sky would fade away.

As the world lay in a state of darkness and chaos, the earth itself would begin to give way. Sensing the tremors, the giant wolf Fenrir would break the enchanted collar that bound him to the earth. Foaming at the mouth with vengeful thoughts, Fenrir would head toward the battle plain of Vigrid to kill the gods. The earth would tremble under his feet as his claws dug deep into the land. Three cocks would crow to wake the warriors for battle. The first, Fjalar the Red, would wake the sleeping giants. Gullinkambi, the golden cock, would alert the warriors in Odin's hall, Vallhalla. Finally, the third cock, whose name was not documented, would crow in Niflheim, waking the dead under the rule of dreaded Hel.

Fenrir's howls would awaken his slumbering brother Jormungand, the World Serpent. With dreadful poison rising in his vile mouth, the great snake would cause tidal waves as he moved toward Vigrid. Hyrm, the giant, would sail his great ship made from the nails of the dead. His ship would hold the legions of giants bent on the destruction of the gods. Loki would break free from his bonds and finally bend his gifts in opposition to the gods.

Jormungand and Fenrir would join together, causing havoc upon the earth as they came to the battle, destroying all that came in their way. Finally, the fire demons of Muspellheim, led by the dreaded Surt and his flaming sword, would enter the fray. As they crossed the rainbow bridge, Bifrost, they would destroy it and close off the entrance to the battle. The giants, Jormungand, Fenrir, Hel and her army, Loki, and the fire demons would all be led by the bright flame of Surt's sword.

Heimdall, the guardian of the gods, would sound his great horn and announce the beginning of Ragnarok. Odin would mount his eight-legged steed, Sleipnir, and travel to the great well of wisdom to get information. As he passed the world tree Yggdrassil, he would see the last two humans entering a hole in its trunk. Meanwhile, all of the gods and the great warriors of Vallhalla would arm themselves and get ready for battle. Odin would return with his great spear Gungnir and lead them to the final battle.

The horrific encounter would result in the gruesome deaths of many of the gods. Then Surt would take his flaming sword and set the world on fire. Every-thing would begin to burn—The giants, the gods, the elves, and the dwarves destroyed, and even Surt and his demons consumed by the flames. Then the scorched earth would falls into the sea.

Eventually the earth would rise again and the stars would reappear. In this rebirth of the world, grass and plants grow again and the great tree Yggdrassil shoots forth new leaves. Birds and animals roam the skies and fields again. From their hiding places, a few of the gods return, including Vidar and Vali, the warrior sons of Odin. Magni and Modi, the sons of Thor, emerge with their father's great hammer, Mjolnir. Last to arrive is Honir, Hod, and Balder, who return from the dead to bring new life and ensure the change of seasons for the new world. They find relics from long lost Asgard and reminisce about the times of great glory and the final battle.

One day they look down at the great tree Yggdrassil and see its trunk part slightly. Out from its core the humans that Odin saw entering the tree ages ago reemerge. These humans enter the brilliant sunlight, having slept all these ages, and they look about in wonder at the new world that is theirs to populate and shape. They remember the times before the fall of Asgard and they pass the tales on in story and song.

Numerous post-apocalyptic movies tell the tale of a mass extinction, followed by the rag-tag remnants of the human race carving a life from the ruins of their ancestors, just like the gods after Ragnarok. They sift through the artifacts of ages long past and figure out how to use them for new purposes. So, too, are the changes in our lives. From infancy to childhood, adolescence to adulthood, and so on, we encounter and remember our "old selves" and try to glean some meaning on a personal scale to apply to our present and future selves.

Numerous novels and movies have been made using the post-apocalyptic earth as a desolate and harsh world where survival is the only goal. The 1988 movie *The Seventh Sign* provides an account of the last days of humanity. Demi Moore stars as a pregnant woman who believes the world is ending. In 1984, the movie *The Terminator* showed a future where the last remnants of humanity are battling against crushing odds for survival. The classic science fiction novel *A Canticle for Leibowitz* by Walter Miller (1959) and the movie *Mad Max* (1979) do not show us the apocalypse, but they certainly give us a glimpse into the world after the fall. In the 1999 film *The Matrix*, humankind destroys its own world in an attempt to defeat computers.

At the end of the Norse myth of Ragnarok, there is a new beginning. One can look for all sorts of meaning in this story, or one can simply understand that the end is also the beginning. The theme of the apocalypse fascinates hu-mankind. Although violent and horrific, the end of the world is often portrayed as a means to a rebirth.

Romulus and Remus

M yths surrounding the lives of twins seem to appear in almost every culture. The Romans were no exception. The tale of Romulus and Remus is a political, or state historical myth. It describes the founding of Rome and links the first inhabitants of the city to divine beings. The lineage and events leading up to their birth are an important backdrop to the story.

King Numitor of Alba Longa had only one child, a girl named Rhea Silvia who grew up to be a beautiful woman. The king's brother, Amulius, was jealous of Numitor's power and desired the throne for himself. Through a series of politically underhanded actions, Amulius deposed Numitor and took the throne of Alba Longa. Fearing that an heir might be born by Rhea Silvia, he forced her to become a vestal virgin. This is very similar to the custom of putting a young woman in a nunnery to shelter her from men.

Amulius ruled and all seemed well, but the gods had a different plan for the family. Mars, the Roman god of war, trespassed in the sacred groves of Vesta and raped Rhea Silvia. She became pregnant from this encounter and gave birth to twin boys, Romulus and Remus. Angered and frightened at the thought of possible threats to his rule, Amulius ordered his servants to kill the twins. The servants could not bring themselves to perform the act. Instead, they placed the twins in a trough and set it afloat on the River Tiber. This part of the myth mirrors the story of Oedipus so closely that most scholars believe the Romans used the Oedipal myth as a source for their story. Note also the similarity to the story of the infant Moses.

But unlike Oedipus and Moses, the twins were not found by a human. As the story goes, the trough washed ashore and the infants crawled out into the lair of a she-wolf. Rather than killing the infants, the she-wolf suckled them and took them as her own. The story mentions that a woodpecker also helped in the feeding and care of the infants. Interestingly enough, the wolf and the woodpecker are both sacred animals of the war god Mars, father of the boys. The infants grew to become strong and good natured, if not a bit too wild for their own good. Eventually, the boys, who were still unnamed, were discovered by the shepherd Faustulus. He was wandering when he came upon the boys sleeping in the lair of the wolf. Surprised and touched by the plight of the two boys, he brought them home to his wife and they took them as their own children.

Romulus and Remus, as they were named by their adoptive parents, learned to speak, build, plant, and fight. They were more than simple shepherds. They were natural-born leaders. Word began to spread of their abilities and eventually reached the ears of the long deposed King Numitor. Numitor guessed the real identity of the boys and cried for joy that they had not perished in the Tiber. He quickly packed up and journeyed to reunite with his grandsons and tell them of their lineage and the tragedy that had befallen their real family. The twins moved to Alba Longa and quietly observed the political situation. They hid their identities in order to find all those who had counseled Amulius to kill them. Chief counselor to Amulius was a priest named Camers. It was he who had told Amulius to drown the twins. Once they knew the truth, the twins gathered up their arms and launched an attack upon the rule of Amulius. The battle ended with the twins triumphant. The heads of the traitors were put on spears and Numitor was returned to the seat of power.

Things were fine for a time, but the twins were now men and wished to find land of their own. They decided to leave Alba Longa in search of their own kingdom. Their search brought them to what is now Rome. The boys split the land, but Romulus got a sizably larger area than Remus. Jealousy began to grow between the two, yet they remained faithful to each other's wishes. Romulus built a wall around his area and claimed that no man could enter Roma, as he now called it, without his permission. Remus looked at the wall and said "This wall is too low and not worth building." He jumped the wall and mocked Romulus. With this, Romulus flew into a rage. His law had been broken. He attacked Remus and killed him. Thus, the first blood to be spilled in Rome was that of the brothers.

Romulus knew that he needed to have people in his lands to protect them and help his kingdom grow, so he allowed criminals and loners to settle there. Over time, it became evident that there were no women to be had in his lands. Without women, Rome would never grow to greatness. With this goal in mind, Romulus and his men raided nearby countries and took the women back to Rome to make them wives and mothers. The women were treated kindly and fairly once they were in Rome. When the men of the neighboring countries came to take the women back, they found them happy and unwilling to leave.

Rome was established and growing. Each year the crops became fuller and the number of actual Roman children increased. Lands were apportioned and an army was gathered and trained under the direct leadership of Romulus. Many new lands were taken and Rome was successfully defended against all threats. Rome had become a famous and respected city. Romulus ruled wisely and fairly in times of war and peace alike and legend has it that he never actually died, but was swept upward, into the realm of the gods. Many believed that he became a god himself and was worshipped under a different name.

Romulus and Remus is a classic story of sibling rivalry that bears similarity to the Cain and Abel story in the Bible. It is a story that has been taken up by John Steinbeck in his book *East of Eden*, which was later adapted into a movie starring James Dean. Other movies follow this similar theme, including *The Krays*, *The Mambo Kings*, and *The Fabulous Baker Boys*. In each of these movies, two brothers work together to create a successful venture, such as a criminal empire in *The Krays* or a better life as musicians in America in *The Mambo Kings*, but then the brothers wrestle with their loyalty toward and jealousy of each other, just as Romulus and Remus did.

Although Romulus and Remus serve as an archetype for sibling rivalry, it is Romulus' legacy that lives on in the most obvious way. His name was used for the city that would become the center of the Roman empire. Today ten U.S. cities are named Rome, including cities in Maine, Kentucky, Illinois, New York, and Georgia.

Sibling Rivalry

Anyone who has a sibling knows that at some point in time a little competition is going to erupt. There are numerous examples of sibling rivalry in myth and as with all mythological accounts of human nature, the situations are larger than life to make the point very clear to the audience. The most well known is the story of Cain and Abel, brothers who were so different that one felt the need to kill the other. Other famous myths about sibling rivalry include Jacob and Esau, who competed for their father's blessing, and Romulus and Remus, who battled over the land that would become Rome.

For every story of sibling rivalry, there also exists a story of the bond between siblings. The twin brothers Castor and Pollux were so close that Zeus made both of them a constellation. But as sweet as the happy stories of sibling bonds are, it seems that the battles between siblings are the more celebrated of the myths. One of the most bitter and sorrowful stories of sibling rivalry involves the children of Oedipus. Their stories are told in the stories *The Seven against Thebes* and *Antigone*.

Oedipus was cursed by fate to kill his father and marry his mother. His children were equally cursed because of their father's actions. Because Oedipus refused to declare an heir, his sons Eteocles and Polynices wondered who would get control over the city of Thebes after their father had abdicated the throne and left the city in self-imposed exile. Fearing that they would come to battle over the city, the brothers decided to take turns ruling Thebes. Each year they were to trade positions so that both would be the ruler. This seemed an amicable agreement and both were excited about the prospects of a cooperative and healthy future.

Unfortunately, once power had been tasted, it is hard for Eteocles to give it up. He refused to relinquish the throne when his term ended and he had

Polynices exiled from Thebes. Polynices traveled to Colonus to meet with his father. He had hoped to gain his fathers support, but instead, Oedipus cursed his sons once again. He told them that they would kill each other and neither would rule.

Polynices, dejected and angry, traveled to the kingdom of Argos. When he arrived, he tried to find a bed in which to sleep. The only bed that was available was also being sought out by another exile, Tydeus, who had fled from Calydon and was not going to give up this bed without a fight. The two began to fight and the battle became so furious and loud that it attracted the whole kingdom, including the king, Adrastus, who stopped the fight and noticed that their shields were emblazoned with a boar and a lion. He had been told that a boar and a lion would fight, and then come together to honor his kingdom.

Believing these combatants' shields were a sign, he quickly married the two men to his daughters and promised that his kingdom would help to restore each of them to their rightful positions. Unfortunately, the people of Argos were not thrilled at the prospect of going into war over the two exiles. A coalition was formed to take back the throne of Thebes and the march toward war began.

As it turned out, only seven warriors of note were involved in the siege of Thebes. These seven excelled in various arts of war. Each was a specialist of sorts. Unfortunately, although they took Thebes by force, Eteocles and Polynices killed one another as their father had foreseen. The curse became truth.

In their absence, Creon took the throne and proclaimed that the body of Polynices should be left unburied and never be given the rites needed to go to the underworld. He did this because Eteocles had portrayed his brother as a traitor. Meanwhile, Antigone, the sister of the dead brothers, mourned the loss of Polynices. She knew what had happened and believed Creon was being unjust. She could not bear to let her brother's soul wander aimlessly without a home. She could not do that to her family, no matter how dysfunctional it was. Knowing fully well that she would be put to death by being sealed in a tomb, Antigone chose to honor Polynices' body. She buried him and suffered a horrible death, thereby ending the curse on her side of the family for good. Creon's family would soon perish as well.

Two famous films are based on the "Seven of Thebes" part of this myth. Akira Kurosawa's film *Shichinin no samurai* (Seven Samurai) (1954) features seven outcasts, each with amazing skills. They face overwhelming odds to become the heroes of a small town. The 1960 movie, *The Magnificent Seven*, Americanizes Kurosawa's movie. It centers on a group of seven gunmen who defend a Mexican peasant village from an army of more than one hundred bandits.

Broken trust is a potent theme for all kinds of films and works of literature. In the film *The Godfather*, a brother is forced to have his sibling killed for crimes that his sibling committed against him. Numerous mafia-style films use the theme of family as the bond that cannot be broken. Ultimately, the same members who pledge allegiance to the family are the same ones who must kill a family member who breaks the oath.

Steven King's novel *The Dark Half* tells the story of a twin brother who exacts revenge on his unwitting sibling. Numerous evil twin plots have been used in so many ways that the device seems to have become a joke. Sibling rivalry is a common theme in soap operas. These shows live off of the theme of a man or woman turning sisters and brothers against one another. The popularity of sibling rivalry in modern culture speaks to its timeless quality.

Sisyphus

~

The myth of Sisyphus is representative of the great capabilities and mental prowess of man and the dire consequences of using those abilities in a way that is against the nature of humanity.

Sisyphus was the son of the king of Thessaly. He was known for his quick mind and crafty nature. For example, Sisyphus owned a large herd of cattle, while his neighbor Autolycus had a much smaller herd. Autolycus had won the favor of Hermes and in return, the god gave him the ability to change the form of any animal. The shifty Autolycus took advantage of his power and stole his neighbor's cattle by changing their color and disguising them among his own herd. Sisyphus soon noticed the shrinking size of his herd and the growing size of Autolycus' herd. Although Sisyphus knew his neighbor was up to something, he didn't know what. To catch Autolycus, Sisyphus carved his initials into the hooves of his animals. When more of them disappeared, Sisyphus went to his neighbors herd and found the animals. Autolycus complained that he had been framed, but Sisyphus took revenge against his neighbor by kidnapping his daughter Anticlia and marrying her.

Sisyphus' craftiness helped him learn secrets the gods assumed that mankind was incapable of figuring out. One of these secrets was Zeus' abduction of a daughter of the river god Asopus. Sisyphus foolishly revealed Zeus' indiscretion to Asopus, who then hunted down Zeus and attacked him. Although Zeus was able to fend off his assailant, he became angry with Sisyphus for compromising him. As revenge and punishment, Zeus sent Thanatos, the god of death, to take Sisyphus to the underworld.

The ingenious Sisyphus tricked Thanatos and actually kept the god of death prisoner. Sisyphus escaped to the real world and lived his life normally. Because he had officially died, he was able to take a new wife, Merope. The gods began to notice that no one was dying. The god of death couldn't do his job from inside his own prison. The gods soon found out what Sisyphus had done and decided that killing him was the only way to deal with the problem.

Sisyphus could not accept his fate. Instead he persuaded his wife, Merope, to leave his unburied body in the town square and forgo all of the funeral rituals like the funeral feast and preparing the body for the trip to the underworld. To ensure entrance into the underworld, Greeks would perform sacrifices to Hades or his wife, Persephone, and a coin would be place under the dead person's tongue to pay Charon for the boat trip across the river Styx.

When the gods killed Sisyphus, he was sent before Hades. Sisyphus convinced Hades that it was unfair to keep him in the underworld until his body was properly buried, as dictated by tradition. Hades agreed to let Sisyphus return to the upper world in order to make sure his body would receive the proper burial rites.

Sisyphus returned and decided to reenter his body. He also decided that he was not interested in returning to the underworld. No one was allowed to defy the law of the underworld and Sisyphus had done so twice. These transgressions, when added to the insult to Zeus, were too much for the king of the gods. Zeus was fed up and condemned Sisyphus to Tartarus, the prison of the Titans, for all of eternity. To show Sisyphus the error of his scheming ways, Zeus decreed that Sisyphus must push a huge rock up a hill. Each time the rock reached the crest of the hill, it would topple and roll back to its starting position. This lesson was designed to show Sisyphus the futility of attempting to get the better of the gods.

This myth graphically demonstrates the origin of the Christian concept of Hell. The irony of the punishment to fit the crime is seen in Milton's *Paradise Lost* and Dante's *Divine Comedy*. Sisyphus has found his way into literature, such as Albert Camus' *The Myth of Sisyphus*, which likens the absurdity of existence to eternally rolling a boulder up a hill. Today, the name Sisyphus is used to refer to someone who is engaged in a futile task.

Tantalus

~

Imagine being submerged in water up to your neck and every time you lower your parched lips to take a drink, the water recedes. Also imagine a limb of delicious juicy fruits above your head, just out of your reach. It sounds like a fate worse than death, and for Tantalus it was.

According to Greek myth, Tantalus was a mortal son of Zeus, which gave him special treatment from the gods. In addition, he was the king of Sipylus, a region in western Asia. His elevated status made him arrogant and he was just as prone to misbehaving as the gods. The Olympians accepted their own squabbles and misconduct, but they did not appreciate that kind of behavior from humans. They quickly punished misbehaving humans in many cases, such as when Gaia killed Orion for boasting that he was a better hunter than her. Like these other unfortunate humans, Tantalus' transgressions and disrespect earned him the wrath of the gods.

Myths about Tantalus diverge on the content of his crime, but its nature is the same: disrespecting the gods. In some versions, Tantalus stole ambrosia and nectar, which were the food and drink of the gods, and he tried to serve them to his mortal friends. Today ambrosia lends its name to a fruity dessert and is used to refer to anything that tastes or smells delicious. The word "ambrosial" describes anything that is sweet, fragrant, or fit for the gods. Nectar refers to any sweet beverage or the liquid in flowers used by bees to make honey.

Tantalus' misdeeds did not stop at stealing ambrosia. In some accounts of the myth, he reveals secrets that he had overheard from the gods. Other versions tell of Tantalus' theft or collusion in the theft of Zeus' golden dog. His final indiscretion involved cutting up his own son, Pelops, cooking him into a stew, and serving it to the gods. The omniscient gods were not fooled for a minute, but Demeter, the goddess of harvest and fertility who was deeply mourning the loss of her daughter Persephone to Hades in the underworld, absentmindedly took a bite from Pelops' shoulder before she realized what she was doing.

Tantalus' contempt of the gods was quickly and thoroughly punished. First, Zeus killed him by crushing him beneath a mountain. Then he was sent to Tartarus, the lowest level of the underworld, for eternal punishment. There, he was submerged in water he could not drink and tantalized by fruit he could not reach. In fact, the word "tantalize" is derived from Tantalus. In addition, he lends his name to tantalum, a metallic chemical element that is used in light filaments and surgical instruments. Tantalum is named for him because it does not absorb acid, just as Tantalus could not drink water.

The gods took pity on Pelops and Zeus restored his life, but the bite that Demeter had taken from his shoulder remained. She replaced it with an ivory shoulder, and his descendents were said to have ivory shoulders. Pelops' brother and sister did not learn from their father's mistakes. Niobe, who was as arrogant as her father, boasted that she had more children than the goddess Leto, and her children were better. As one might imagine, Leto did not take this insult lightly, so she sent her children Apollo and Artemis to kill every one of Niobe's twelve children. Devastated by her punishment, Niobe could not stop weeping, which eventually turned her to stone. Niobe's brother Broteas refused to honor Artemis, so the goddess of the hunt drove him mad. In his state of madness, Broteas thought he was impervious to fire and he leapt into a fire and died.

The story of Tantalus is clearly a morality tale. It reminded the ancient Greeks to respect their gods and understand their place in society. Like Sisyphus' continually rolling the boulder up the hill, Tantalus' unquenchable thirst and "tantalization" with fruit helped form our modern idea of punishment in the afterlife.

The Trickster

Loki

Among the many recurring characters in mythology, the trickster seems to be the most intriguing as well as confusing from the reader's point of view. Trickster myths can be found in almost every culture. Given the prevalence and distribution of this clown-genius, it stands to reason that the trickster should have an entry in this text.

The trickster archetype takes a variety of forms, which depend on the culture that spawned it. Despite the form the archetype takes, there is one element that remains consistent: the trickster challenges the core beliefs and social values of the people telling the myth. This challenge often comes in the form of a taboo action performed by the trickster that ultimately benefits humankind with a new technology or radical change in worldview.

In many trickster myths, the trickster is capable of truly awesome feats but remains astoundingly foolish at times. More confusing is the fact that, just when the reader of the myth has become quite comfortable with the foolishness of the trickster, the fool shows actual genius in its actions. This dual nature is the very essence of the trickster. It is the trickster's job to point out the absolute duality of the universe. Many scholars claim that mythology is simply a primitive mending and explanation of the paradoxes that lie behind our very existence.

The trickster myths tend to exploit the duality, rather than make sense of it. The trickster relishes the paradox and in many ways is the personification of duality. Wisely foolish and disgustingly alluring, the trickster captures our imagination and snaps us back into reality all at once. Shrouded in mystery and capable of powerful magic, the trickster stands as one of the most primal and potent of mythological figures.

Among the Norse myths, Loki, the doer of good and evil, takes on the role of trickster. He possesses a gift that seems fairly common to all tricksters: shapeshifting. The ability to alter oneself both physically and morally helps illustrate the trickster's ever-changing and unpredictable nature. Although he is vilified throughout the Norse mythos and he is compared to Satan by many Western readers, Loki serves as a catalyst for growth and change for the entire universe. Dubbed the god of fire by the Norse, he serves as the spark that begins the eventual burning of the world, but just as the world ends, so it also begins anew and fresh. Without Loki acting as a catalyst, this would never happen and the universe would remain static and unchanging.

The fire theme is extremely interesting in that it seems that the trickster is irrevocably tied to that element. As Loki controlled fire, so Prometheus brought fire to humankind as a gift to make their lives easier. In doing so, he had to break the edict of Zeus and pay the price. Prometheus acted foolishly, according to common wisdom, but ultimately his actions provided a great benefit to man. One of the Native American tricksters, Raven, stole fire sticks from the gods and gave them to humans, and the spider Anansi of African myth stole fire and brought it to humans in a small basket on her back.

The trickster takes on different forms in different cultures. The Native Americans portrayed the trickster as three different animals: the raven, coyote, and rabbit. Interestingly enough, this triad encompasses the food chain. Grass is eaten by rabbit the vegetarian, who is eaten by coyote the predator, who is fed upon by raven the scavenger, who eventually dies and feeds the grasses. These three tricksters survive and rely on each other.

Most interesting is the way these three tricksters have been embraced and employed by mainstream America. Raven the trickster lives on in the cartoon duo of Hekyll and Jekyll. These two fulfill the role of trickster in that they are duality personified. There are two of them, yet they act as one. They are obviously quite intelligent but consistently get in trouble for doing rather foolish things. In the end, however, all is well in their world and the audience has learned something from them.

Coyote the trickster lives on in the Looney Tunes Roadrunner and Coyote series. Constantly scheming and creating rather sophisticated machinery, the Coyote is doomed to failure each time due to a fatal flaw in his plan, or by being outwitted by Roadrunner. Coyote plays the fool because he expends more and more energy and time—and presumably racks up a huge credit debt with Acme Products—to catch the elusive Roadrunner. The audience knows that he will fail every time, yet he fails to learn the lessons that he inadvertently teaches them.

Finally, the most well known and true to the mythical archetype of the tricksters must be Bugs Bunny. He is the clown prince of tricksters, eminently witty and full of surprises, yet prone to putting himself in situations that are dangerous. His nonsensical behavior and language twisting abilities leave the audience mixed up, yet somehow feeling an order to the chaos.

In medieval times, the court jester played the role of the trickster. These clowns were one of the few people who could point out injustices and class differences without fear of reprisal from the court. Their job was to bring to light the silliness of the feudal system while paying homage to the king in a simultaneous fashion.

To this day we still honor the tricksters who entertain us while also pointing out harsh realities. Comedians rarely get a laugh if they do not point out a specific quirk that all people can relate to. They are appreciated precisely for the wittiness of their stabs at the collective human experience. In particular, the movie *The Mask* showcases Jim Carrey and exploits the dual nature of the trickster in the main character's alter-ego.

The trickster appears in literature as well. Tom Sawyer, the character immortalized in the books *Huckleberry Finn* and *Tom Sawyer*, is a classic trickster who flows through a series of events causing trouble but ultimately doing good. Those benefits are the ultimate outcome that the trickster neither strives for nor is aware of. The trickster gets where he or she does not by virtue of a great plan or forethought, but simply by being him or herself. That alone is a lesson we would do well to learn.

The Trojan War

Achilles versus the River God

The myth of the Trojan War has origins in history. Long before ancient Greece was filled with city-states and cultural icons, it was an amalgamation of war bands whose similarities were limited to language and geography. Historians believe that the Greeks, under the leadership of King Agamemnon of Mycenae, probably set on a mission to plunder the Troads, a group who resided in what is now Turkey. Around 1184 B.C., the war led to the siege and capture of the city of Troy by the Greeks.

Unlike the greed that originated the real Trojan War, the mythical war began on a much more supernatural note. It began with the wedding of Peleus and Thetis. Peleus was the leader of the Myrmidions, a fierce group of warriors, and Thetis was a Nereid, one of the many daughters of Poseidon. Because Thetis was a goddess, the wedding guests were an elite group, mostly gods and goddesses. One of those in attendance, Eris, the goddess of discord, threw a golden apple into the crowd. The words "for the fairest" were inscribed upon the apple. Quickly a debate arose as to who should receive the apple: Hera, Athena, or Aphrodite. These three goddesses were powerful, important, and beautiful. No one wanted to make the decision and risk offending the other two goddesses. Finally, it was decided that Paris, a member of the royal family of Troy, would decide who should get the apple.

The three goddesses rushed to influence his decision. Hera offered him power, Athena offered him wisdom and military glory, and Aphrodite offered him the most beautiful woman in the world as his wife. Paris favored Aphrodite's bid and awarded the apple to her. The other two goddesses were not pleased and promised retribution. To make matters worse the most beautiful woman in the world was Helen, the wife of a king named Menelaus.

Long before Helen married the king, she had been abducted by Theseus, who had hoped to marry her. Unfortunately for the young hero, Helen's brothers came looking for her. A man named Akadēmos revealed Theseus' hideout to the brothers. For his honorable act, a park and gymnasium near Athens was named after Akadēmos. It was called the Akadēmeia, and Plato founded his school on the spot. The school is the source of our modern word "academy."

Years later, Paris met Helen while acting as an ambassador to Sparta. He and Helen fell in love and ran away together, taking a great deal of the city's treasure with them to Troy. The Greeks would not let Paris steal Helen so easily. First they sent a delegation to Troy to convince the Trojans to oust the lovers, but the Trojans refused to drive them out. Undeterred, the Greeks declared war and assembled 1,000 ships to sail for Troy. Helen is said to have "the face that launched a thousand ships."

Cassandra, the daughter of King Priam of Troy, had been given the gift of prophecy from Apollo, the god of fine arts and medicine. She knew of the impending attack by the Greeks and she tried to warn her people. Unfortunately, she had made the mistake of spurning Apollo's advances and he punished her by commanding that her prophecies go unheeded. As she desperately pleaded with Trojans to prepare from the imminent assault, they dismissed her as crazy. Today the word "Cassandra" is used to describe a prophet of doom.

When the war started, the gods got involved and chose their sides. Aphrodite, Artemis, and Apollo all sided with the Trojans. Hera and Athena still felt the sting of the slight that Paris delivered them when he chose Aphrodite as the most beautiful. They naturally favored the Greeks. Hephaestus, Hermes, and Poseidon sided with the Greeks as well. Ares, the god of war, was driven by his passion for battle and supported both sides to extend the length of the war. Several of the gods, including Zeus and Hades, remained neutral.

Commanding one of the ships was Achilles, the son of Thetis and Peleus, at whose wedding this story began. Achilles is one of the central figures in the war and he has an interesting past. As the son of Thetis, Achilles was not your average human. In fact, Thetis had worked very hard to protect him from the frailties of humanity. She dipped him in the magical River Styx to protect his body from weapons. The only part that remained dry and unprotected was the heel by which Thetis held him. Additionally, Achilles had been trained as a warrior by Chiron, a centaur renowned for his battle techniques. Achilles was the best warrior Greece had to offer. The Greeks would need him, for they would be battling the fierce Trojans and their champion, Hector.

The battle went on for nine years without a decisive victor, but the tenth year changed that. The turning point in the war began when King Agamemnon abducted the daughter of one of Apollo's prophets because he wanted slaves. As the god of music and archery, Apollo was insulted by Agamemnon's actions, and in retribution, he sent a plague on the Greek army. When a council was called to solve the problem, Agamemnon and Achilles argued. Agamemnon punished Achilles for arguing with him and took one of Achilles' slave girls as a price for the argument. Achilles got so mad, he decided not to fight in the war anymore. Achilles' anger did not stop there. He went so far as to ask his mother to tell Zeus to help the Trojans as payment for the insult. Zeus owed Thetis a favor so he did her bidding.

With the added help of Zeus, the Trojans began to take a toll on the Greek army and the Trojan champion Hector called out to challenge Achilles to battle him. Achilles was still refusing to fight and so his best friend, and possibly lover, Patroclus, donned the armor of Achilles and fought Hector. Hector killed Patroclus and when he found out it was not Achilles, he stripped the body of armor, as was the custom, and sent it back for burial.

Achilles flew into a rage but soon realized it was his stubbornness that had caused Patroclus' death. He asked the god Hephaestus to forge him new armor and he returned to the war and wreaked havoc on the Trojans. With the return of Achilles, the Greeks fought with renewed vigor. They fought so fiercely that some of the gods who had sided with the Trojans actually got into the fight.

Finally, Achilles got revenge when he faced Hector in battle and killed him. He was so enraged that he dragged Hectors body behind a chariot until it was terribly mutilated. He sacrificed Trojans and made the men perform funeral games in honor of Patroclus. Then he refused to give the body of Hector back to his family. Finally he gave them the body for money. His brutal acts deeply offended the Trojans, the Greeks, and even the gods. By committing them, Achilles doomed himself.

This element of blind revenge has served as a central plot for many movies. In the *Death Wish* series, Charles Bronson's character, Paul Kersey, gets revenge on the men who killed his family. Mel Gibson is the archetypal revenge hero in movies like *Payback*, *Lethal Weapon*, and *The Patriot*. The comedy *The Princess Bride* parodies the archetype with the character Inigo Montoya, played by Mandy Patinkin. Seemingly motivated solely by revenge, he introduces himself by saying, "Hello, my name is Inigo Montoya. You killed my father; prepare to die." The popularity of these characters illustrates the timeless interest in revenge.

According to Homer, author of *The Iliad*, Hector was the bravest and most valiant of the Trojan soldiers. He is portrayed by Homer as a devoted son of King Priam, brother of Paris, and husband of Andromache. Until the seventeenth century, brave warriors were known as "hectors." At that time the meaning of the word changed. By the later half of the century, the rowdy thugs who tormented people on London streets were known as hectors. While they perceived themselves as brave warriors, their victims saw them as boastful tormentors. Soon the word began to be used broadly to mean braggart or bully. Then it began to be used as a verb, so "to hector" meant "to harass." In this form, the word is still used today.

Pandarus, another Trojan warrior, has added a word to our language as well. He was an archer with an admirable reputation. In the original Greek myth, he is cited as breaking the truce between the Trojans and Greeks by firing on the king of Sparta, Menelaus. In medieval stories he becomes a go-between in the love affair between Troilus, a Trojan prince, and Cressida, the daughter of a Greek priest. This popular tale of ill-fated love first appeared around 1338 in Boccaccio's *Il Filostrato*. His work became the inspiration for Chaucer's *Troilus and Criseyde*, which was written in the fourteenth century. Around 1601, William Shakespeare used Chaucer's work as a basis for his drama, *Troilus and Cressida*. In Shakespeare's version, Pandarus is more of a self-interested procurer than a well-intentioned intermediary in the affair.

From his role in the lover affair, Pandarus is the basis for the word "pander." At first it described a go-between in a love affair and then evolved to mean a pimp. The word progressed again to describe someone who aids an evil-doer or one who exploits the weaknesses of others. At the same time, the word began to be used as a verb and took on the same meaning as it has today: to attend to the base desires or motives of others.

As the tenth year wore on, more forces came to the aid of the Trojans only to be killed by Achilles. Meanwhile, the gods Apollo and Poseidon were plotting against him. They collaborated with Paris to kill Achilles by helping Paris fire an arrow at Achilles one vulnerable spot: his heel. This story is the origin of the terms "Achilles tendon" and "Achilles heel."

Knowing that the war would rage on indefinitely, the Greeks devised a plan to build a giant wooden horse as a fake offering to the Trojans. They pretended to leave Troy, but in fact many great warriors sealed themselves inside the Trojan horse. The Trojans accepted the gift horse and wheeled it into their city for a party that left them all passed out drunk. In the middle of the night Odysseus and the warriors of Greece emerged from the horse and slaughtered the Trojans in their own town. They killed innocents and sacked the town and its temples. Today, the phrase "a Trojan horse" is commonly used to refer to someone or something that infiltrates from within. The adjective "Trojan" is used to describe someone who is determined and energetic.

The unusually cruel behavior of the Greeks' Trojan horse offended the gods, and each of the kings, including Agamemnon and Odysseus, met with great adversity or a tragic death. For example, when Agamemnon arrived home his wife Clytemnestra stabbed him to death. Each king's story is the center of an epic or plays written by the Greeks.

The Trojan War served as the plot for Robert Wise's movie *Helen of Troy* (1956). Wise, who also directed the classic musicals *West Side Story* and *The Sound of Music*, devoted himself to developing a Hollywood spectacular on the scale of Cecil B. DeMille's *The Ten Commandments*. Thousands of extras clothed in elaborate costumes filled expansive sets to create the most ambitious portrayal of Greek myth.

The Trojan War has richly contributed to our lexicon and it is one of the most colorfully told events in our history. Homer tells the events near the end of the war in *The Iliad*, while Apollodorus reviews all ten years of the war in *Epitome* and Euripides describes the events in *The Trojan Women* and *Helen*. The myth of this historical event reminds us that myths are rooted in reality, however fantastical they may seem.

The World Tree

Yggdrassil

We climb them in our youth, take a nap in their shade, build our homes from their bodies, and use them as fuel for warmth. Trees provide fruit and clean the very air we breathe. Growing from a single seed, a tree can live for hundreds of years, providing for the people and animals that live near or in its branches. Giant redwoods tower over landscapes while choruses of birch trees sway and rustle by the thousands on mountainsides. Each fall they change from green to almost every warm color imaginable, then drop their leaves to feed the ground around them. The spring brings new buds and the trees explode with green again to herald the coming summer. They are a natural calendar and historic preserver. Looking at their rings, one can see the past climates, year to year. For all of their noble beauty above ground, they are equally magnificent underground. Complex root systems spread out through the soil, anchoring a tree's mass to the earth and drawing water and nutrients to feed its growth. The root system can be just as expansive of the branches topside.

With each of these ideas in mind, it should come as no surprise that people from ancient cultures recognized and valued trees. Trees were worshiped, given special status, and made the subject of myths in almost every culture. They stand as a symbol of strength, longevity, giving, and duality. From the Maya of ancient South America to the Norse to the Buddhists of the Orient, the tree is seen as the center of the world, an axis upon which all existence is connected.

The Maya of ancient South America were avid astronomers and based a great deal, in fact most, of their mythology on the movement of the stars and planetary bodies. The Milky Way itself was seen as a huge tree that blossomed with great shining flowers. They believed that the Great Tree of Life was actually the source of life itself. In the world tree were animals that had specific duties for and against mankind.

Almost all so-called primitive cultures venerated the tree. Evidence of this is found in Asia, Australia, and North America as well. We need only to look to the Druids of Britain and Gaul to see the importance they attached to oaks and various other trees. Leaves were used as an alphabet and lives were centered on the woods themselves. Sacred groves became the sites for ritual. In ancient Greece, certain oaks were said to carry the words of Zeus within their trunks. The ancient Hebrew Kabbalists used the tree as a symbol of spiritual growth for humans. Siddartha Gautama, a prince of India who would later become the Buddha, attained enlightenment while sitting at the base of the bohdi tree, and in the Garden of Eden the fruit of a special tree was capable of giving knowledge to those who tasted it, even though they were forbidden to do so.

One of the most famous mythical trees is Yggdrassil, the great tree of life. Yggdrassil was seen by the Norse as the connection between all of the realms. This huge ash tree had branches that could bring shade to any area in all of the nine worlds. Its roots touched the earth in all nine worlds as well. Its three main support roots tapped into special areas. One reached into Niflheim, the land of the dead. A spring called Hvergelmir began at this root and leads to the many great rivers of the world. A horrible dragon, Nidhogg, gnawed at the root to maintain its own strength and keep the tree from growing too fast. When not feeding on the tree's roots, the dragon punished and tormented the dead.

Another root tapped the Ginnungagap, from which all life began and passed through the land of the giants. Its root taps Mimir's Well, where wisdom itself was located. Odin gave his eye to this well in exchange for the knowledge and power of runic magic. Another root reached into heaven and directly into a very special well. Here stood the three Norns that wove humankind's fate. According to the myths, answers to all questions could be found here and drinking from the well changed the drinker entirely. The water was so pure that the drinker became pure white and clean, incapable of decay. Here the first swans resided, swimming in the water that made them white.

All kinds of animals lived within the branches of the trees. Stags ran along its great branches and fed upon its leaves. At the top stood an eagle and on the eagle's head, a hawk was perched. The hawk could see all that transpired in the nine worlds from this vantage point. A chatty squirrel ran from the top of the tree all the way to the lair of Nidhogg, bringing insults from the eagle to the dragon, and then headed back up to deliver the dragon's retort. All life was represented by the tree Yggdrassil. In fact, it became the safe haven for the last two humans during Ragnarok, which was the Norse's end of the world. These two humans, Lif and Liftrasir, lived deep within the tree and were fed by morning dew and sap from Yggdrassil. Yggdrassil was the only thing capable of withstanding the scorching fires that would destroy the earth, proving once more why the tree was such a powerful symbol of life, strength, and abundance.

In today's society, we have a version of the World Tree in the concept of a family tree. Instead of representing the branches of animal life, the family tree illustrates the interconnection and relationship of human life. One of the roots of the World Tree has a parallel in modern culture as well. The root that reached into heaven is similar to a fountain of youth, with its ability to prevent decay.

Appendix A
Mythology in Nature

The Diving God

⟡ Plants

Agave
Any of a number of related plants of the amaryllis family.
Origin: from Agauē, the daughter of Cadmus, who was the Greek founder of Thebes.

Amaryllis
Any of a number of related bulb plants bearing several lilylike flowers on a single stem.
Origin: from a shepardess in poems by Virgil and Theocritus.

Anemone
Any number of related plants with cup-shaped flowers, usually white, purple, or red.
Origin: When Adonis was killed by a wild boar, anemones sprang from his drops of blood. Christians adopted the symbolism and used anemones to represent the blood shed by Christ.

Arethusa
A variety of orchid, usually with one long, narrow leaf and one rose-purple flower.
Origin: from a woodland nymph named Arethusa, who was changed into a stream by Artemis, the Greek goddess of the hunt. The goddess transformed her so that she could escape her persuer, the river god Alpheus.

Artemisia
Any of a number of related aromatic plants of the composite family, with small yellow or white flowers.
Origin: from Artemis, the Greek goddess of the moon, wild animals, and hunting.

Calypso
Any of a number of related orchids found in bogs bearing on each stem a single white flower with purple or yellow markings.
Origin: from Calypso, the nymph who detained the Greek hero Odysseus for seven years, prolonging his journey home.

Cypripedium
Any of a group of orchids with showy, drooping flowers.
Origin: from the Greek *kypris* meaning Venus, the goddess of love, and *podion* meaning slipper.

Daphne
1. The laurel tree; 2. a kind of shrub having fragrant flowers.
Origin: from Daphne, a nymph in Greek mythology who escaped from the pursuing Apollo (the god of music) by turning into a laurel tree.

Flora
1. A flower; 2. the plants of a specified region or time
Origin: from Flora, the Roman goddess of flowers.

Hercules'-club
A small, very spiny tree of the ginseng family, found in the Eastern United States.
Origin: named for Hercules, the Greek hero.

Hesperidin
1. A fruit that is related to the orange; 2. a crystalline glycoside found in most citrus fruits
Origin: from Hesperides, the nymphs in Greek mythology who guarded the golden apples that were given to Hera as a wedding gift by Gaia.

Hyacinth
Any group of plants of the lily family with long, narrow leaves and spikes of fragrant, bell-shaped flowers.
Origin: from a Greek youth named Hyacinthus. Apollo, the god of music, fell in love with the young man and accidentally killed him. According to the myth, Apollo grows the hyacinth flower from the boy's blood.

Iris
Any of a large group of bulb plants with sword-shaped leaves and a prominent flower composed of three petals.
Origin: from Iris, the Greek goddess of the rainbow.

Narcissus
Any of a number of related bulb plants with smooth leaves and clusters of yellow, white, or orange flowers.
Origin: from Narcissus, a Greek youth. When he rebuffed Echo, Nemesis punished him by causing him to fall in love with his own image. After he wasted away from staring at himself, Nemesis transformed him into the flower.

Nymphaeaceous
Belonging to the water lily family.
Origin: from nymphs, minor Greek goddesses who populated rivers, mountains, and trees.

Peony
Any of a number of related plants with large colorful flowers.
Origin: from Paiōn, the epithet of Apollo, who was the physician of the gods. It was named for him because the flower was originally used for medicinal purposes.

Silenaceous
A genus of plants.
Origin: from Silenus, a god of the forest in ancient Greek mythology.

Sterculiaceous
Of a family of mainly tropical trees and shrubs, including the cacao and kola
nut trees.
Origin: from Sterculius, the Roman god of manure.

Venus flytrap
A white-flowered plant having leaves with hinged blades, which close up
around insects.
Origin: from Venus, the Roman goddess of love.

Venushair
A delicate maidenhair fern.
Origin: from Venus, the Roman goddess of love.

∾ Animals and Insects

Arachnid
Any of a large group of arthrodos with four pairs of legs, including spiders,
scorpions, and mites.
Origin: from the myth about the Greek maiden Arachnida, who was turned
into a spider after smugly defeating Athena in a weaving contest.

Argonaut
A paper nautilus.
Origin: from Jason and the men who sailed the *Argo* to search for the Golden
Fleece.

Argus
An East Indian bird resembling the peacock.
Origin: from the Argos, a hundred-eyed monster in Greek mythology.

Cecropia moth
Name of a genus of mulberry trees; a large silkworm moth having wide wings,
each with a crescent-shaped spot of white edged with red.
Origin: from Cecrops, the founder of Athens. He was first represented as half-
man, half-dragon.

Centaury
Any of a group of small plants of the gentian family.
Origin: named because the centaur Chiron is said to have discovered the me-
dicinal properties of the plant.

Cygnet
A young swan.
Origin: named after Cygnus, the mythical king who changed into a swan and was placed among the stars.

Fauna
The animals of a specified region or time.
Origin: from Fauna, the sister of Faunus, who was the Roman god of animals.

Halcyon
A kingfisher.
Origin: named after Alcyone, the daughter of Aeolus, who was the king of the winds. According to Greek myth she was turned into a kingfisher at death.

Harpy eagle
A large tropical American eagle.
Origin: named after harpies, the hideous winged monsters of Greek mythology with women's heads.

Hyacinth
A water bird with purple feathers.
Origin: from a Greek youth named Hyacinthus. Apollo, the god of music, fell in love with the young man and accidentally killed him.

Hydra
Any of a group of very small freshwater animals with a tubelike body and a mouth surrounded by tentacles.
Origin: named after the Hydra, a water serpent, that according to Greek mythology possessed nine heads, each of which, if cut off, would grow back as two.

Io moth
A large American moth with an eyelike spot on each hind wing.
Origin: according to Greek mythology, Io was a maiden who was pursued by Zeus and she was transformed into a heifer by Zeus' jealous wife, Hera.

Nemertean
Belonging to a group of brightly colored marine worms living in coastal mud or sand.
Origin: from the Greek Nēmertēs, the name of a sea nymph.

Nymphalid
Any of a group of butterflies with very short forelegs.
Origin: from nymphs, the group of Greek and Roman minor goddesses who lived in rivers, mountains, and trees.

Philomel

A nightingale.

Origin: from Philomele, a princess in Greek mythology who was raped by her brother-in-law Tereus. After he cut out her tongue, her sister avenged the attack and she was transformed into a nightingale.

Phoebe

A small bird, one of the American flycatchers.

Origin: named after Phoebe, another name for Artemis, the Greek goddess of the moon.

Pierid

A family of small or medium-sized butterflies.

Origin: named for the nine Greek maidens who challenged the Muses to a singing contest and lost. They were transformed into magpies for their boasting.

Promethea moth

A silkworm moth having reddish-brown wings.

Origin: named for Prometheus, a Titan in Greek mythology stole from heaven and gave it to humankind.

Python

Any of a group of very large, nonpoisonous snakes that crush their prey to death.

Origin: named for an enormous serpent that lurked in the cave of Mount Parnassus and was killed by Apollo.

Rhea

Any of a group of large South American nonflying birds comprising the American ostriches.

Origin: named after Rhea, the mother of Zeus.

Rhesus monkey

A short-tailed brownish-yellow monkey often used in medical research.

Origin: named for the Greek mythical king, Rhesus. His horses were captured by Odysseus and Diomedes to keep them from drinking from the Xanthus River. An oracle foretold that if the horses drank from the river, Troy would not fall.

Saturniid

Any of a family of large moths with a small head, broad wings, and a hairy body.

Origin: from Saturn, the Roman god of agriculture.

Satyr

Any of a group of butterflies with gray or brown wings often marked with eye-like spots.

Origin: from the satyrs of Greek mythology. These woodland creatures attended
to Dionysus, the god of vegetation and wine.

Siren
A small, slime-coated, eel-shaped animal with internal lungs and external gills.
Origin: named after the Sirens of Greek myth. These sea nymphs were part-
women, part-birds who lured sailors to death with their seductive singing.

Triton
A kind of sea snail with a long spiral shell.
Origin: named for Triton, the Greek sea god who was the son of Poseidon and
Amphitrite.

∾ Elements

Cadmium (symbol: Cd)
A blue-white, malleable, ductile, metallic chemical element occurring as a sul-
fide or carbonate in zinc ores.
Origin: Cadmus, the founder of Thebes, who, according to Greek legend, killed
a dragon that was sacred to Mars, the god of war. He sowed the
dragon's teeth in the soil and armed men sprung up from them.

Cerium (symbol: Ce)
A gray, metallic element of the rare-earth group.
Origin: named after the asteroid Ceres, which had been named after the Roman
goddess of agriculture.

Helium (symbol: He)
A very light, inert, colorless gas.
Origin: named for the Greek god of the sun, Helios.

Mercury (symbol: Hg)
A heavy silver-white metallic element that remains liquid at ordinary temper-
atures.
Origin: named after Mercury, the Roman messenger of the gods.

Neptunium (symbol: Np)
A chemical element produced by irradiating uranium atoms with neutrons.
Origin: named for Neptune, the Roman god of the seas.

Niobium (symbol: Nb)
A rare metallic chemical element.
Origin: named after Niobe, the mother whose boasting prompted Artemis and
Apollo to kill all of her children. The weeping mother transformed into
stone from which tears continued to flow.

Plutonium (symbol: Pu)
A radioactive chemical element formed from neptunium.
Origin: named after Pluto, the Roman god of the Underworld.

Promethium (symbol: Pm)
A metallic chemical element of the rare-earth group.
Origin: named for Prometheus, the Greek Titan who gave fire to humans.

Tantalum (symbol: Ta)
A rare steel-blue metallic element.
Origin: named after Tantalus, the mortal man who was punished in the afterlife
    by being tantalized with food and drink always out of his reach.

Tellurium (symbol: Te)
A rare, tin-white, brittle nonmetallic element.
Origin: from Tellus, the Roman goddess of the Earth.

Titanium (symbol: Ti)
A dark-gray, lustrous chemical element.
Origin: named after the Titans, the predecessors to the Greek gods.

Uranium (symbol: U)
A very hard, heavy radioactive metallic chemical element.
Origin: Named for Uranus, the Greek personification of heaven and father of
    the Titans.

∾   Other

Amethyst
A purple or violet variety of quartz or corundum.
Origin: from a Greek nymph named Amethyst who changed into a pure white
    stone to save herself from Dionysus. When Dionysus realized his cruelty
    toward the nymph, his wine-stained tears soaked the stone and turned
    it purple.

Atropine
A poisonous crystalline alkaloid obtained from belladonna and similar plants. It
    is used to relieve spasms and dilate the pupil of the eye.
Origin: from Atropos, one of the three Fates from Greek mythology who is
    represented as cutting the thread of life.

Hyacinth
Any of the reddish-orange varieties of zircon, garnet, or topaz.
Origin: from a Greek youth named Hyacinthus. Apollo, the god of music, fell
    in love with the young man and accidentally killed him.

Morphine

A bitter crystalline addictive narcotic used in the form of a soluble salt as an analgesic and sedative.

Origin: from Morpheus, the Greek god of sleep.

Appendix B
Mythology in Brand Names

Companies often look to mythology for inspiration when naming products or even the company itself. This is a selected list of brands that take their names from mythology.

Ajax (a brand of cleaner). He was a Greek hero in the Trojan War.

Amazon (a dot-com marketplace). The Amazons were a race of female warriors.

Green Giant (a brand of frozen vegetables). Giants were the legendary humanlike beings of great size and strength from Greek mythology.

Hyperion (a book publishing company). Hyperion was the ancient Greek god of the sun.

Janus (a brand name of a watch; an investment company). Janus was the Roman god of beginnings and doorways.

Mars (a brand of candy bar). Mars was the Roman god of war.

Mercury (a music recording label; a make of car). Mercury was the Roman god of merchandise, trade, and theft.

Midas (a muffler repair business). Midas was the king of Greek myth whose touch turned everything to gold.

Nike (a brand of athletic shoe). Nike was the Greek goddess of victory.

Olympus (a photography equipment company). Mount Olympus was the mountain-top home of the Greek gods.

Oracle (a database software company). A cryptic prophecy delivered by a priest or priestess. Oracles play an important role in many myths.

Orion (a motion picture production company). Orion was a hunter who was slain by the Greek goddess Artemis.

Saturn (a make of car). Saturn was the Roman god of agriculture.

Trident (a brand of gum). Trident was the three-pronged spear used by Poseidon and Neptune, the Greek and Roman gods of the sea.

Appendix C
Mythology in the Solar System

∾ The Nine Planets of the Solar System

Other than earth, each of the planets of the solar system is named after a Roman or Greek god.

Mercury
The closest planet to the sun is named after the Roman god of commerce and theft. He was also the messenger to the gods.

Venus
The second planet from the sun is named for the Roman goddess of love.

Mars
The fourth planet from the sun, often called the "Red Planet," is named for the Roman god of war.

Jupiter
The fifth planet from the sun is the largest and named after the chief Roman god.

Saturn
The sixth planet from the sun is named for the Roman god of agriculture. Saturn was also the father of Jupiter.

Uranus
The seventh planet from the sun is named after the Greek personification of the sky. He was also the father of the Titans, the hundred-handed Giants, and the Cyclopes.

Neptune
The eighth planet from the sun is named after the Roman god of the sea.

Pluto
The farthest planet from the sun is named for the Roman god of the underworld.

∿   Planetary Features

In addition to planet names, mythical figures have loaned their names to a variety of planetary features.

Aphrodite Terra
This highland along Venus' equator was named after the Greek goddess of love. The area is roughly the size of South America.

Cerberus
This large dark spot on the surface of Mars was named after the ferocious three-headed dog that guarded the gate of Hades.

Olympus Mons
The largest volcano on Mars was named after the mythical home to the gods and goddesses.

Rhea Mons
This volcano on Venus was named after Rhea, who was the daughter of Uranus and Gaia. Her relationship with her brother Cronus resulted in six Olympians including Zeus, Poseidon, Hades, Hera, Hestia, and Demeter.

Theia Mons
This volcano on Venus was named after one of the Greek Titans, Theia. Like Rhea, she was the daughter of Uranus and Gaia. She and her brother Hyperion had three children, Helius, Selene, and Eos.

∿   Constellations—The Twelve Signs of the Zodiac

Aries (Ram)
Aries is a cluster of sixty-six stars in the Northern Hemisphere. To the Syrians and Hebrews, the constellation represented a lamb. The Arabs called it Alhamal, meaning "sheep." The Egyptians believed it was the ram-headed figure of their sun god. The ancient Greeks thought it was a ram as well. There are two stories of its origin. In the first story, Dionysus, the god of wine, was leading his followers across the desert with no food or drink. Dionysus summoned a ram and alongside the ram was a spring. The second story asserts that the ram is the golden

fleeced one that tries to save Nephele's children and whose fleece is sought after by Jason and the Argonauts.

Taurus (Bull)

Taurus is comprised of ninety-eight stars. The ancient Egyptians associated this constellation with Osiris, the god of fertility. The Chinese thought it was either a white tiger or a bridge. The Greek association with a bull is derived from two stories. In the first, Zeus seduces Europa by transforming himself into a bull. In the second, King Minos' wife Pasiphaë seduces a beautiful bull and gives birth to the half-man–half-bull Minotaur.

Gemini (Twins)

There are forty-seven stars that make up Gemini. Although today's version of Gemini depicts the sign as twins, earlier zodiacs depicted them as pairs. For example, in ancient Egypt, it was illustrated as a man and woman. In Greece, it was Apollo and Hercules.

Cancer (Crab)

Cancer is made up of twenty-three visible stars. The Arabs and Syrians knew the sign as "The Holder," while Tibetans described it as a frog. Egyptians deciphered it as a scarab and the Hindus and Chinese illustrated it as a crab.

Leo (Lion)

Fifty-two stars comprise the constellation of Leo. In the Greek myth of Hercules, he slays the Nemean lion in one of his labors and then wears the skin of the lion.

Virgo (Maiden)

Virgo is a cluster of fifty-eight stars. In the Assyrian and Babylonian zodiacs, Virgo represents Ishtar, their goddess of fertility and love. Virgo is also associated with the Greek goddesses Dike and Demeter and the Roman goddess Ceres.

Libra (Scales)

There are thirty-five stars that make up Libra. The Hebrews called this constellation the "weighing scales" and the Arabs described it as the "purchase." The Greeks called it "the claw," but the Romans gave it its modern interpretation of scales.

Scorpio (Scorpion)

Sixty-two stars comprise Scorpio. This sign has long been seen as associated with dark and evil things. While Arabs called it the Scorpion, the Sumerians described it as the outlaw. Even the Mayans called it "god's death sign." According to Greek mythology, the scorpion was sent to the heavens after Artemis, the goddess of the hunt, sent it to kill Orion, a hunter who was sent to the heavens as well.

Sagittarius (Archer)

Sagittarius is comprised of sixty-five stars. It is one of the oldest identified shapes. The Babylonians illustrated the constellation as a mounted bowman. The Greeks believed that the constellation represented Chiron, the centaur who taught Hercules and Jason.

Capricorn (Goat)

There are thirty-one stars in Capricorn. Babylonians thought this constellation represented Ea, their god of subterranean water, but the Greeks had a more fanciful interpretation of the constellation. They believed it represented Pan, who had the ability to change into different animals. Once in the midst of a battle, he was in the shape of a goat when he jumped into the river to escape an enemy. When he entered the water, the lower half of his body turned into a fish. For this reason, the ancient Greeks believed that the constellation represented Pan in his half-goat–half-fish form.

Aquarius (Water bearer)

Aquarius is a cluster of fifty-six stars. Babylonians believed that Aquarius was located in the part of the sky that they called "the sea." Ancient Greeks had another interpretation. They thought that it depicted Ganymede, the youth that Zeus had abducted to be cupbearer to the gods.

Pisces (Fish)

Fifty-one stars make up the constellation Pisces. The Greeks associated this constellation with Aphrodite and Eros' escape from Typhon. They jumped into the river and turned into fish.

⸰ᵕ⸰   Other Constellations

Andromeda

Andromeda was the wife of the Greek hero Perseus. She was placed among the stars by Athena out of reverence for the feats of Perseus.

Aquila

Aquila was Zeus' eagle that brought Ganymede to Olympus to be Zeus' cupbearer.

Ara

Ara was the altar on which Zeus and the other gods swore their allegiance in the battle against Cronus and the Titans.

Argo

Argo was the ship on which Jason and the Argonauts sailed in their quest of the Golden Fleece.

Auriga

Erichthonius was the first person to harness horses to a chariot. Zeus honored the innovator by placing his chariot in the stars.

Cassiopeia

Cassiopeia was the mother of Andromeda. Poseidon put Cassiopeia in the heavens as a punishment for her vanity. According to the myth she is tied to a chair that turns upside down.

Centaurus

This constellation was named after the centaur, the half man–half horse in Greek myth.

Cetus

Cetus was the daughter of the sea and earth. This sea monster was depicted as having a dog's head and a whale's body

Cygnus

Cygnus means swan and represents Zeus when he took the form of a swan to seduce Leda, who then gave birth to Helen of Troy.

Delphinus

This constellation represents the dolphin that helped Poseidon find Amphritrite when he wanted to marry her. When the dolphin brought her back to Poseidon, the god of the sea was so overjoyed the he immortalized the dolphin in the stars.

Draco

This constellation depicted the serpent that guarded the golden apples. When it was slain by Hercules, Hera put it up in the stars.

Hercules

This constellation illustrates the Greek hero Hercules.

Hydra

This creature from Greek mythology was a water serpent with nine heads.

Lyra

This constellation represents the lyre of the Greek Muses.

Ophiuchus

Asclepius used his art of healing to raise the dead and was put into the stars at Apollo's request to Zeus.

Orion
Orion was a giant hunter in Greek mythology. He was killed by Artemis, the goddess of the hunt.

Pegasus
Pegasus was the great winged horse in Greek mythology.

Perseus
This constellation depicts Perseus, the Greek hero who killed Medusa.

Pleiades
The constellation of seven stars that represents the daughters of Zeus.

～ Satellites

Adrastea
A satellite of Jupiter, named after the daughter of Melissa, who was entrusted by Rhea with rearing Zeus.

Amalthea
A satellite of Jupiter, named after a nymph who helped rear Zeus.

Atlas
A moon of Saturn, named after the Titan Atlas, who was forced to hold the heavens on his shoulders for eternity.

Callisto
A moon of Jupiter, named after the nymph attendant of Artemis, who was punished for having a love affair with Zeus. She was changed into a bear and unknowingly killed by Artemis.

Calypso
A satellite of Saturn, named after the nymph who kept Odysseus on Ogygia for seven years.

Charon
A satellite of Pluto, named after the ferryman who transported the souls of the dead across the River Styx.

Deimos
A satellite of Mars, named after the son of Ares.

Dione
A satellite of Saturn, named after one Zeus' lovers.

Enceladus
A satellite of Saturn, named after giant who was buried under Mount Etna after warring with the gods.

Epimetheus

A satellite of Saturn, named after the brother of Prometheus and husband of
  Pandora.

Europa

A moon of Jupiter, named after the sister of Cadmus, who was abducted by
  Zeus while he was in the form of a bull.

Galatea

A moon of Neptune, named after a sea nymph who was courted by Polyphemus.

Ganymede

A moon of Jupiter, named after the youth who was carried off to Olympus by
  an eagle that was ordered by Zeus. He became the cupbearer of the
  gods.

Hyperion

A moon of Saturn, named after the father of Helios, Selene, and Eos.

Iapetus

A satellite of Saturn, named after the Titans who was the father of Atlas, Epimetheus, and Prometheus.

Io

A moon of Jupiter, named after Zeus' lover who was transformed into a heifer
  to escape Hera.

Janus

A moon of Saturn, named after the Roman god of beginnings.

Juno

One of the brightest asteroids in the solar system, named after the wife of
  Jupiter.

Leda

A satellite of Jupiter, named after one of Zeus' lovers.

Metis

A moon of Jupiter, named after one of the Titans who was the mother of
  Athena.

Mimas

A satellite of Saturn, named after one of the Gigantes who was killed by Hercules.

Naiad

A moon of Neptune, named after the nymphs who were associated with bodies
  of water in Greek myths.

Pandora

A satellite of Saturn, named after the first woman in Greek mythology.

Pasiphaë

A moon of Jupiter, named after the wife of Minos and mother of the Minotaur.

Phobos

A satellite of Mars, named after the son of Ares.

Prometheus

A satellite of Saturn, named after the Titan who stole fire from heaven and gave it to mankind.

Proteus

A satellite of Neptune, named after a shape-changing sea god in Greek mythology.

Rhea

A satellite of Saturn, named after the mother of Zeus.

Tethys

A moon of Saturn, named after the wife of Oceanus.

Thalassa

A satellite of Neptune, named after the personification of the sea in Greek mythology.

Thebe

A satellite of Jupiter, named after the daughter of Asopus and Metope who was abducted by Zeus.

Titan

A moon of Saturn, named after the children of Uranus and Gaia. The Titans ruled over the earth until they were overthrown by the Olympians.

Triton

A satellite of Neptune, named after the son of the sea god Neptune and Amphitrite.

Vesta

One of the brightest asteroids in the solar system, named after the Roman goddess of the hearth.

Appendix D
Mythology in the Calendar

∾ Months

January
Named for Janus, the Roman god of beginnings.

March
Named for Mars, the Roman god of war.

April
Derived from an abbreviation for Aphrodite, the Greek goddess of love.

May
Named for Maia, the mother of Hermes, the Greek messenger of the gods.

June
Named for Juno, the Roman goddess of women. Her Greek equivalent is Hera.

Not all of the months were named after gods:

February
Derived from the Latin word meaning "month of purification."

July
Named after Julius Caesar, a Roman emperor whose legacy, some might argue, has reached mythic proportions.

August
Named after the Roman emperor Caius Julius Caesar Octavian.

September
Derived from the Latin word for "seven" because September was once the seventh month of the year.

October
Derived from the Latin word for "eight" because October was once the eighth month of the year.

November
Derived from the Latin word for "nine" because November was once the ninth month of the year.

December
Derived from the Latin word for "ten" because December was once the tenth month of the year.

～   Days of the Week

Sunday
Named after the Sun. In the Romance languages, the names for this day mean "Lord's day" (e.g., *domingo* [Spanish] and *dimanche* [French]).

Monday
Means "moon's day."

Tuesday
Named for Tiu, the Germanic god of war and sky, which is another form of Tyr, the Norse god. In cultures that base the names of the days of the week on Latin etymology, Tuesday is named after the Roman god of war, Mars, (*Martes* [Spanish] and *Mardi* [French]).

Wednesday
Named for Woden, the chief Germanic god, which is another form of Odin, the Norse god. In cultures that base the names of the days of the week on Latin etymology, Wednesday is named after the Roman messenger of the gods, Mercury (*Miercoles, Mercredi*).

Thursday
Named for Thor, the Norse god of thunder. In cultures that base the names of the days of the week on Latin etymology, Thursday is named after Jupiter, the king of the Roman gods, who was also called Jove (*Jueves, Jeudi*).

Friday
Named for Frigga, the Norse goddess of married love and the hearth. In cultures that base the names of the days of the week on Latin etymology, Friday is named after the Roman goddess of love, Venus (*Viernes, Vendredi*).

Saturday
Named for Saturn, the Roman god of agriculture.

Note: Our modern notion of a seven-day week is derived from the Egyptians, who based the seven days on the seven planets that they believed re-volved around the earth. From the farthest to the nearest, the Romans called these seven planets Saturn, Jupiter, Mars, Sol, Venus, Mercury, and Luna, with Sol and Luna being the sun and moon respectively. The Egyptians believed that the planets governed different hours of the day. If the planet ruled the first hour of the day, the day was named after the planet. So Saturn day became Saturday, and so on.

Appendix E
Mythology in Common Words

academy

n. 1. A place of higher learning; 2. an association of learned persons for advancing art, literature, and science; 3. a private secondary school.

The word "academy" emerged from a park near Plato's school. The park was called Akadēmeia and was named after Akadēmos. According to Greek myth, Akadēmos revealed Theseus' hideout when he had abducted Helen.

Achates

n. A loyal friend.

In Virgil's *Aeneid*, Achates was Aeneas' loyal friend.

Adonis

n. A very handsome young man.

Adonis' beauty made him a favorite of the Greek goddess Aphrodite. When he was killed by a wild boar, Zeus allowed him to live for four months each year with Aphrodite, four months with Persephone in the underworld, and four months wherever he chose.

aegis

n. 1. Protection; 2. sponsorship.

An aegis was a shield used by the Greek god Zeus and his daughter Athena.

Aeolian

adj. Carried or produced by the wind.

Aeolus, the Greek god of the winds and forefather of Aeolis (a region in Northwestern Asia Minor), is the origin of the word "Aeolian."

Amazon
n. 1. A woman or girl warrior; 2. a large, strong, masculine woman; 3. a river in South America.
According to Greek mythology, Amazons were a race of female warriors.

ambrosia
n. Anything that tastes or smells delicious.
Ambrosia was the food of the Greek and Roman gods.

ambrosial
adj. 1. Of or fit for the gods; 2. delicious or fragrant.
From "ambrosia," the food of the Greek and Roman gods.

aphrodisiac
adj. Arousing or increasing sexual desire.
n. Any drug, food or other agent with aphrodisiac qualities.
Aphrodisiacs are named after the Greek goddess of love, Aphrodite.

Argonaut
n. 1. An adventurer engaged in a quest; 2. a person who took part in the California gold rush of 1848–1849.
According to Greek myth, Argonauts were the men who sailed with Jason to search for the Golden Fleece.

argosy
n. 1. A large ship, especially a merchant ship; 2. a fleet of large merchant ships.
An "argosy" was named after the Argo, which was the ship of the Greek hero, Jason.

Argus
n. An alert watchman
An Argus is named after the Argos, a hundred-eyed monster in Greek mythology.

Argus–eyed
adj. Vigilant or intensely observant.
The adjective Argus-eyed comes from the Argos, a hundred-eyed monster in Greek mythology.

athenaeum
n. 1. A literary or scientific club; 2. any building or hall used as a library or reading room.
The original athenaeum was the temple of Athena the Greek goddess of wisdom and warfare. Scholars and writers met at her temple.

atlantean
adj. Strong.
Atlantean comes from the Greek legend Atlas, a giant who was responsible for holding up the heavens on his shoulders.

Atlas

n. 1. Any person who carries a great burden; 2. a book of maps; 3. the top vertebra of the neck.

The modern use of the word "atlas" comes from the Greek giant Atlas, who held the heavens on his shoulders. The word became standard for books of maps when sixteenth-century cartographer Gerhardus Mercator included an illustration of Atlas holding up the heavens on one of his map books and called it *Atlas*.

augean

adj. 1. Extremely difficult task; 2. filthy.

The word "augean" has origins in one of the tasks of the Greek hero, Hercules. He was charged with cleaning the horribly neglected stables of King Augeas.

aurora

n. 1. Dawn; 2. the beginning or early period of something; 3. luminous bands of light appearing in the night sky including the Aurora Australis and Aurora Borealis.

Our modern word aurora has its origin in the Roman goddess of dawn.

bacchanal

adj. Carousing.

n. 1. A drunken carouser; 2. a drunken party; 3. an orgy.

Bacchanal comes from the drunken worshippers of the Roman god, Bacchus.

boreal

adj. 1. Northern; 2. of the north wind.

The word boreal owes its origins to Boreas, the Greek god of the north wind.

by Jove

A phrase used to express surprise or agreement.

Jove was one of the names of Jupiter, the most powerful of the Roman gods.

calliope

n. A musical instrument with a series of steam whistles that is played using a keyboard.

When A. S. Denny invented the calliope around 1850, he named it in honor of the Greek muse, Calliope, whose name meant "beautiful voice."

calypso

adj. Designating of songs improvised and sung by the natives of Trinidad.

Calypso was a nymph who detained the Greek hero Odysseus for seven years, prolonging his journey home.

capitol

n. 1. The building in which the United States Congress meets; 2. the building in which a State legislature meets.

Capitol was the name of the temple of the Roman god, Jupiter.

Cassandra

n. 1. A person whose warnings of misfortune are disregarded; 2. a person who predicts misfortune or disaster.

Cassandra comes from the Greek myth of the Trojan War. King Priam's daughter Cassandra had been given prophetic power from Apollo, the god of prophecy and music. When she spurned his advances, he punished her by making everyone disbelieve her prophecies.

cereal

n. 1. Any grain, such as wheat or oats; 2. any grass producing such grain; 3. food made from grain, especially breakfast food.

Cereal is named after the Roman goddess of agriculture.

Charon

n. A ferryman: humorous usage.

In Greek mythology, Charon is the ferryman who transported the souls of the dead across the River Styx in the underworld.

Cimmerian

adj. Dark and gloomy.

The Greek poet Homer described the Cimmerians as mythical people living in a realm of mist and gloom.

cliometrics

n. The application of methods developed by other fields to the study of history.

Cliometrics is derived from Clio, the Greek muse of history.

cupid

n. A representation of Cupid as a naked, winged boy often holding a bow and arrow.

Cupid is the Roman god of erotic love.

Cupid's bow

n. A bow that consists of two convex curves.

Cupid is the Roman god of erotic love.

cyclopean

adj. Huge, gigantic, enormous or massive.

According to Greek mythology, the Cyclopes were a race of giants with one eye in the middle of their foreheads.

Cyprian

n. A prostitute.

adj. Wanton or licentious.

Cyprus was the supposed home of Aphrodite, the Greek goddess of love.

daedal

adj. 1. Skillful in workmanship or ingenious; 2. finely adorned, intricate, ornate.

Daedalus was the legendary builder of the labyrinth that housed the Minotaur in Greek mythology. When he was trapped in the labyrinth, he made wings so that he and his son Icarus could escape imprisonment.

Delphic

adj. Obscure or ambiguous.

Delphi was a Greek city and the site of a great oracle of Apollo.

Delphic utterance

n. A comment or response to a question that is ambiguous or difficult to understand.

Delphi was a Greek city and the site of a great oracle of Apollo.

Dionysian

adj. Being of a frenzied or orgiastic character.

Dionysus was the Greek god of wine and vegetation. His followers were known for engaging in orgiastic revelry.

east

n. 1. The direction to the right from a person who is facing North; 2. a region in or toward this direction.

adj. In, of, to, toward, or facing the east.

adv. In an easterly direction.

The word "east" is derived from Eos, the Greek goddess of dawn.

echo

n. 1. The repeating of a sound, caused by the reflection of sound waves from of a surface; 2. any repeating or imitation of words, style, or ideas.

Echo was a nymph in Greek myth who pined away for the love of Narcissus until nothing was left but her voice.

Egeria

n. Any woman adviser.

Egeria was a nymph who advised and dictated laws to the legendary Roman king Numa.

Electra complex

n. The unconscious tendency of a daughter to be attached to her father and hostile toward or jealous of her mother.

In Greek legend Electra was the daughter of Agamemnon and Clytemnestra. She convinced her brother Orestes to kill their mother and her lover, who together had killed Agamemnon.

elysian

adj. Happy, blissful, delightful.

Elysium was the place where virtuous people went after death in Greek myth.

Elysium

n. Any place or condition of ideal bliss or complete happiness; paradise.

Elysium was the place where virtuous people went after death in Greek myth.

erogenous

adj. The zones or parts of the body where the stimulation of which tends to arouse sexual desire.

Eros was the Greek god of sexual love.

erotic

adj. Having to do with sexual love; of or causing sexual feelings or desire.

n. 1. a person abnormally sensitive to sexual stimulation; 2. an erotic poem.

Eros was the Greek god of sexual love.

giant

n. 1. An imaginary being of human form but super human size and strength; 2. a person or thing of great size, strength, or intellect.

adj. Like a giant; of great size, strength, or intellect.

In Greek mythology giants were a race of huge humanlike beings who warred with the gods.

gorgon

n. Any ugly, terrifying, or repulsive woman.

Gorgons were three snake-haired sisters in Greek mythology whose appearance turned men to stone.

Hades

n. A euphemism for hell.

Hades was the Greek god of the underworld and a name for the underground world of the dead.

Halcyon Days

n. 1. Tranquil, happy, unruffled; 2. the seven days before and after the winter solstice.

Alcyone was the daughter of Aeolus, the king of the winds. According to Greek myth, she was turned into a kingfisher at death. This myth was from the popular belief that the bird hatched its young in a nest floating on the sea during the halcyon days of the solstice when Aeolus caused fourteen windless days.

harpy

n. 1. A relentless, greedy person; 2. a shrewish woman.

A half-woman–half-bird in Greek mythology. They carried off the souls of the dead.

hector

n. A bully or braggart.

v. 1. To pester, tease; 2. to browbeat or bully.

Hector was a hero in the Trojan War who was killed by Achilles. In early
popular drama, he became a bully and a braggart.

Hellene

n. Greek.

According to Greek myth, Hellen was the son of Deucalion and ancestor of
the Greeks.

hellenize

v. To become Greek or Hellenistic

According to Greek myth, Hellen was the son of Deucalion and ancestor of
the Greeks.

Herculean

adj. 1. Having the great size and strength of Hercules; 2. calling for great
strength, size, or courage.

Hercules was a mythical Greek hero known for his great strength and for performing the twelve labors imposed on him by Hera.

Hermaphrodite

n. A person, animal, or plant with the sexual organs of both the male and female.

Hermaphroditus was the son of Aphrodite and Hermes. He merged with the
nymph Salmacis to become one two-sexed creature.

hermetic

adj. 1. Magical, alchemical; 2. completely sealed by fusion soldering, etc., to
keep air or gas from getting out; airtight.

The word "hermetic" is derived from Hermes Trismegistus, which was the
Greek name for the Egyptian god Toth. He was the reputed founder
of alchemy and other occult sciences. He is somewhat associated with
Hermes, the Greek messenger of the gods.

hygiene

n. 1. A science of health and its maintenance; 2. a system of principles for the
preservation of health and prevention of disease.

Hygeia was the Greek goddess of health.

hymen

n. The thin mucous membrane that usually covers part of the opening of the
vagina in a virgin.

Hymen was the Greek god of marriage.

hymeneal

adj. Of a wedding or marriage.

n. A wedding song or poem.

Hymen was the Greek god of marriage.

hypnosis

n. A psychically induced sleeplike condition in which the subject loses consciousness and responds to suggestions by the hypnotist.

Hypnos was the Greek god of sleep.

hypnotic

adj. 1. Causing sleep; 2. inducing hypnosis.

Hypnos was the Greek god of sleep.

irenic

adj. Promoting peace.

Irene was the Greek goddess of peace and daughter of Zeus and Themis.

iris

n. 1. Rainbow; 2. the round pigmented contractile diaphragm portion of the eye.

Iris was the Greek goddess of the rainbow. According to the *Iliad*, she was the messenger of the gods.

Janus-faced

adj. Two-faced, deceiving.

Janus was the Roman god of portals, beginnings, and endings. He is depicted as having two faces, one in the front of his head, and the other in the back.

jovial

adj. Full of playful, hearty humor.

Jove was one of the names of Jupiter, the most powerful of the Roman gods.

Juno

n. A stately or regal woman.

Juno was the wife of the Roman god Jupiter, as well as the goddess of light, birth, women, and marriage.

junoesque

adj. Stately and regal like Juno.

Juno was the wife of the Roman god Jupiter, as well as the goddess of light, birth, women, and marriage.

lethe

n. Oblivion or forgetfulness.

Lethe was the river of forgetful in the Greek and Roman underworlds. Its waters caused drinkers to forget their pasts.

lethean

adj. Causing forgetfulness or oblivion.

Lethe was the river of forgetful in the Greek and Roman underworlds. Its waters caused drinkers to forget their pasts.

lethargy

n. 1. An abnormal drowsiness, or great lack of energy; 2. total indifference or apathay.

Lethe was the river of forgetful in the Greek and Roman underworlds. Its waters caused drinkers to forget their pasts.

martial

adj. 1. Of or suitable for war; 2. warlike, brave, soldierly; 3. of the army, navy, or military life.

Mars was the Roman god of war.

mercurial

adj. 1. Having the qualities of the god Mercury; eloquent, clever, shrewd; 2. having the qualities suggestive of mercury; quick-witted, volatile, changeable, fickle.

Mercury was the Roman god of merchandise, trade, and theft, as well as the messenger of the gods.

Midas touch

n. An ability to make money in every venture.

The legend of King Midas tells of a the king's power to turn everything he touched into gold.

Minoan

adj. Of or relating to a Bronze Age culture of Crete (3000 B.C.–1100 B.C.).

King Minos was the son of Zeus and mythical king of Crete. His wife mated with a bull to produce the half-man–half-bull Minotaur.

mnemonic

adj. 1. Helping the memory; 2. of memory.

Mnemosyne was the Greek goddess of memory and mother of the nine Muses.

muse

n. 1. The spirit regarded as inspiring a poet or other; source of genius or inspiration; a meditation.

v. To think or consider deeply and at length.

According to Greek mythology the Muses were nine sister goddesses who presided over song and poetry and the arts and sciences.

museful

adj. Meditative.

According to Greek mythology the Muses were nine sister goddesses who presided over song and poetry and the arts and sciences.

musing

n. Meditation; reflection; contemplation.

According to Greek mythology the Muses were nine sister goddesses who presided over song and poetry and the arts and sciences.

museum

n. A building or room for preserving, studying, and displaying artistic, historical, or scientific objects.

In Greek myth, a museum was a place where the Muses could study. They were nine sister goddesses who presided over song and poetry and the arts and sciences.

music

n. The art and science of ordering vocal and instrumental tones or sounds in varying rhythms, melodies, or harmonies.

In Greek myth, music was any art presided over by the Muses. They were nine sister goddesses who presided over song and poetry and the arts and sciences.

Myrmidon

n. An unquestioning follower or subordinate.

A Myrmidon was a member of the Thessalian people who, according to Greek legend, accompanied his king Achilles in the Trojan War.

narcissism

n. 1. Self-love; excessive interest in one's own appearance; 2. in psychoanalysis, the arrest or regression to the first stage of sexual development, in which the self is an object of sexual pleasure.

According to Greek myth Narcissus was a beautiful youth who shunned Echo. In punishment, Nemesis made him fall in love with his own reflection.

nemesis

n. 1. Just punishment; 2. someone who imposes retribution.

Nemesis was the Greek goddess of retributive justice or vengance.

nestor

n. A wise old man.

In Greek legend, Nestor was a wise old counselor who fought with the Greeks at Troy.

night

n. 1. The period from sunset to sunrise; 2. the darkness of this period; 3. any period or condition of darkness or gloom.

The word night is derived from Nyx, the Greek god of the night.

nymph

n. 1. A lovely young woman.

Nymphs were a group of minor Greek and Roman nature goddesses who lived in rivers, mountains, and trees.

nymphet

n. A sexually attractive pubescent girl.

Nymphs were a group of minor Greek and Roman nature goddesses who lived in rivers, mountains, and trees.

nympholepsy

n. A violent emotional state, which the ancient Greeks thought was caused by nymphs.

Nymphs were a group of minor Greek and Roman nature goddesses who lived in rivers, mountains, and trees.

nymphomania

n. An abnormal and uncontrollable sexual desire in women.

Nymphs were a group of minor Greek and Roman nature goddesses who lived in rivers, mountains, and trees.

ocean

n. 1. The body of salt water that covers more than two-thirds of the earth's surface; 2. any great expanse or quantity.

Oceanus was the ancient Greek god who ruled over the seas before Poseidon.

odyssey

n. Any extended wandering or journey.

Homer's epic poem, *The Odyssey*, recounts the long wanderings of Odysseus, a king of Ithaca and Greek leader in the Trojan War. After ten long years of wandering, he reached home.

Oedipus complex

n. The unconscious tendency of a child to be attached to the parent of the opposite sex and hostile toward the other parent.

According to Greek legend, Oedipus was the son of Laius and Jocasta who abandoned him because of an oracle. When he grew up, he unknowingly killed his father and married his mother.

olympian

adj. Like an Olympic god; exalted celestial; majestic.

Mount Olympus was the home of the Greek gods.

orphic

adj. Mystical, occult, oracular.

Orpheus was a mythical Greek musician whose ability on the lyre affected animals and inanimate objects. He was almost able to rescue his wife Eurydice from Hades by charming Hades and Persephone with his lyre.

pander

n. 1. A pimp; 2. a person who provides the means of help to satisfy the ambitions or vices of another.

v. To act as a pander; provide gratification for the desires of others.

Pandarus was a Lycian archer in the Trojan War. In medieval romance he acts as a go-between in love intrigues.

Pandora's box

n. A source of untold troubles.

The Greek gods sent a box to Pandora, the first woman. She was instructed
   not to open the box, but she could not contain her curiosity. When
   she opened the box, she let all of the evils into the world.

panic

adj. Of sudden fear.

n. 1. A sudden unreasoning hysterical fear; 2. a widespread fear of the collapse
   of the financial system.

v. To affect with panic.

The word panic is derived from Pan, the Greek god of fields, forests, wild
   animals, and flocks. Originally panic meant fear inspired by Pan.

pan-pipe

n. A primitive wind instrument made of a row of reeds or tupes of graduated
   lengths bound together lengthwise and played by blowing across the
   open ends.

Pan was the Greek god of fields, forests, wild animals, and flocks.

parnassian

adj. Relating to poetry.

Parnassus is a mountain in Greece that was sacred to the Greek god Apollo and
   the Muses.

parnassus

n. 1. Poets or poetry collectively; 2. any center of poetic or artistic activity.

Parnassus is a mountain in Greece that was sacred to the Greek god Apollo and
   the Muses.

phaeton

n. A touring car.

Phaethon was the son of Helios. He drove his father's sun chariot through the
   sky, but lost control and was struck down by Zeus' thunderbolt.

phoenix

n. 1. Immortality; 2. rebirth.

According to Egyptian myth, the phoenix was a bird of great beauty, the only
   one of its kind. It would live 500 or 600 years, consume itself in fire,
   and rise from its ashes in the freshness of youth and live through another
   cycle.

pierian

adj. Of the Muses or the arts.

Pieria in ancient Macedonia was where the Muses were once worshipped.

plutonian

adj. Of or like Pluto and the underworld.

Pluto was the Roman god of the underworld.

priapic

adj. 1. phallic; 2. relating to virility.

Priapus was the Greek and Roman god of male procreative power. He was the son of Aphrodite and Dionysus.

priapism

n. A condition characterized by the persistent erection of the penis.

Priapus was the Greek and Roman god of male procreative power. He was the son of Aphrodite and Dionysus.

Promethean

adj. Life-bringing, creative, or courageously original.

According to Greek myth, Prometheus was the Titan who stole fire from heaven and gave it to humankind. Zeus punished him by chaining him to a rock where a vulture came each day to eat his liver.

procrustean

adj. Designed to secure conformity at any cost; drastic in reference to methods.

Procrustes was an evil giant in Greek mythology. He would force travelers to fit into his bed by stretching their bodies or cutting off their legs.

procrustean bed

n. A format or configuration into which someone or something is arbitrarily forced.

Procrustes was an evil giant in Greek mythology. He would force travelers to fit into his bed by stretching their bodies or cutting off their legs.

proteus

n. A person or thing that readily changes appearance, character, principles, etc.

Proteus was a Greek sea god who attended Poseidon and had the ability to change his own form at will.

protean

adj. Very changeable; readily taking on different shapes and forms.

Proteus was a Greek sea god who attended Poseidon and had the ability to change his own form at will.

psyche

n. 1. The human soul; 2. the mind.

According to Greek myth, Psyche was a beautiful princess who was loved by Cupid. She personified the human soul.

psychedelic

adj. 1. Causing extreme changes in the conscious mind, such as hallucinations or delusions; 2. stimulating auditory or visual effects of the psychedelic.

n. A drug.

According to Greek myth, Psyche was a beautiful princess who was loved by Cupid. She personified the human soul.

psychiatry

n. The branch of medicine concerned with the study and treatment of the disorders of the mind.

According to Greek myth, Psyche was a beautiful princess who was loved by Cupid. She personified the human soul.

psychic

adj. 1. Of the mind; 2. beyond natural or known physical processes.

According to Greek myth, Psyche was a beautiful princess who was loved by Cupid. She personified the human soul.

pythonic

adj. 1. Prophetic, oracular; 2. of or pertaining to pythons; 3. gigantic or monstrous.

According to Greek myth, Python was an enormous serpent that lived in the cave of Mount Parnassus. It was killed by Apollo, the messenger of the gods.

rhadamanthine

adj. Inflexibly just.

Rhadamanthus was the judge of the underworld in Greek mythology.

salutary

adj. Promoting or conducive to health.

Salus was the Roman goddess of health and prosperity.

Saturnalia

n. A period of unrestrained, often licentious revelry.

Saturn was the Roman god of agriculture.

Saturnalian

adj. Riotously merry or orgiastic.

Saturn was the Roman god of agriculture.

Saturnian

adj. Used to describe a period that is prosperous, contended, happy, or peaceful.

Saturn was the Roman god of agriculture. Saturnian refers to the Saturn's rule, which was a golden age of peace.

Saturnine
adj. Sluggish, gloomy, morose, grave, taciturn.
Saturn was the Roman god of agriculture. The word Saturnine refers to someone born under the supposed influence of the planet Saturn.

satyr
n. A lecherous man.
Satyrs were woodland diety with legs, hooves, and horns of a goat. They attended Dionysus, the Greek god of wine and vegetation.

satyriasis
n. Excessive or uncontrollable sexual craving in a man.
Satyrs were woodland diety with legs, hooves, and horns of a goat. They attended Dionysus, the Greek god of wine and vegetation.

Scylla and Charybdis
Facing difficulty on either side; between two evils, neither of which can be evaded without risking the other; between a rock and a hard place.
According to Greek myth, Scylla was a nymph who had been transformed into a sea monster. In reality, Scylla was a hazardous rock off the coast of Italy that was opposite Charybdis, a deadly whirpool.

sibyl
n. Witch, sorceress, fortune-teller.
In Greek mythology, Sibyl was a prophetess.

siren
n. 1. A seductive woman; 2. a warning device that produces a sound.
Sirens were Greek sea nymphs who were part women, part birds. They lured sailors with their seductive singing.

siren song
n. A seductive utterance or appeal, especially one that is deceptive.
Sirens were Greek sea nymphs who were part women, part birds. They lured sailors with their seductive singing.

Sisyphean
adj. Endless and difficult.
Sisyphus was a legendary Greek king who was condemned to Hades to eternally repeat the cycle of rolling a heavy rock up a hill, only for the rock to roll down again as it neared the top.

somnambulate
v. To sleepwalk.
Somnus was the ancient Roman god of sleep.

somniferous
adj. Inducing sleep.
Somnus was the ancient Roman god of sleep.

sphinx
n. A person whose character is deep and mysterious.
In Greek mythology, the sphinx was a winged monser with a lion's body and
the head and breasts of a woman. She asked her riddle of everyone that
passed by and killed those who could not answer it.

stamina
n. Staying power or endurance.
According to Greek myth, the stamen was the thread of life spun by the Fates.

stygian
adj. 1. Infernal, dark, gloomy; 2. inviolable, completely binding.
The word "stygian" is derived from the River Styx. This was the principal river
surrounding the underworld in Greek mythology. Those whose crossed
the river had to take an unbreakable oath.

tantalize
v. Arouse in hope and then disappoint; tease.
Tantalus was a king in Greek mythology who was condemned to remain for
the rest of eternity standing chin-deep in water with fruit hanging just
above his head. Every time he would attempt to quench his thirst or
alleviate his hunger, the water and fruit would move out of his reach.

tantalus
n. A stand with decanters that are plainly visible but cannot be removed until
the bar that locks them in place is raised.
Tantalus was a king in Greek mythology who was condemned to remain for
the rest of eternity standing chin-deep in water with fruit hanging just
above his head. Every time he would attempt to quench his thirst or
alleviate his hunger, the water and fruit would move out of his reach.

telluric
adj. Of or arising from the earth's soil.
In Roman mythology, Tellus is the Roman goddess of the earth.

terpsichorean
adj. Having to do with dancing.
Terpsichore was one of the Greek Muses. She ruled dancing and choral song.

thanatophobia
n. An abnormally great fear of death.
Thanatos was the personification of death in Greek mythology.

thanatopsis
n. A musing about death.
Thanatos was the personification of death in Greek mythology.

thersitical
adj. Loud, abusive, and scurrilous.
According to *the Iliad*, Thersites was an ugly, foul-mouthed Greek soldier who
      was killed by Achilles.

Thyestean banquet
n. A banquet at which human flesh is served.
According to Greek myth, Thyestes unknowingly ate the flesh of his own sons
      when his brother and rival, Atreus, fed them to him as punishment for
      committing adultery with the wife.

titan
n. Any person or thing of great size and strength.
In Greek myth, there were many Titans, and they were a family of giants born
      to Uranus and Gaia. They ruled the earth until they were overthrown
      by the Olympian gods.

titanic
adj. Of great size, strength or power.
In Greek myth, there were many Titans, and they were a family of giants born
      to Uranus and Gaia. They ruled the earth until they were overthrown
      by the Olympian gods.

titanism
n. The spirit of revolt or defiance.
In Greek myth, there were many Titans, and they were a family of giants born
      to Uranus and Gaia. They ruled the earth until they were overthrown
      by the Olympian gods.

tychism
n. The theory that chance has objective existence in the universe.
Tyche was the Greek goddess of chance.

uranography
n. The branch of astronomy dealing with the descriptions of the heavens.
Uranus was the Greek god who was the personification of heaven.

uranometry
n. The measurement of the heavens.
Uranus was the Greek god who was the personification of heaven.

venerate
v. To worship; to look upon with deep feelings of respect.
The word "venerate" was derived from Venus, who was the Roman goddess
      of love and beauty.

venereal

adj. 1. Having to do with sexual intercourse; 2. transmitted by sexual intercourse with infected people.

The word "venereal" was derived from Venus, who was the Roman goddess of love and beauty.

Venus

n. A beautiful woman.

Venus was the Roman goddess of love and beauty.

vesper

n. 1. Evening; 2. an evening prayer.

adj. Of the evening.

Hesperos was the Greek god of evening.

vestal

adj. Chaste, pure.

n. 1. A chaste woman; virgin; 2. a nun.

Vesta was the Roman goddess of the hearth. The sacred fire in her temple was tended by the six vestal virgins.

volcanic

adj. 1. Of, thrown from, caused by, or characteristic of a volcano; 2. violently and powerfully explosive or capable of explosion.

Vulcan was the Roman god of fire and metalworking.

volcano

n. A vent in the earth's crust through which rocks, dust, ash, and liquid magma are expelled.

Vulcan was the Roman god of fire and metalworking.

vulcanian

adj. Having to do with metalworking.

Vulcan was the Roman god of fire and metalworking.

vulcanite

n. A hard rubber made by treating crude rubber with a large amount of sulfur and subjecting it to intense heat; used in the manufacture of combs, buttons, and for electrical insulation.

Vulcan was the Roman god of fire and metalworking.

vulcanization

n. The process of treating crude rubber with sulfur and intense heat to give it greater elasticity and strength.

Vulcan was the Roman god of fire and metalworking.

west

n. 1. The direction to the left of a person facing north; 2. a region or district
in or toward this direction.

adj. In, of, to, toward, or facing the west; designating the western part of a
continent, country.

adv. In or toward the west.

The word west is derived from the Greek god of the evening, Hesperos.

zeal

n. Eager interest and enthusiasm; ardent endeavor or devotion.

Zelos was the Greek god of zeal or emulation, and the brother of Nike.

zephyr

n. 1. The west wind; 2. a soft, gentle breeze, 3. something light, airy, or un-
substantial.

Zephyros was the Greek god and personification of the west wind. He was
considered the most mild and gentle of all of the wood deities.

Bibliography

Ayto, John. *Dictionary of Word Origins*. New York: Arcade Publishing, 1990.

Bailey, Adrian. *The Caves of the Sun*. London: Pimlico, 1998.

Bolle, Kees W. *The Freedom of Man in Myth*. Nashville, TN: Vanderbilt University Press, 1968.

Campbell, Joseph. *The Hero with a Thousand Faces*. Princeton, NJ: Princeton Bollingen, 1968.

———. *Historical Atlas of World Mythology: The Way of the Animal Powers*. New York: Harper & Row, 1983.

———. *Historical Atlas of World Mythology: The Way of the Seeded Earth*. New York: Harper & Row, 1983.

———. *The Mythic Image*. New York: MJF Books, 1974.

Cavendish, Richard, ed. *Man, Myth, and Magic: An Encyclopedia of the Supernatural*, 13 vols. New York: Marshall Cavendish Corporation, 1970.

Colum, Padraic. *Nordic Gods and Heroes*. New York: Dover Publications, 1996.

Condos, Theony. *Star Myths of the Greeks and Romans: A Sourcebook*. Grand Rapids, MI: Phanes Press, 1997.

Doty, William G. *Mythography: The Study of Myths and Rituals*, 2nd ed. Tuscaloosa: University of Alabama Press, 1986.

Eliot, Alexander. *The Timeless Myths*. New York: Continuum, 1996.

Eliot, Alexander. *The Universal Myths*. New York: Penguin Books, 1976.

Frazer, Sir James George. *The Golden Bough*. New York: Macmillian, 1922.

Hendrickson, Robert. *The Facts on File Encyclopedia of Word and Phrase Origins*. New York: Checkmark Books, 1997.

Hollander, Lee M., trans. *The Poetic Edda*. Austin: University of Texas Press, 1996.

Jung, C. G. *Man and His Symbols*. New York: Bantam, 1968.

Kerenyi, C. *The Gods of the Greeks*. New York: Thames & Hudson, 1979.

Levi-Strauss, Claude. *The Savage Mind*. Chicago: University of Chicago Press, 1966.

Macrone, Michael. *By Jove! Brush Up Your Mythology*. New York: Cader Books, 1992.

McDonald, Marianne. *Tales of the Constellations: The Myths and Legends of the Night Sky.* New York: Michael Friedman Publishing, 1996.

Moses, Robert, ed. *American Movie Classics Classic Movie Companion.* New York: Hyperion, 1999.

Ovid. *The Metamorphoses of Ovid.* Translated by A. E. Watts. San Francisco: North Point Press, 1980.

Philip, Neil. *Myths and Legends: The World's Most Enduring Myths and Legends Explored and Explained.* New York: DK Publishing, 1999.

Reynolds, Richard. *Super Heroes: A Modern Mythology.* Jackson: University Press of Mississippi, 1998.

Snodgrass, Mary Ellen. *Signs of the Zodiac: A Reference Guide to Historical, Mythological and Cultural Associations.* Westport, CT: Greenwood Press, 1997.

Squire, Charles. *Celtic Myth and Legend.* Hollywood, CA: Newcastle Publishing, 1975.

Wickersham, John M., ed. *Myths and Legends of the World*, 4 vols. New York: Macmillan, 2000.

Zimmerman, J. E. *Dictionary of Classical Mythology.* New York: Bantam, 1966.

Index

About the Authors and Illustrator

AMY T. PETERSON is Director of Course Development at American InterContinental University and is one of the authors of *In an Influential Fashion* (Greenwood, 2002).

DAVID J. DUNWORTH has taught courses in Art, Mythology, and Literature for high school, college, and online courses.